Bakhtin, Stalin, and Modern Russian Fiction

Recent Titles in
Contributions to the Study of World Literature

Bakhtin, Stalin, and Modern Russian Fiction

Carnival, Dialogism, and History

M. Keith Booker
and Dubravka Juraga

Contributions to the Study of World Literature, Number 58

GREENWOOD PRESS
Westport, Connecticut • London

Library of Congress Cataloging-in-Publication Data

Booker, M. Keith.
    Bakhtin, Stalin, and modern Russian fiction : carnival, dialogism,
and history / M. Keith Booker and Dubravka Juraga.
        p.   cm.—(Contributions to the study of world literature,
ISSN 0738–9345 ; 58)
    Includes bibliographical references and index.
    ISBN 0–313–29526–3 (alk. paper)
    1. Russian fiction—20th century—History and criticism.
2. Russian fiction—Political aspects.   3. Bakhtin, M. M. (Mikhail
Mikhailovich), 1895–1975.   4. Criticism—Soviet Union.   5. Stalin,
Joseph, 1879–1953.   I. Juraga, Dubravka.   II. Title.   III. Series.
PG3098.4.B66   1995
891.73′409—dc20   94–24572

British Library Cataloguing in Publication Data is available.

Library of Congress Catalog Card Number: 94–24572
ISBN: 0–313–29526–3
ISSN: 0738–9345

First published in 1995

Greenwood Press, 88 Post Road West, Westport, CT 06881
An imprint of Greenwood Publishing Group, Inc.

Printed in the United States of America

Copyright Acknowledgment

The authors gratefully acknowledge the University of Texas Press for
permission to quote from *The Dialogic Imagination* by M. M. Bakhtin. Ed.
Michael Holquist. Trans. Caryl Emerson and Michael Holquist. Austin:
University of Texas Press, 1981. Copyright 1981 by the University of
Texas Press.

For Adam Booker

For Milja Mulić

za Nadu i Marka Juraga

Contents

Introduction: Bakhtin, History, and Russian Literature

One of the chapters of Andrei Sinyavsky's autobiographical novel *Goodnight!* (1984) centers around the appearance of the ghost of the recently deceased Stalin to a clairvoyant, the implication apparently being that Stalin's ghost was still stalking Russia at least as late as the publication of Sinyavsky's book. Indeed, if there is a specter haunting modern Russian fiction, it is the specter of Stalinism. In the quarter of a century during which Stalin ruled the Soviet Union with his iron hand, his government exerted a powerful and direct control over the production of art and literature in the Soviet state. Not only were the works of artists and writers strictly monitored for ideological consistency with the official Party line, but a highly formulaic socialist realism became during this time the only officially sanctioned artistic mode. This development had especially powerful consequences given the radical contrast between the tenets of socialist realism and the artistic practices of the great nineteenth-century predecessors of twentieth-century Soviet writers. As a result, from about 1929, the formal experimentation, biting satire, and fantastic imagery generally associated with the works of writers like Pushkin, Gogol, and Dostoevsky—and with much postrevolutionary literature of the 1920s—virtually disappeared from Soviet literature. This situation began to ease to a certain extent after Stalin's death in 1953, but Sinyavsky's 1965 arrest and incarceration—simply for the nature of his writing—served as a grim reminder to Russian writers of the mid-1960s that the dark days of Stalinist censorship were far from being swept away by the famous "thaw." Meanwhile, Stalin's impact on

Russian literature was so strong that it could still be felt even twenty years after the notorious arrests of Sinyavsky and Daniel. Stalin continued to be a major presence in contemporary Russian fiction, appearing directly as a character in works like *Goodnight!*, Vladimir Voinovich's *Pretender to the Throne*, Alexander Zinoviev's *The Yawning Heights*, and Sasha Sokolov's *Astrophobia* and exerting a powerful influence on numerous other works, from the grimly realistic accounts of Solzhenitsyn to the fantastic science fiction of the Strugatsky brothers.

Stalin is also a major defining presence in the work of Mikhail Bakhtin, probably the most important Russian literary thinker of the Stalinist era. However, this presence has been insufficiently appreciated in the West, where Bakhtin's work has been so influential. Bakhtin's ongoing preoccupation with questions of history and identity clearly marks him as a representative Russian thinker whose concerns are similar to those of many modern Russian writers. And Bakhtin's career began amid the exciting and tumultuous artistic and intellectual climate of the Soviet 1920s, a fact of considerable importance to a thorough understanding of his thought. For example, though Bakhtin's continuing interest in artistic innovation and experimentation clearly echoes the earlier work of the Russian Formalists, Bakhtin's insistence on the political and social dimension of artistic and literary strategies owes a great deal to the renewed awareness of such issues in postrevolutionary Russia. Moreover, Bakhtin's particular approach to these issues has much in common with that of many postrevolutionary Russian artists and writers. Meanwhile, Bakhtin's most important work was done during the later Stalinist years, when he was forced to cope with the restrictions and limitations that brought the postrevolutionary period of innovation in Russian art and literature to a screeching halt.

Western critics who have employed Bakhtin's theories have typically emphasized two central aspects of his thought—dialogism and carnival. Thus, R. B. Kershner, in a Bakhtinian study of the early fiction of James Joyce, introduces Bakhtin by noting that "Bakhtin's importance rests on two key concepts, *dialogism* . . . and *carnivalization*" (15, Kershner's emphasis). Elsewhere, Michael Holquist has suggested dialogism as Bakhtin's master concept, arguing that the term can be applied to an "interconnected set of concerns that dominate Bakhtin's thinking" throughout his career (*Dialogism* 15). Holquist emphasizes that in this sense "dialogism" is an extremely complex and subtle concept that involves an interconnecting network of ideas about language, epistemology, and human existence in general. Meanwhile, in their influential critical biography of Bakhtin,

Holquist and Katerina Clark argue for Bakhtin's consistent lifelong focus on dialogic relations between self and other, a focus that already takes shape in his early "architectonics of answerability" project of the 1920s. On the other hand, Gary Saul Morson and Caryl Emerson have challenged this rather static view of Bakhtin's ethical and intellectual concerns. In their excellent recent survey of Bakhtin's work, Morson and Emerson argue that Bakhtin's ideas and interests change dramatically from one period to another in his long intellectual career. However, Morson and Emerson suggest that there are certain "global concepts" that are of central importance in attempting to understand Bakhtin's work. These concepts include "prosaics," "unfinalizability," and "dialogue," but Morson and Emerson specifically seek to downplay the importance of the carnivalesque in Bakhtin's thought, believing that this aspect of Bakhtin's work represents something of an anomaly that has probably been overemphasized, especially by Western critics.

The insistence of Morson and Emerson on the dynamic and evolutionary quality of Bakhtin's thought is consonant with their emphasis on history and historical change as central elements of his work. These elements have not been sufficiently appreciated in Western appropriations of Bakhtin's work, even though an intense concern with history characterizes Bakhtin's entire career. Bakhtin himself described the main thrust of his work as an attempt to create an "historical poetics," and in fact all of Bakhtin's major concepts include an historical dimension. For example, his studies of genre place crucial importance on issues of history and temporality. In particular, a concern with such issues forms a central part of Bakhtin's highly influential theories of the novel as a genre. Probably the most fundamental of the many reasons for which Bakhtin considers the novel a special genre is the novel's ability to grow and evolve in time, responding to and participating in the process of history. Rather than functioning according to rigidly defined principles, the novel by its very nature challenges its own principles and conventions and thereby remains open to change. As a result, parody is for Bakhtin the novelistic strategy *par excellence*, a fact that echoes the earlier work of the Russian formalists and that anticipates the central use of parody in the work of recent Russian writers like Voinovich, Zinoviev, Andrei Bitov, Vassily Aksyonov, and Sasha Sokolov.

Bakhtin's concern with history (especially as figured in crucial notions like the "chronotope") should thus be added to dialogism and the carnivalesque as the central conceptions of Bakhtin's career as it relates to literary criticism. On the other hand, Bakhtin's work, like Russian literature, is extremely diverse, and any attempt succinctly to summarize that work is in danger not only of oversimplifying

Bakhtin's thought but of doing considerable violence to the complex and avowedly nonsystematic nature of his project. Even Clark and Holquist, who have been criticized (particularly by Morson and Emerson) for trying to fit all of Bakhtin's work into a single mold, insist that Bakhtin's own emphasis on multiplicity implies that "to claim that any version of him is the correct one would be to straitjacket the philosopher of variety, to 'monologize' the singer of 'polyphony'" (4). Similarly, they approvingly cite L. E. Pinsky near the end of their book to the effect that "Bakhtin's work is exciting precisely because of its contradictoriness and ability to spark different and unexpected interpretations, and that one should thus be careful not to assign his writings any single, authoritative interpretation" (344).

This warning is particularly crucial given that Bakhtin himself practices what he preaches, writing in a dialogic (and often parodic) mode that makes it impossible to appreciate the significance of his statements unless they are read in conjunction with other statements to which they respond and with potential responses that they themselves might be expected to invoke. The very heart of dialogism is a movement beyond monological modes of "either-or" logic which demand that a given interpretation of a text (or of the world) be either accepted or rejected. Similarly, the most important aspect of the spirit of carnival is its ambivalence, its refusal to allow simple choices between opposing alternatives. Finally, Bakhtin's historical vision crucially relies on a sense of continual becoming which requires that final conclusions and interpretations be perpetually deferred in favor of an ongoing potentiality.

In addition, interpretations of Bakhtin's work are always complicated by the fact that, writing within the context of the Stalinist Soviet Union, Bakhtin was not necessarily free to say or write what he wanted. In reading Bakhtin, then, one must remain alert to absences that might have been caused by the exigencies of political reality in the Soviet Union. Moreover, it is almost certain that what Bakhtin *does* say is distorted by this reality, both because some of his points must be made obliquely in order to skirt controversy and because many of them are in fact subtly subversive commentaries on Stalinism itself. The most obvious example of this distortion is the way (widely recognized by critics) Bakhtin employs medieval Catholicism in *Rabelais and His World* at least partially as a cipher for Stalinism. But it is also clear that a great deal of Bakhtin's more general commentary on the intrinsic multiplicity and ideological diversity of language and on the evolutionary nature of history can also be read as responses to Stalinist totalitarian utopianism.

This study presents a survey of Bakhtin's ideas that attempts to remain aware of these complications in reading his work. As a result, we suggest no final interpretations of Bakhtin's writings. Indeed, given the availability of general studies like those by Morson and Emerson and by Clark and Holquist, we attempt no direct summary of Bakhtin's ideas at all. After all, Bakhtin himself remained suspicious of all-encompassing systems throughout his career, seeing them as an instance of the kinds of monological and centripetal forces that he so strongly opposed. We simply proceed from the assumption that Bakhtin's complex body of work is informed by a number of key concepts, including carnival, dialogism, and historicism. In the first chapter, we introduce these concepts in relation to Bakhtin's historical context, paying particular attention to the ways this context, along with Bakhtin's own dialogic mode of discourse, complicates the interpretation and application of Bakhtin's work. In the second chapter, we continue this introduction to some of the most important concepts in Bakhtin's thought, using the work of Aksyonov to introduce the application of Bakhtin's work on carnival, dialogism, and historicism to literature. Aksyonov was chosen for this chapter both because his writing exemplifies many of Bakhtin's comments about literature and because Aksyonov's postStalinist work provides vivid illustrations of the continuing response of Russian literature to the legacy of Stalinism.

In the remainder of the book, we turn to more detailed Bakhtinian readings of some important works of modern Russian fiction. We begin with a discussion of the work of the satirists Ilf and Petrov, whose work received official approval and achieved widespread popularity in the early Stalinist years. We argue that the satire of Ilf and Petrov is far more complex than it has generally been considered by critics: while this satire is ostensibly directed at lingering bourgeois tendencies in Soviet society, it can also be read as a subtle criticism of certain tendencies in Stalinism. Moreover, their work recalls nineteenth-century Russian literature in subtle ways that are potentially subversive of the official Stalinist privileging of the future. Finally, the narrative structure of the novels of Ilf and Petrov suggests a vision of history far different from the official Stalinist one.

In the fourth chapter we examine the work of the satirist Mikhail Zoshchenko, an almost exact contemporary of Bakhtin. Zoshchenko is still best known for the early satirical stories that he wrote in the postrevolutionary 1920s, but we concentrate on his later work, using Bakhtin's theories of the novel as genre (and particularly of its ability to incorporate and parody other genres) to provide useful insights into enigmatic texts like *Youth Restored* and *Before Sunrise*. These texts (like most of Bakhtin's own) were generally written in the shadow of Stalinism and are clearly informed by that fact.

The remainder of this study focuses on postStalinist writers who have in one way or another addressed the Stalinist attempt to manipulate history and the disruption in Russian cultural tradition brought about by the Stalinist years. For example, the novels of Yuz Aleshkovsky are overtly political, functioning largely as direct parodies of the ideology of Stalinism. Aleshkovsky's two major works, *The Hand* and *Kangaroo*, are both usefully read within the context of Bakhtin's discussions of carnival, dialogism, and history. Meanwhile, Andrei Bitov's *Pushkin House* draws its energies from nineteenth-century Russian literature while treating the themes of history and subjectivity in ways reminiscent of Western postmodernism. Bitov's dialogues with other literary texts provide illuminating enactments of Bakhtin's commentary on literary intertextuality. Read through Bakhtin, Bitov's highly literary work has powerful, though subtle, political implications. Finally, we end our study with Sasha Sokolov's highly Menippean *Astrophobia*, which again comments on the Stalinist manipulation of history, but which also parodies the attempts of Solzhenitsyn and other recent Russian writers to unveil the historical "truth."

Together, the readings in this study are intended to provide a useful illumination of the attempts of Bakhtin—and of modern Russian writers of fiction—to cope with the difficulties of modern Russian history and to maintain a sense of Russian cultural tradition amid the many events that have disrupted that tradition in this century. The dialogues in this study between Bakhtin and modern Russian fiction help to illuminate the impact of modern Russian history (especially the Stalinist years) on Bakhtin's work and on modern Russian culture as a whole. This approach also usefully highlights Bakhtin's intense concern with history and cultural tradition, an aspect of his work that has received inadequate attention in Western appropriations of his work. In addition, our approach helps to identify links between the modern Russian literary tradition established by writers from Zamyatin to Sokolov and the great nineteenth-century tradition of writers like Pushkin, Gogol, and Dostoevsky, especially in the way all of these writers work to use literature as a force for cultural and historical stability. This delineation of an important common ground between modern Russian writers and their illustrious predecessors also suggests a potentially powerful role for literature in the attempts of Russian society to define its cultural and political identity in the tumultuous postSoviet years.

Bakhtin, Stalin, and
Modern Russian Fiction

1

Reading Bakhtin Dialogically

In their important study *The Politics and Poetics of Transgression*, Oliver Stallybrass and Allon White acknowledge their debt to Bakhtin's theories of the carnivalesque, noting that Bakhtin has in fact been the major figure in a widespread fascination with the notion of carnival among Western critics in the latter decades of the twentieth century. The Rabelais book, Stallybrass and White suggest, "catalysed the interest of Western scholars . . . around the notion of carnival" (6). There are, of course, a number of reasons for the enthusiastic reception of Bakhtin's presentation of the transgressive potential of carnivalesque imagery. Probably the most important of these reasons (especially if viewed in the light of Bakhtin's own continual insistence on the importance of historical context) is the ability of *Rabelais and His World* to respond so well to the needs and interests of Western critics when it was first introduced to them in the 1970s. In particular, the exuberant, exorbitant, transgressive, emancipatory rhetoric and imagery that most critics have associated with Bakhtin's readings of Rabelais closely parallel those that informed the oppositional political movements of the 1960s, movements which themselves had a major formative influence on Western literary critics in subsequent decades.

There is, however, a danger associated with this appropriation of Bakhtin's work on Rabelais to provide a vocabulary and theoretical framework within which to express the concerns of American and Western European critics of the 1970s and 1980s. For one thing, there is a possibility that Bakhtin's extremely complex body of work might be reduced to a series of slogans and clichés–a situation suggested by Edward Said's remark in a published dialogue with Raymond Williams that he hates even to use the word "dialogical" because of its associations with the "cult of Bakhtin." Bakhtin's own historical situation was, after all, vastly different from that of most of the critics who would later adopt his work. *Bakhtin and His World* was written primarily in the late 1930s in the Stalinist Soviet Union, a context hardly comparable to England or the United States in the 1960s. Reading the book with a sensitivity to Bakhtin's own historical context thus suggests that we approach its carnivalesque rhetoric with a certain amount of caution and skepticism. Indeed, close attention to Bakhtin's Soviet background suggests potential readings of the Rabelais book that differ substantially from the typical Western vision of it as an unequivocal celebration of the subversive energies of the carnival.

The Stalinist 1930s were certainly anything but a carnivalesque decade, and it is now widely accepted among Bakhtin scholars that the description of the rigid, humorless, and authoritarian practices of the medieval Catholic Church put forth by Bakhtin in *Rabelais and His World* is at least partially a veiled comment on Stalinism. In his prologue to the English translation of the book, Michael Holquist points out that it is important to consider the "obvious parallels between Bakhtin's scathing references to the Catholic church in the sixteenth century and Stalinism in the twentieth" (xv). In the double-voiced mode that he himself praises in the work of writers like Rabelais and Dostoevsky (and somewhat in the Russian tradition of Aesopian language), Bakhtin's description of a sterile, monological society in *Rabelais and His World* thus refers simultaneously to a medieval world of the distant past and to a Soviet world of his own Stalinist present. Indeed, Bakhtin scholars have become more and more aware in the past decade of the submerged critique of Stalinism in Bakhtin's Rabelais book. Richard Berrong has even gone so far as to conclude that *Rabelais and His World* "is an allegorical work of political criticism and theory" that shows admirable courage in its assault on Stalin, but that the book has no "real value as historical criticism" in its account of Rabelais (109). But simply to dismiss Bakhtin's book as an Aesopian diatribe against Stalin that has little or no relevance to Rabelais does not do justice to the double-voicing of the book, which manages to comment on *both* Stalin and Rabelais in useful ways. Thus Samuel Kinser (who finds Berrong's own figuration of Rabelais's historical context inadequate) concludes that Bakhtin's book is in fact "inspiring" as a study of Rabelais, even if its status as a contemporary political polemic requires that some of its specific descriptions of Rabelais and his context are not necessarily accurate.

Among other things, the hidden polemic against Stalin in *Rabelais and His World* calls attention to the fact that all of Bakhtin's important work was done under conditions in which published works had to meet the demands of severe censorship and published authors were in danger of imprisonment or even execution should their works turn out even retroactively to appear to challenge the authority of Stalin's Soviet regime. As a result, one should always keep in mind that Bakhtin was not free to say what he wanted and that his work is almost certainly distorted in one way or another by the ubiquitous presence of the Soviet censors and the secret police. Such distortions are perhaps especially strong in the Rabelais book, which was written in the latter part of the worst years of the Stalinist terror. Moreover, this book was originally written as a doctoral dissertation, so that Bakhtin also had to worry about having his work approved by an academic committee that was itself under considerable political pressure. As it was, Bakhtin had a great deal of difficulty in getting his dissertation approved, and we know for a fact that it underwent substantial revisions in the process. For example, a section on Gogol (eventually deleted from the published text) caused particular difficulties in getting the dissertation approved, perhaps because commentary on a Russian writer hit too close to home.[1]

Bakhtin's historical context, especially in relation to the carnivalesque imagery of revolution in *Rabelais and His World*, should include not only the 1930s, but also the 1920s, that complex decade of explosive revolutionary energy (and concomitant conservative reaction) in which many of Bakhtin's ideas were originally formed. During most of the tumultuous first decade after the Revolution, Russian artists and writers were able to pursue their work with relatively little (especially compared to the later Stalinist years) official interference, a situation that combined with the general spirit of radical change associated with the Revolution to produce an explosion in artistic and literary innovation and creativity analogous to contemporary Western cultural phenomena like modernism and the avant-garde. Poets like Mayakovsky, Blok, and Esenin, dramatists and directors like Tretiakov, Kharms, Vvedensky, and Meyerhold; satirists like Zoshchenko and Bulgakov; novelists like Zamyatin, Pilnyak, Olesha, and Platonov; painters like Malevich and Tatlin; and filmmakers like Eisenstein and Protazanov all participated in a Russian artistic revolution that might have rivaled in importance the political revolution it accompanied had it not been squelched by the growing oppression of the Soviet regime and by the eventual Stalinist aversion to experimental art of all kinds.[2]

As Stites points out, the atmosphere in the early years of the Soviet Union was often highly carnivalesque, "marked by spontaneous celebration, light-hearted buffoonery in the midst of violent political struggle, constantly self-creating forms of art and entertainment, and the movement of these forms onto the streets and into the villages." At the same time, Stites notes that the unleashing of traditional folk energies in the streets of modern Russia triggered a conservative reaction informed by a counterrevolutionary fear "that the masses, if left to their own ludic and Dionysian impulses, would unleash chaos" (79). In this conservative reaction, one can perhaps find the seeds of Stalinism, though the exact alignment of different cultural and political forces during this period was extremely complex. In any case, one can certainly find in the confrontation of opposing cultural forces in postrevolutionary Russia an anticipation of the agonistic vision of society that consistently informs Bakhtin's work.[3] Indeed, as Fitzpatrick notes, confrontations among violently opposed cultural forces (of which the confrontation between Communism and bourgeois culture was paradigmatic) were the fundamental informing characteristic of the Soviet Union in its early years, Lenin's famous question "*Kto kogo*?" (roughly, "Who will beat whom?") serving as an paradigm of this situation (*Cultural* 2).[4]

Bakhtin's initial popularity in the West may have owed a great deal to his anticipation of the oppositional cultures of the 1960s, but if there is a modern instance of carnivalesque energy to which *Rabelais and His World* refers, it is clearly not the West of the 1960s, but the Soviet Union of the decade after the Revolution. Bakhtin, after all, was not yet twenty-two years old when the October Revolution occurred, and the unique atmosphere of postrevolutionary Russia no doubt exercised a powerful influence on the formation of his subsequent thought. However, given that the heady days of postrevolutionary Russia led not to universal emancipation but to the ascendancy of Stalin, the Soviet 1920s serve as a rather problematic image of the political power of carnival. In addition, numerous critics of Bakhtin have seen the medieval carnival as a highly unsatisfactory metaphor for revolution because the carnival was in fact an officially sanctioned event whose very purpose was to release potentially subversive energies in politically harmless ways and thus to *prevent* revolution. Terry Eagleton, for example, expresses a strong skepticism toward the subversive potential of Bakhtin's notion of the carnival, pointing out that carnival is "a *licensed* affair in every sense, a permissible rupture of hegemony, a contained popular blow-off as disturbing and relatively ineffectual as a revolutionary work of art" (*Walter Benjamin* 148, Eagleton's emphasis). In addition, Bakhtin's apparent treatment of the carnival as an unequivocal image of emancipation seems to ignore the important fact that carnivalesque violence was often directed not at official authority but precisely at the kinds of oppressed and marginal groups who would presumably be liberated by carnivalesque subversion of authority.

Bakhtin's discussion of the carnival, combined with his frequent references to the antiauthoritarian power inherent in language itself, have led many critics to charge him with an unwarranted, even naive, optimism. Michael Gardiner, for example, grants that Bakhtin may use his discussion of the medieval carnival at least partially as a commentary on Stalinism. He also acknowledges a strong element of irony in much of Bakhtin's writing. Yet he nevertheless argues that Bakhtin "projects an almost entirely positive—indeed, utopian—image of carnival and related folk-festive practices" (181). Further, Gardiner sees a similar utopian optimism in Bakhtin's discussion of the novel, concluding that the "central shortcoming" of Bakhtin's thought is that he "seriously overestimates the capacity of dialogic literature and popular culture to effect the liberation of human consciousness from the grip of monologism" (176).

But Gardiner's apparent equation of utopianism with naiveté is highly debatable. One need only consider the insistence of Marxist critics like Fredric Jameson that a utopian notion of a desirable alternative future is necessary to empower meaningful political action in the present. Jameson thus notes that in our contemporary social climate "[t]he Utopian idea . . . keeps alive the possibility of a world qualitatively distinct from this one and takes the form of a stubborn negation of all that is" (*Marxism* 111). Elsewhere, Jameson emphasizes the importance of utopian impulses both to bourgeois society and to Marxist critiques of that society:

all class consciousness—or in other words, all ideology in the strongest sense, including the most exclusive forms of ruling-class consciousness just as much as that of oppositional or oppressed classes—is in its very nature Utopian. (*Political* 289)

Of course, Jameson's insistence on the power and ubiquity of utopianism is made partially out of his embattled recognition of the extreme suspicion toward utopian impulses shown by many modern thinkers, who have equated utopian ideals with nostalgia, conservatism, and a desire to escape from the contingency of history.

Jameson's defense of utopianism is, in short, highly dialogic: it participates in an ongoing debate over the value of utopian thought.

But Bakhtin's treatment of the carnival and of the emancipatory power of language is likewise a response to specific preexisting conditions. It is certainly true that the rhetoric of *Rabelais and His World* celebrates transgression and revolution. But the emancipatory tone of the book can be seen as an attempt to revive revolutionary energies that had been lost under Stalin. Holquist thus sees the Rabelais book as a suggestion that under Stalin the Russian Revolution had "lost touch with its roots in the people" and as Bakhtin's attempt to "remind his fellow countrymen what Revolution still could mean" ("Bakhtin" 17). Importantly, however, this reading (though Holquist himself does not draw this conclusion) potentially makes the Rabelais book less a celebration and glorification of revolutionary success than a sort of elegy to a revolution that has failed. Bakhtin's consistent emphasis on the revolutionary power of popular culture and dialogic language may thus represent less a naively optimistic faith in such power than a desperate (and valuable) attempt somehow to keep hope alive amid the terrors of Stalinism.

Bakhtin, in any case, must have been perfectly well aware of the authorized nature of the medieval carnival. After all, his interest in the carnival was far from unprecedented in the context of the Soviet thirties in which the Rabelais book was conceived. As early as 1931 Anatoly Lunacharsky anticipated Bakhtin by launching a project for the study of the history of satire by pointing out the importance of the institution of the carnival to the development of satirical genres. But Lunacharsky anticipated critics like Eagleton by noting that the carnival merely acted as a sort of safety valve that would allow for the release of social tensions that might otherwise lead to genuine subversion. Given Lunacharsky's prominence as the Minister of Enlightenment in the new Soviet regime, Bakhtin would likely have been aware of his comments on the carnival, though Lunacharsky is not actually referenced in the Rabelais book.[5] Clark and Holquist thus suggest that Bakhtin probably read Lunacharsky's published comments on carnival and that this reading "could account for the appearance of the word 'carnival' in his [Bakhtin's] own work" (313). Most readings of Bakhtin's figuration of the carnival have resembled Holquist's conclusion that carnival for Bakhtin is "not only not an impediment to revolutionary change, it is revolution itself" (Prologue xviii). On the other hand, if one reads Bakhtin's discussion of the revolutionary potential of the carnival as a commentary on the progress of modern Soviet history, then his use of the carnival as a metaphor for revolution is consistent with Lunacharsky's comments. It is also precisely appropriate. In the medieval carnival, oppressive conditions were momentarily relieved by an outburst of seemingly transgressive energies, followed by a restoration of the normal order. In the Soviet Union, the oppressive tsarist past was interrupted by the emancipatory excitement of the postrevolutionary 1920s, only to see oppression restored under the rule of Stalin. Bakhtin's treatment of the carnival thus becomes not a naively optimistic paean to the power of revolution, but a reminder of just how difficult revolutionary change can be.

Within the dialogic complexity of Bakhtin's writing, then, medieval Catholicism stands in both for the tsarist past that was disrupted by the Bolshevik Revolution and for the Stalinist aftermath in which the emancipatory hopes that accompanied the Revolution were crushed. Similarly, the carnival represents aspects of both potential resistance to Stalinism and Stalinism itself. This potential doubleness in Bakhtin's use of the carnival metaphor is perhaps indicated in his insistence in both *Rabelais and His World* and *Problems of Dostoevsky's Poetics* on ambivalence as a central characteristic of carnivalesque imagery. This ambivalence can clearly be taken to include the relationship between Catholic authority and the medieval carnival: far from existing in polar opposition, the Church and the carnival in fact work in close complicity. But the same can be said for the relationship between the carnival and Stalinism. Gardiner points out that Stalin himself employed a number of openly carnivalesque strategies, a fact that for Gardiner compromises Bakhtin's use of the carnival as an antiStalinist metaphor. But, if one reads this metaphor as double-voiced, then Stalin's carnivalism actually reinforces Bakhtin's complex use of the carnival as an image of both liberation and oppression.

Conventional readings of Bakhtin's figuration of the carnival merely as a metaphor for revolution and emancipation thus encompass only one side of carnivalesque ambivalence. Such readings, in fact, rely largely on a notion similar to what Michel Foucault has called the "repressive hypothesis" in relation to the work of Sigmund Freud on sexuality and society.[6] Freud's various comments on the inherent conflict between the desires of individuals and the demands of society suggest that human sexual desire arises from natural instinctive impulses and that the orderly conduct of civilization requires that these impulses be repressed, then sublimated into socially productive areas like politics, science, or art. Following Freud's lead, thinkers like Georges Bataille, Herbert Marcuse, and Norman O. Brown have in their various ways figured sexuality as a locus of inherently transgressive energies, regarding the attainment of sexual liberation as an important step toward a more general freedom from social and political repression. Indeed, this Freudian "repressive hypothesis" seems to have been accepted as almost axiomatic in most modern analyses of the role of sexuality in society. On the other hand, Foucault mounts a very influential challenge to this notion. Foucault argues, *pace* Freud, that modern society seeks not to repress or even to extirpate sexuality, but instead to administer it and turn sexual energies to its own advantage. In short, sexuality does not necessarily stand in direct opposition to official power and may in fact directly support it: "Pleasure and power do not cancel or turn back against one another; they seek out, overlap, and reinforce one another" (*History* 48).

For Foucault, sexuality is not so much a matter of natural instinctive impulses as of socially and discursively conditioned responses. He describes sexuality as "an especially dense transfer point for relations of power" (*History* 103). In particular, sexuality functions as a focal point for an entire array of practices through which modern society has attempted to constitute the individual as a subject of administrative control. Psychoanalysis itself is one of these practices, and Foucault especially argues that the psychoanalytic project of categorizing certain sexual practices as normal and others as deviant contributes to general strategies for the manipulation of individual behavior in modern society. Thus society does not seek to eliminate even "deviant" or marginal sexual behaviors; on the contrary it is in the interest of society to assure that such behaviors continue in order to provide negative models against which to define proper conduct. For Foucault, then, sexuality can be a tool of official power rather than being inherently transgressive, just as the carnival for Bakhtin can be an image of oppression as well as liberation.

Morson and Emerson, like most other readers of Bakhtin, apparently accept the "Freudian" interpretation of *Rabelais and His World*, but in order to do so they are forced to argue that the emphasis on the disruptive and transgressive aspects of carnivalesque imagery in this book differs substantially from the tone of Bakhtin's other texts, including the related chapter on carnival and Menippean satire in *Problems of Dostoevsky's Poetics*. Morson and Emerson thus conclude that the attitude shown in the Rabelais book represents a temporary phase through which Bakhtin quickly passed. This point is a crucial one: the book on Rabelais is clearly the single work that did the most initially to popularize Bakhtin's ideas in the West, and if the book is inconsistent with Bakhtin's other work the ensuing widely held critical picture of Bakhtin as a thinker of wildly subversive carnivalesque emancipation probably represents a distortion of the real emphases of Bakhtin's career. However, if *Rabelais and His World* in fact indicates the difficulty of revolutionary change, then the treatment of carnival in the book is much more consistent with Bakhtin's far more somber and restrained thoughts elsewhere, as in the discussion of carnival in *Problems of Dostoevsky's Poetics*.

There is, of course, no reason why we should necessarily expect Bakhtin's long and diverse career to remain entirely consistent. Indeed, there is no question that the tone and emphasis of *Rabelais and His World* are quite different from those of, say, *Problems of Dostoevsky's Poetics*. We would suggest, however, that these very real differences can to a large extent be attributed to differences between Dostoevsky and Rabelais themselves. It is our belief that Bakhtin's own highly dialogic critical practice was such that he often adapted his voice to fit the material at hand, allowing his style in the Dostoevsky book to be influenced by Dostoevsky's own, and likewise for the Rabelais book. In this way, Bakhtin lets the voices of Dostoevsky and Rabelais sound in his own texts, thus avoiding a monological and univocal appropriation of their work for his own purposes. Granted, Morson and Emerson have suggested in another context that viewing Bakhtin's writings as instantiations of his theories represents a "suspiciously anachronistic" projection of contemporary American critical practice onto Bakhtin's Russian work of decades before (110-111).[7] But it is not inappropriate to see Bakhtin as enacting his theories in his writings, especially as such a strategy would be so consistent with the nature of those theories.

In fact, Morson and Emerson themselves often read Bakhtin this way. For example, noting that Bakhtin's earlier philosophical writings can be "turgidly polemical," they argue that Bakhtin in *Rabelais and His World* "strives for the effervescent critical apostrophe" (90). Indeed, their argument that the Rabelais book is something of an aberration in Bakhtin's career rests largely on the fact that Bakhtin's style and tone change dramatically in this work, moving toward "Rabelaisian excess and the ecstatic" (91). They go on to note that in the Rabelais book "[t]he claims Bakhtin offers for carnival laughter are themselves extravagant and 'Rabelaisian'" (93). Indeed, Bakhtin's rhetoric in the Rabelais book is highly Rabelaisian, tending toward hyperbole and expressions of greatness in size and scope. The book begins, for example, with the categorical statement, "Of all great writers in world literature, Rabelais is the least popular, the least understood and appreciated" (1). Similarly, Bakhtin insists that the "size and importance" of the medieval culture of laughter "were immense," and so on (4). Favorite adjectives throughout the book include "powerful," "profound," "acute," "extreme," "mighty," and "great."

Among other things, the Rabelaisian character of *Rabelais and His World* implies that many of Bakhtin's comments about texts like *Gargantua and Pantagruel* pertain to Bakhtin's book as well. We should, for example, pay careful attention to Bakhtin's numerous suggestions that Rabelais's writing must be carefully perused for suggested meanings that go well beyond the literal. The difficulty that he cites in relation to Rabelais's work, for example, arises largely because "it contains a great number of allusions, which were often understood only by his contemporaries and sometimes by his closest friends alone" (110). The complexity of signification in Rabelais goes beyond allegory as well, and Bakhtin warns against simplistic "historic-allegorical" (i.e., Aesopian?) methods of reading involving lists of "keys" explaining the meaning of various images in Rabelais's texts. Bakhtin even goes so far as to end the book with a potentially important reminder that his reading of Rabelais's work is relevant not just to medieval Europe, but also "to other ages," presumably including Bakhtin's own (474).[8]

Kinser, in fact, argues that Bakhtin's real theme in *Rabelais and His World* concerns not Rabelais's use of the folkloric tradition as a weapon against authority so much as Rabelais's signifying practice, which involves a complex "systematization of images" and an "encouragement of oblique readings of text" (257). In particular, Kinser argues that Bakhtin's reading of Rabelais reveals a subversive potential of literature that lies not in populist content but in literary style. Bakhtin thus shows "fiction's capacity—and hence also criticism's capacity, in dealing with such fiction—for bewildering recursive communication (who is the author? where is the reader?) and bitingly ambivalent polysemy (how does a text refer, coordinate, mean?)" 258). For Kinser, then, Bakhtin uses Rabelais to make points not only about both Rabelais and Stalinism, but also about the relationship between written texts and historical contexts in general.

Clearly, the capability for "recursive communication" and "ambivalent polysemy" that Bakhtin locates in Rabelais resides in Bakhtin's own texts as well. These texts, in fact, are informed by an almost astounding rhetorical complexity: rather than conventional discursive statements, Bakhtin's writing involves elaborate dialogues among Bakhtin, his readers (including the Stalinist censors), and the subject matter at hand. In short, Bakhtin's texts enact the complex interactive structure that he attributes to the process of linguistic communication as a whole. In the essay "The Problem of the Text," Bakhtin argues that both the speaker and the addressee play a constitutive role in the formulation of any utterance. But he also insists that an "invisibly present" third party, which he labels the "superaddressee," plays such a role because all utterances are spoken or written with the imagined response of this listener in mind. Bakhtin characterizes this addressee as an ideal listener "whose absolutely just responsive understanding is presumed, either in some metaphysical distance or in distant historical time" (*Speech* 126). He offers a number of potential examples of superaddressees, including God, absolute truth, the court of dispassionate human conscience, the people, the court of history, and science. These examples tend to have positive connotations, and Morson and Emerson interpret this passage as one of Bakhtin's "few openly theological notes." Interestingly, however, all of these representations of the superaddressee carry resonances that one might associate with Stalinism: "God" suggests the religious aura that Stalin sought to create around his regime, "absolute truth" suggests the absolutism of Stalin's rule, the legal implications "court" references suggest official power, and both "the people" and "science" are keywords in Stalinist rhetoric. One might then suggest that Stalin and his successors constitute a central superaddressee in Bakhtin's Soviet context. In any case, it is certainly true that a speaker or writer in Stalinist Russia needed to be aware of the potential reactions to his utterances by Stalin, the censors, and the police.

Given this complexity, it clearly makes no sense to attempt to determine the "real" meaning of Bakhtin's texts or to draw general conclusions about the implications of Bakhtin's theories for our reading of literature: that meaning and those implications do not exist apart from a dynamic interaction with a variety of other texts and contexts, including that of the reader. Bakhtin's meaning does not belong to him alone, but also to all of those who would read his work and about whom he writes. One cannot, for example, come to an authoritative conclusion concerning the "message" of *Rabelais and His World* with regard to the subversive potential of carnivalesque literature or the political potential of revolution. One can, however, place Bakhtin's book in dialogue with other texts that treat similar issues. These "texts" might include the writings of Rabelais himself, the Stalinist ideology that is so clearly a factor in Bakhtin's reading of Rabelais, and any works that a critic might wish to illuminate via that reading.

Bakhtin's key notion of dialogism has most frequently been employed by Western critics as a reminder of the inherent richness of language and of the inevitable multiplicity of meaning, yet critics have consistently paid too little attention to the implications of this richness and multiplicity for our understanding of Bakhtin's own writing. Moreover, it should be emphasized that readings of dialogism as an expression of linguistic multiplicity cannot be separated from

Bakhtin's Stalinist context, in which any such antiauthoritarian visions of language have specific political implications that should not be ignored. Indeed, one can find potential critiques of Stalinism not just in Bakhtin's description of medieval Catholicism in *Rabelais and His World*, but also in a great deal of his commentary on literature, language, and culture. Clark and Holquist, for example, note that Bakhtin's continual emphasis on linguistic energy and diversity had special resonances in a Stalinist context that was characterized by official attempts to limit and control language:

The official language had become homogenized and dominated all aspects of public life. Most literature and literary scholarship were mere subfunctions of the official rhetoric and myths. Official pronouncements were absolutely authoritative and final. (267)

That Bakhtin's general emphasis on openness, change, and multiplicity runs directly counter to the ideology of Stalinism should be obvious. Moreover, close reading frequently reveals potential subtle commentary on Stalinism even in some of the most technical aspects of Bakhtin's writing on literature and language. For example, in his discussion of what he sees as two different lines of "stylistic development" in the history of the novel, Bakhtin associates the "First Line" novel with attempts to suppress heteroglossia and to establish a unified and monological literary voice. The "Second Line" novel, on the other hand, openly embraces heteroglossia and draws its most important energies directly from the diversity of styles, discourses, and ideologies that inform society as a whole. This "stylistic" distinction—like all of Bakhtin's distinctions—is not purely formal, but implies specific ideological differences as well. And these differences are clearly relevant to Bakhtin's Stalinist context. Novels of the First Line, Bakhtin argues, "approach heteroglossia from above." Novels of the Second Line, on the other hand, "approach heteroglossia from below: out of the heteroglot depths they rise to the highest spheres of literary language and overwhelm them" (*Dialogic* 400).

Second Line novels, in short, enact a sort of literary revolution against pretentiousness and formal sterility: the resemblance to Bakhtin's later description of the Rabelaisian carnival is unmistakable. Further, if the Second Line novel functions as a sort of literary reenactment of proletarian revolution, the First Line novel functions as a sort of counterrevolutionary force that operates in a way similar to the official medieval culture that Bakhtin would describe in the Rabelais book. The appropriation of heteroglossia by the imperial voice of the First Line novel is also suspiciously similar to the drive toward industrialization in the cities and collectivization on the farms that characterized Stalin's first Five-Year Plan (1929-1932), an attempt to transform society by government edict that has frequently been described as a "revolution from above."

Some of Bakhtin's most seemingly esoteric comments on literature can be found in the essay "Forms of Time and Chronotope in the Novel," yet even here one can find a number of potential references to Stalin and Stalinism. For example, there is clearly a potential subversive commentary on the Stalinist cult of the family in Bakhtin's comments on the fusion of the family and the state in classical Rome, where "religious cults of the family or clan . . . function as a direct extension of the cults of the state." Meanwhile, for Bakhtin this cult of the family results in a situation where "the national ideal is represented by ancestors," suggesting a mode of hero worship that is suspiciously similar to the glorification of Stalin, which frequently involved comparisons to forerunners like Ivan the Terrible, Peter the Great, and Lenin (*Dialogic* 137). There is also a potential critique of the Stalin personality cult in Bakhtin's comments on the Rabelaisian hero in this essay. Bakhtin insists that the folkloric Rabelaisian giants Gargantua and Pantagruel remain fundamentally human despite their many fantastic aspects. "The great man in Rabelais is profoundly democratic. In no sense is he opposed to the mass, as something out of the ordinary, as a man of another species. On the contrary, he is made of the same human stuff as are all other men." Moreover, Bakhtin specifically contrasts Rabelais's depiction of heroism with "all other heroisms, which oppose the hero to the mass of other men as something out of the ordinary" (*Dialogic* 241).

Bakhtin's commentary on the heroicization of Stalin (and the association of Stalin with predecessors like Ivan the Terrible and Peter the Great) merges with his association of Stalin with the carnival in his discussion in *Rabelais and His World* of Ivan as a carnivalesque figure who opposed "Russian feudal sanctimonious traditions" (270). Bakhtin even figures the *oprichina* (Ivan's special police and bodyguard, forerunners of Stalin's NKVD) as a carnivalesque force. But Ivan and his *oprichina* are hardly plausible as figures of emancipatory opposition to official power, and their association with the carnival indicates the problematic nature of the carnival as an image. Meanwhile, Bakhtin immediately follows with an equally problematic presentation of Peter as a figure of carnival, claiming that under Peter "the jingling of the jester's bells almost entirely drowned the sound of church bells" (270-71). For Bakhtin, again, carnival is often associated not with liberation but with the most daunting forms of official Russian power.

In their discussion of Bakhtin's references to Ivan the Terrible in *Rabelais and His World*, Morson and Emerson conclude that it is difficult to tell whether Bakhtin is parodying Stalin's own idealization of Ivan or whether he is "providing us with a counteridealization of his own" (447-8). In the same way, many of Bakhtin's specific statements about literature, read using straightforward monological methods of interpretation, seem dogmatic and simplistic. But such statements can also be read as parodies of or counters to the statements of other critics and theorists—and of the official representatives of the Stalinist government. For example, Bakhtin has often been faulted for his seemingly stubborn insistence on the generic superiority of the novel to poetry and drama as a site of dialogic energy. Indeed, Bakhtin frequently makes statements that depict both poetry and drama as the unitary and monological representations of the consciousness of their authors, as opposed to the novel, which is able to reflect multiple points of view in a single work. In *Problems of Dostoevsky's Poetics*, for example, Bakhtin responds to Lunacharsky's suggestion that the plays of Shakespeare are polyphonic by insisting that drama can *never* be polyphonic (*Problems* 34).

This dismissal of drama seems absolute. It has, for example, provoked Jennifer Wise to defend the genre against Bakhtin's characterization of it. Wise suggests that Bakhtin's emphasis on the contemporaneity of the novel (as opposed to the irreducible anteriority of the epic) derives directly from Goethe's and Schiller's 1797 essay (published in 1827) "On Epic and Dramatic Poetry." In this essay, Goethe and Schiller contrast the strong sense of current action in drama with the epic sense that all action is occurring in the past. In particular, they suggest that the drama is informed by "progressive" motifs (motifs leading to the furthering of action and plot development), while the epic relies principally on "regressive" motifs that retard action and slow the plot. Wise argues that Bakhtin's contrast between the novel and the epic is largely a reinscription of Goethe's contrast between drama and the epic.[9]

Indeed, apparently incensed by Bakhtin's privileging of the novel over drama, Wise virtually accuses Bakhtin of plagiarizing this distinction from Goethe, referring to Bakhtin's essay "Epic and Novel" as a "generically purged version" of Goethe's essay which has "effaced all traces of the dramatic accents so definitive of Goethe's original discourse" (16).

Wise does not mention, however, that Bakhtin specifically cites Goethe and Schiller as a source of his characterization of the epic (*Dialogic* 13). Indeed, Bakhtin's appropriation of the argument of Goethe and Schiller is an exemplary case of the reaccentuation of the words of others that Bakhtin's sees as central to all language use. Further, such statements must be read in their own dialogic context. For one thing, the discussion of drama in *Problems of Dostoevsky's Poetics* is part of a direct dialogue with Lunacharsky and other critics. Moreover, while it is true that Bakhtin often seems unfairly to dismiss the dialogic potential of drama (and poetry) it is also true that Bakhtin's apotheosis of the novel is part of a complex rhetorical strategy that is designed to counter a centuries-old critical tendency to consider the novel as an inferior or even subliterary genre. Indeed, Goethe himself has quite frequently been depicted as considering the novel inferior to drama or to lyric poetry.[10]   Finally, Bakhtin's seemingly cavalier dismissal of the polyphonic potential of drama must be viewed in light of his suggestions elsewhere that essentially any genre can be infused with the spirit of dialogism and therefore "novelized."

Bakhtin conducts a similar dialogue with the critical history of poetry when he declares in the important essay "Discourse in the Novel" that "the language of the poetic genre is a unitary and singular Ptolemaic world outside of which nothing else exists and nothing else is needed" (*Dialogic* 286). But the dismissal of poetry in "Discourse in the Novel" follows an extensive section in which Bakhtin reviews the work of previous critics who have dismissed the novel as aesthetically inferior to poetry and drama. Bakhtin specifically cites the work of critics like Viktor Vinogradov and Gustav Shpet, who suggest that artistic prose is not poetic, but purely rhetorical, and thus "utterly denies the novel any aesthetic significance" (*Dialogic* 268). Bakhtin then proceeds to respond by denying any dialogic significance to poetry, opening himself to charges that he unwittingly reproduces in reverse the error he attributes to Shpet, Vinogradov, and other critics. But such a charge would miss the point of Bakhtin's rhetorical strategy entirely. Given Bakhtin's emphasis on the inherent dialogism involved in the appropriation of the words of others, it seems likely that he echoes Shpet's stance intentionally.   Indeed, Bakhtin's response to Shpet can be seen as a form of what Bakhtin calls the "hidden polemic," in which

the author's discourse is directed toward its own referential object, as in any other discourse, but at the same time every statement about the object is constructed in such a way that, apart from its referential meaning, a polemical blow is struck at the other's discourse on the same theme, at the other's statement about the same object. (*Problems* 195)

Bakhtin's subsequent apotheosis of the novel can thus be read not only as a response to such critics, but as a parody of their narrow-minded rejection of the novel. In the same way, Bakhtin's sweeping rejection of poetry can be read as a parody of the totalizing proclamations and condemnations of Stalinism. Indeed, Bakhtin (who so often praises the power of parody) himself writes quite frequently in a parodic mode, so that one must be especially careful to avoid jumping to conclusions concerning the implications of his work.[11]

Philosophically, dialogism implies a fundamental rejection of the "either-or" logic of the Aristotelian tradition in favor of a richly multiple reconceptualization of the notion of truth itself. This new notion of truth implies, among other things, that one should avoid coming to final conclusions about Bakhtin's work: faced with a choice of competing interpretations we must always choose both, as difficult and unsatisfying as that might be to our monological habits of thought. In the debate over the novel, for example, the point is not to decide between Shpet's dismissal of the novel and Bakhtin's apotheosis of it. Rather, the confrontation between Shpet and Bakhtin should make us aware that the novel can be seen in varying ways depending on one's own project and position. Importantly, however, the complexity of Bakhtin's notion of dialogue goes well beyond a confrontation between the voices of individuals: the individuals themselves are always already dialogized. For Bakhtin, the self develops through an ongoing dialogue with others and with the external world, consistent with his vision of subjectivity as a boundary phenomenon between different consciousnesses, as something that arises not prior to intersubjective exchange but as a dynamic product of that ongoing exchange.

But if the subject is the product of dialogue, then that subject should itself be dialogic, an implication highly consistent with Russian experience. James Billington, for example, suggests that "the kind of debate that is usually conducted *between* individuals in the West often rages even more acutely within individuals in Russia" (ix). This vision of the dialogic self often recurs in Bakhtin's work, though it is probably presented most explicitly by V. N. Voloshinov in the "disputed" texts *Marxism and the Philosophy of Language* and *Freudianism*. In the latter, an extended neoMarxist polemic against Freudian psychoanalysis, Voloshinov describes the Freudian psyche as a sort of formalist self-contained entity, and opposes to that notion a model in which subjectivity is generated through social experiences with language.[12] Voloshinov dispenses with Freud's vision of psychological depth, replacing the notion of separate conscious and unconscious minds with that of a continuum of "official" and "unofficial" consciousnesses, both operating according to similar linguistic principles. Official consciousness is reflected in outward speech, while unofficial consciousness expresses itself through "inner speech," which is still a thoroughly social phenomenon:

Every utterance is *the product of the interaction between speakers* and the product of the broader context of the whole complex *social situation* in which the utterance emerges. . . . Nothing changes at all if, instead of outward speech, we are dealing with inner speech. Inner speech, too, assumes a listener and is oriented in its constitution toward that listener. (*Freudianism* 79)[13]

This dialogic model of selfhood thus posits a model in which speech is irreducibly social and subjectivity is meaningless apart from intersubjectivity: "Consciousness becomes consciousness only once it has been filled with ideological (semiotic) content, consequently, only in the process of social interaction" (*Marxism* 11). The psyche is thus not a *thing* that exists internally in an individual so much as an *event* that occurs in the process of intersubjective relations: "By its very existential nature, the subjective psyche is to be localized somewhere between the organism and the outside world, on the *borderline* separating these two spheres of reality" (*Marxism* 26).

   This vision of subjectivity as a social phenomenon is often reflected in Bakhtin's discussions of characterization in the novel, especially in *Problems of Dostoevsky's Poetics*. According to Bakhtin, in a sense Dostoevsky's characters have virtually no psychological depth, despite Dostoevsky's reputation as a psychological novelist.[14] Rather than attempt to probe the psychological depths of his characters, Dostoevsky stays on the surface, showing us the self-conscious images of his characters as they believe others perceive them externally. With a Dostoevsky character, "[w]e see not who he is, but *how* he is conscious of himself; our act of artistic visualization occurs not before the reality of the hero, but before a pure function of his awareness of that reality" (*Problems* 49). What we see of any Dostoevsky character is determined at least partially by the Other: Dostoevsky does not create and describe fully formed and finalized characters; instead, he lets those characters evolve in dialogue with their author and with the other characters. Dostoevsky's novels are thus "polyphonic" because they are so fundamentally informed by dialogues among multiple consciousnesses.

   In *Problems of Dostoevsky's Poetics* Bakhtin discusses this mode of characterization as specific to Dostoevsky, but he argues elsewhere that one of the key differences between the epic and the novel as genres lies in the way epic characters are unified and whole, as

opposed to the relatively unstable and provisional identities of the
characters in novels. He suggests that "[t]he epic wholeness of an
individual disintegrates in a novel" and goes on to argue that in the
novel "[a] crucial tension develops between the external and the
internal man, and as a result the subjectivity of the individual
becomes an object of experimentation and representation" (*Dialogic*
37). Bakhtin envisions the individual in the novel (and in the social
world) not as a fixed identity, but as an ongoing process of
development: "As long as a person is alive he lives by the fact that he
is not yet finalized, that he has not yet uttered his ultimate word"
(*Problems* 59).

Bakhtin's emphasis on intersubjectivity points toward a communal
vision of selfhood that potentially serves as a counter to the
fragmented and alienated subject of capitalist society. At the same
time, Bakhtin's dialogic subject bears many resemblances to the split
subject of capitalism. Further, the dynamic and evolutionary quality
of the self in Bakhtin's model can potentially lead to an unstable sense
of self, especially if the individual has a problematic relation to
history. Indeed, Bakhtin's emphasis on the dynamic nature of the
individual subject links up with the intense concern with historical
process that informs all of his writing, a concern that again has special
connotations in Bakhtin's Russian context. In his study (strongly
influenced by Bakhtin) of the fiction of Dostoevsky, Holquist
emphasizes the importance of history in the writings of Dostoevsky
and other nineteenth-century Russian authors. In particular, Holquist
argues that the fragile and unstable identities of Dostoevsky's
characters reflect an uncertain sense of cultural identity in nineteenth-
century Russia as a whole. Despite the strength of nineteenth-century
Russian literature, Holquist suggests that "doubts about the existence
of a national literature, not pious affirmations of Russian culture,
carried the day in the early nineteenth century" (*Dostoevsky* 13). He
then illustrates this point with reference to the work of nineteenth-
century thinker Pyotr Chaadaev, noting that Chaadaev's work

cut to the heart of all doubts about the history of particular Russian
institutions, political as well as cultural, by declaring, in effect, the
Russians had no history at all: "Historical experience does not exist for
us. Generations and ages have passed without benefit to us. With
regard to us it is as if the general law of mankind had been suspended.
. . .." He goes on to speak of the Russians as "being somehow out of
time." (14)

Holquist further observes that the attempts of Dostoevsky's characters to employ narrative as a means to develop a viable sense of self parallel the broader nineteenth-century Russian project of developing historical narratives to supply a viable sense of national identity. Indeed, for Holquist literature in general functions as a particularly important site for attempts to establish a stable Russian cultural identity in the nineteenth century. As a result, "history was more often than not in Russia equated with literary history" (28). Meanwhile, though writers like Derzhavin and Karamzin had struggled to find a Russian literary voice, the special exigencies of Russian history left early-nineteenth-century writers like Pushkin and Gogol with virtually no native Russian literary tradition upon which to draw. Such writers were thus forced to attempt to create their own traditions and conventions, a fact that does much to explain the particularly innovative and experimental quality of much nineteenth-century Russian literature.

The Russian sense of being outside history that Holquist cites can be attributed at least partially to the results of the attempts of Peter the Great a century earlier to transform his essentially medieval Russia along lines suggested by the Western Enlightenment. Peter's project did in fact bring great changes to Russian society, though Russia's participation in the cultural and political life of Europe remained marginal and secondary at best. Meanwhile, the radical rupture in the flow of Russian history effected during Peter's reign separated Russians from their own native cultural and political traditions as well, eventually contributing to the nineteenth-century sense of historical estrangement described by Holquist. During the course of the nineteenth century, however, writers like Pushkin, Gogol, Dostoevsky, Lermontov, and Turgenev had begun to establish a Russian literary tradition that was formidable indeed, and this tradition became even more firmly installed with the work of Silver Age writers like Chekhov, Gorky, Bely, Bunin, and Mayakovsky in the late nineteenth and early twentieth centuries.

This high level of literary achievement was not, however, accompanied by social or political stability, and by 1917 increasing tensions had erupted in the Bolshevik Revolution, thus instituting a second rupture in Russian history. Meanwhile, subsequent events in the twentieth century did little to stabilize the already unsteady Russian sense of national and personal identity. The flurry of artistic activity in the postrevolutionary 1920s may have offered the potential of developing a new cultural identity appropriate to life in the new Soviet state, but this potential was not to be realized. The Stalinist years then effected still another violent upset in the flow of Russian

history. Official intrusions into the world of art and literature during
this period, including the installation of socialist realism as the only
sanctioned mode of artistic production, dramatically disrupted the
century-old attempt to establish a Russian cultural identity through
literature and art. Meanwhile, history itself became a prime target of
Stalinist domination; the overt revisionism of official versions of
history during the Stalinist years posed a serious challenge to the value
of genuine human experience, while official attempts to focus
attention on the coming radiant future represented a devaluation not
only of the present, but of the past as well. It is not surprising, then,
that much of the most important Russian art and literature during the
Stalinist years was produced by exiles and émigrés living outside the
boundaries of the Soviet Union. Nor is it surprising that one of the
most important movements in postStalinist Russian literature
(Solzhenitsyn is exemplary here) involved an attempt to recover the
"true" history of the Stalinist period and to reestablish connections
with the Russian cultural identity that had begun to be established in
the nineteenth century.

Bakhtin's work—much of which he himself describes as an attempt
to create an "historical poetics"—clearly participates in the long-time
Russian attempt to establish a meaningful connection with history and
a consequent sense of a stable cultural identity. One might note, for
example, how much of his discussion of the novel as genre is related
to the ability of that genre to participate in the ongoing process of
historical change. Bakhtin's work is in this sense directly descended
from the projects of nineteenth-century Russian writers like
Dostoevsky. At the same time, Bakhtin's focus on history must be
understood within its Stalinist context. It can, in fact, be read largely
as a subtly subversive response to the distinct historical vision that was
so central to the ideology of Stalinism, with its dual apotheosis of the
possibility of radical revolutionary change and of eventual utopian
historical stasis.

Bakhtin's work as a whole is consistently skeptical of utopianism,
and one can read this skepticism as a subtle challenge to the official
utopian goals of Stalinism. Even Bakhtin's presentation of the
medieval carnival in *Rabelais and His World*—which most Western
readers have viewed as highly utopian—can be read as a critique of
utopianism. For example, the discussion of excremental imagery in
Rabelais and His World is in fact closely related to Bakhtin's intense
concern with history. Bakhtin notes traditional attempts to view the
body as a seamless classical whole by denying excremental and other
processes that emphasize the dynamic interaction between body and
world; he then suggests that these attempts represent a denial of

history. But the "unfinished and open body (dying, bringing forth and being born) is not separated from the world by clearly defined boundaries; it is blended with the world, with animals, with objects" (*Rabelais* 26-7). Moreover, the dynamic nature of this blending and of the carnivalesque representation of body functions thrusts the subject directly into the contemporaneous flow of history: "The material bodily lower stratum and the entire system of degradation, turnovers, and travesties presented this essential relation to time and to social and historical transformation" (81). In short, the transfer of physical material from the interior of the body into the outside world (and vice versa) provides a graphic reminder that human beings are part of that world and undermines the Kantian duality of subject and object that underlies conventional Western approaches to the relationship between individuals and their surroundings. Moreover, such physical processes also provide reminders that human beings are biological creatures who live (and die) in time.[15]

In *Rabelais and His World* Bakhtin seems to depict the carnival as a kind of time-out from history, a suspension of the normal flow of events in which the strange and marvelous temporarily become the rule of the day. It is largely for this reason that Morson and Emerson see the book as an aberration in Bakhtin's career—the bulk of his work is concerned with placing humanity in time and history, while the Rabelais book involves a removal, however momentary, from history. In short, for Morson and Emerson the Rabelais book is to Bakhtin's career very much what the carnival itself is to history—a sudden disruption in the ordinary course of affairs. But for Bakhtin the disjunctive nature of time in the Rabelaisian carnival actually shows an engagement with history, because it corresponds to an intense sense of cultural crisis in Rabelais's early Renaissance historical context. Moreover, if one reads Bakhtin's carnival as a metaphor not just for revolution, but also for Stalin's petrification of the revolutionary energies of Bolshevism, then the depiction of the carnival in *Rabelais and His World* as ahistorical potentially becomes a critical commentary on Stalin's derailing of the historical process in the attempt to maintain his power at all costs.

Bakhtin's most direct commentaries on the historical process occur in the essay on the "chronotope"—literally the sense of time and space (and their relation) that informs a literary work. Like all of Bakhtin's key terms, the chronotope is not merely a formal literary device but a reflection of deep-seated attitudes in the society at large. For Bakhtin the most fundamental characteristic of a society is the way it thinks about space and time, and this characteristic is inevitably reflected in one way or another in that society's literature. Moreover,

Bakhtin's emphasis on the chronotope is closely related to his emphasis on genre: "The chronotope in literature has an intrinsic *generic* significance. It can even be said that it is precisely the chronotope that defines genre and generic distinctions" (*Dialogic* 84-5). In particular, Bakhtin notes that the chronotope is of obvious importance to narrative structure. Chronotopes are, he argues, "the organizing centers for the fundamental narrative events of the novel. The chronotope is the place where the knots of narrative are tied and untied" (*Dialogic* 250).

As with so many elements of his thought, Bakhtin's emphasis on the chronotope has special resonances within his Stalinist context. For one thing, Bakhtin's essay enacts a number of dialogues with distinctive chronotope of Stalinism, which was fundamentally informed by claims that the current regime was in the process of completing the radical transformation of Russian society initiated by the 1917 Revolution. Of course, revolution itself can be read as an attempt to short-circuit the historical process, and Bakhtin quite often (in the chronotope essay and elsewhere) espouses the idea that genuine historical change arises not from sudden revolution, but from long, slow, gradual evolution in "great time." Moreover, there are comments in the chronotope essay that seem especially relevant to the Stalinist project of glorifying the revolutionary past as an image of the radiant future to come. Thus Bakhtin strongly disparages the utopian mode of nostalgia that he describes as "historical inversion," which locates all things good and beautiful in an idealized vision of a golden past. As a result, things that can in fact only be achieved in the future are "portrayed as something out of the *past*" (*Dialogic* 147, Bakhtin's emphasis).

In the realm of literature, Bakhtin's comments on the chronotope have special implications for the officially endorsed Soviet mode of socialist realism, the conventions of which clearly reflected distinctive official attitudes toward space and time in the Stalinist Soviet Union. Clark notes that Soviet novels of the 1930s employed a highly consistent (and distinctive chronotope) that employed a dual focus on idealized visions of the past and the future, thereby deflecting attention from the present, which was far too grim to idealize. She argues that the highly formulaic plot of the socialist realist novel is directly related to the dual task that novel had to perform:

It had to recapitulate the conventional myths for maintaining the Stalinist status quo; second, it had to affirm that future progress toward communism as defined by Lenin is assured under the present leadership. ("Political" 231-2)

Moreover, Clark points out that this dual chronotope is the chronotope of Stalinism itself. On the one hand, the Marxist model of history as an inexorable march toward a future Communist paradise suggests a powerful forward movement. On the other hand, the conservative Stalinist regime consistently sought to justify its power by identifying itself as the direct heir of the mythical time of Lenin and the Revolution. Thus, even the highly authoritarian ideology of Stalinism involves a mixture of chronotopes, albeit a rather mechanical one. Bakhtin himself emphasizes that multiple chronotopes can inform a single work, and that these different chronotopes can in fact interact dialogically. Such mixtures of chronotopes are especially obvious in works that openly incorporate different genres that might themselves typically be characterized by very different chronotopes.

In short, there is for Bakhtin no "correct" or "good" chronotope, just as there is no one proper attitude toward history. As elsewhere, Bakhtin's comments on the chronotope finally serve primarily as reminders that many chronotopes are possible—and that attitudes toward space and time can have powerful political implications. In point of fact, each of Bakhtin's major treatments of literature seemingly describes a very different chronotopic vision. In the Rabelais book, Bakhtin emphasizes the carnival as a temporary and atypical removal from the normal progression of historical time. In *Problems of Dostoevsky's Poetics*, on the other hand, Bakhtin insists on the powerfully dynamic nature of the Dostoevskian text, in which the reader is propelled forward by an intense sense of temporal movement. But this temporal flow is jerky, moving forward discontinuously by starts and stops as one moment of crisis leads unpredictably to another—much like Russian history. Dostoevsky, according to Bakhtin, visualizes history not as a smooth progression, but as a series of stages, each of which is the "cross-section of a single moment" (28). Finally, what we have of Bakhtin's work on Goethe shows still another vision of history and temporality. In Goethe's texts, according to Bakhtin, time flows smoothly and continuously, with events developing gradually and continuously through a series of small and continuous developments. Of all authors, in fact, it is Goethe who for Bakhtin has the most profound sense of history and of the mutual involvement of time and space in human events:

Everything—from an abstract idea to a piece of rock on the bank of a stream—bears the stamp of time, is saturated with time, and assumes its form and meaning in time. Therefore, everything is intensive in Goethe's world; it contains no inanimate, immobile, petrified places, no immutable background that does not participate in action and emergence (in events), no decorations or sets. On the other hand, this time, in all its essential aspects, is localized in concrete space, imprinted on it. In Goethe's world there are no events, plots, or temporal motifs that are not related in an essential way to the particular spatial place of their occurrence. (*Speech* 42)

Of course, there is no reason that Bakhtin need maintain the same attitude toward time and history throughout his long career, a career that spanned historical so momentous that it would be almost stunning were Bakhtin's ideas not to change. Indeed, Bakhtin's own insistence on the historicity of all discourse would imply that his work would necessarily change with time. On the other hand, there is more at stake in Bakhtin's variable statements about history than a mere evolution in his thought. For example, the first version of *Rabelais and His World* was written at about the same time as the work on Goethe and the important essay "Forms of Time and Chronotope in the Novel"—the central expressions of Bakhtin's vision of history as a long, slow process of gradual evolutionary change.

One might wonder, then, what was Bakhtin's "real" attitude toward history during this period, but of course that would be the wrong question to ask. Bakhtin's attitudes as a whole cannot be summarized in themselves, but must be read in relation to the other attitudes with which they place themselves in dialogue. In another of his expressions of the complexity of linguistic communication, Bakhtin insists that the meaning of a given utterance is produced by both speaker and listener, as well as by the "hero" or topic of the given utterance. Thus the historical vision expressed in *Rabelais and His World* is clearly the product not only of Bakhtin, but of his "hero" Rabelais, just as the conceptions of history in *Problems of Dostoevsky's Poetics* and "The *Bildungsroman* and Its Significance in the History of Realism" are greatly impacted by Bakhtin's perception of the attitudes of Dostoevsky and Goethe. In short, the historical visions conveyed by Bakhtin's writings are the dialogic products of Bakhtin's engagement with the authors about whom he writes. At the same time, Stalin and the Stalinist censors should be recognized as participants in these dialogues as well, acting as Bakhtinian superaddressees that force Bakhtin to adopt oblique strategies of expression while providing him with a direct target of subversion.

One can see this rhetorical complexity quite clearly in Bakhtin's theories of the novel. The novel for Bakhtin is a special genre for a variety of reasons, probably the most fundamental of which is its ability to grow and evolve in time, participating in processes of historical change. Rather than functioning according to rigidly defined principles, the novel by its very nature challenges its own principles and thereby remains ever new, ever in touch with contemporary reality. In order to maintain this dynamic adaptive ability, the novel must continually challenge predefined notions of what it should be. It is therefore an inherently antiauthoritarian genre, "a genre that is ever questing, ever examining itself and subjecting its established forms to review. Such, indeed, is the only possibility open to a genre that structures itself in a zone of direct contact with developing reality" (*Dialogic* 39). The novel as a genre is "both critical and self-critical, one fated to revise the fundamental concepts of literariness and poeticalness dominant at the time" (*Dialogic* 10). But Bakhtin's own continual insistence—*pace* the Russian formalists—on the social and political implications of literary discourse provide reminders that these challenges to "literariness and poeticalness" include challenges to broader ideological attitudes as well.

Such challenges have special political significance in a Stalinist context in which any challenge to official authority paradoxically gained significance by virtue of the fact that such challenges were strictly forbidden. Under Stalin "concepts of literariness and poeticalness"—like most other concepts—were a matter not of literary convention or taste but of government edict, and Bakhtin's apotheosis of continual innovation and experimentation in the novel stands in stark contrast to the rigidly defined Stalinist principles like the endorsement of socialist realism. Like his figuration of the medieval carnival, his notion of the multiple meanings inherent in any linguistic utterance, and his vision of the evolving interactive subject, Bakhtin's model of the novel as a multivocal and continually evolving genre cannot be understood apart from his dialogic interaction with a variety of other texts, including the broad cultural text constituted by Bakhtin's historical situation in the Stalinist Soviet Union. This does not, of course, mean that Bakhtin's work cannot be productively used by Western critics to illuminate Western literature. Indeed, such appropriations of Bakhtin are themselves quite consistent with his own insistence that no one person or group has an exclusive proprietary right to any statement or concept. At the same time, the profoundly dialogic nature of Bakhtin's own discourse and the intense embeddedness of Bakhtin's work in its Russian cultural context should be carefully contemplated by any critics who would employ Bakhtin's ideas in any way.

NOTES

1. Clark and Holquist argue that the almost total absence of references to Russian literature in the resultant final version of the Rabelais book can be taken as an oblique suggestion of the increased relevance of his commentary to his Russian context (305).

2. Soviet experimental art of the postrevolutionary period has received increasing critical attention in the West in recent years. On Russian avant-garde art of this period, see the collection edited by Roman and Marquardt. On the relationship between culture and politics during this period, see Fitzpatrick (*The Cultural Front*) and Thomson. On the utopian (and often carnivalesque) aspects of postrevolutionary Russian culture, see Stites.

3. Stites, in fact, specifically cites Bakhtin's thought as representative of this tendency in postrevolutionary Russian society (79).

4. On the other hand, Fitzpatrick points out, "It was an axiom of this approach that conflicts had to end in outright victory for one side and total defeat for the other" (*Cultural* 7). Bakhtin's emphasis on the never-ending nature of dialogic confrontation clearly differs dramatically from this insistent all-or-nothing approach and might, in fact, be seen as a critical comment upon it.

5. Bakhtin and Lunacharsky engaged in at least one direct dialogue. When the first version of the Dostoevsky book was published in 1929, Lunacharsky wrote a generally favorable review of it (now available in English as "Dostoevsky's 'Plurality of Voices'" in the collection of Lunacharsky's essays entitled *On Literature and Art*). Bakhtin responded to that review at some length in the later (1963) version of the Dostoevsky book.

6. Given the negative attitude toward Freud's work (and in particular to the notion of the unconscious mind, on which the repressive hypothesis centrally relies) shown in Voloshinov's *Freudianism*, such readings of Bakhtin are clearly questionable at best. Clark and Holquist, among others, believe that Bakhtin was in fact the author of *Freudianism* and the other "disputed texts" of the Bakhtinian *oeuvre*. We do not find this argument of Bakhtin's authorship convincing, but *Freudianism* is not fundamentally inconsistent with the rest of Bakhtin's writing in its treatment of Freud's model of the psyche.

7. Morson and Emerson here refer to arguments that, in order to dramatize his dialogic notion of authorship, Bakhtin might have avoided signing his name to the "disputed texts" initially attributed to his associates Voloshinov and Medvedev.

8. Just before this concluding sentence, Bakhtin cites three lines from Pushkin's *Boris Godunov* that have to do with the silencing of the voice of the people. See Clark and Holquist (306).

9. Wise lists Goethe as the sole author of the essay, though it was cosigned by Schiller.

10. See Blackall for an extended treatment of Goethe's novels which seeks to demonstrate that Goethe did not consider the genre an inferior form of literature and that Goethe's novels participate in the traditions of the genre in more important ways than has generally been recognized. For example, Goethe himself declared the novel a genre worthy of consideration as serious literature and even of comparison with the drama (Blackall 77-9).

11. For a discussion of the applicability of Bakhtin's work to poetry, see my essay "'A War Between the Mind and Sky.'"

12. Interestingly, Alan Singer points to revisionary readings of Freud such as those performed by Samuel Weber and Leo Bersani in arguing for a view of the Freudian subject as dynamically constituted through the conflict of competing drives. To Singer, this view of Freud is quite compatible with Bakhtin. He argues that both Freud and Bakhtin produce a view of the self that is radically opposed to formalist/idealist models ("Dis-position").

13. The notion of "inner speech" recalls the psycholinguistic theories of Lev Vygotsky. In fact, the models of subjectivity of Vygotsky and of the Bakhtin circle converge at many points. Caryl Emerson outlines some of the similarities between the two thinkers and suggests that Vygotsky's *Thought and Language* "can be read as an important predecessor and perhaps even as clinical underpinning to Bakhtin's philosophy of language" ("Outer" 27).

14. Dostoevsky himself insisted that he was not a psychologist, as Bakhtin notes (*Problems* 62).

15. One could also read Bakhtin's insistence on the continuity of communities through the deaths of individuals as a reminder that Stalin himself was mortal and therefore could not rule forever. For example, there is a clear comment on the Stalin cult in Bakhtin's characterization of this communal sense of historicity as denying the need to "immortalize ones own 'I'" (*Dialogic* 203).

2

Carnival, Dialogism, and Chronotope in the Fiction of Vassily Aksyonov: A Bakhtin Primer

If it is impossible to reach definitive conclusions concerning the interpretation of Bakhtin's work, it is also true that it is quite easy to establish dialogues between Bakhtin and a number of modern Russian writers. Many works of modern Russian literature, for example, recall Bakhtin's concept of dialogism in especially obvious ways. Yury Olesha's *Envy*, published in 1927 and typical of the inventive, unconventional art produced in the Soviet Union in the 1920s, illustrates this phenomenon well. Formally, the text is constructed as a diverse assemblage of letters, memos, inserted tales, and other documents. In addition, this combination of textual materials is accompanied by extensive dialogues among different discourses and worldviews, including a central opposition between art and science. Critics of the text have emphasized that it derives a large part of its energy from the violation of the expectations that readers are likely to bring to it. Robert Maguire, for example, notes that many elements of *Envy* invite readers to approach it as a relatively conventional novel of manners, but that the text then radically undermines such readings (344). T. S. Berczynski goes farther, noting that the book's disparate combination of textual materials shows a "baroque disdain for genre lines," so that the book is a novel "only in the loosest sense" (376). Noting such readings, Victor Peppard points out that the dialogic combination of genres that constitutes *Envy* resembles that of a number of postrevolutionary Russian texts. In addition to Olesha, writers like Shklovsky, Pilnyak, and Zamyatin all produced texts that were literally assembled from a variety of materials, including non-literary ones, such as letters and documents (35). Most importantly, Peppard emphasizes that texts constructed in this way can be usefully approached from the perspective of Bakhtin's theories of dialogism. Indeed, Bakhtin's work is highly relevant to the strong tradition of such "assembled" texts that runs throughout modern Russian literature, ranging from Dostoevsky's *Diary of a Writer* through the textual collages of Alexander Zinoviev.

Vassily Aksyonov's works often involve a similarly diverse array of materials. Moreover, with their overt interrogation of the ideological implications of language, these works clearly enact Bakhtin's idea that "[l]anguage in the novel not only represents, but itself serves as the object of representation" (*Dialogic* 49). In his novella "The Steel Bird" (written in 1965 and published in English in the collection *"The Destruction of Pompeii" and Other Stories*) Aksyonov already shows the ability to mix styles and languages that will become so central to his later work. This story is subtitled "A Tale with Digressions & A Solo for Cornet," indicating the way the basic narrative is punctuated by numerous inserted documents such as doctor's reports, building inspectors' reports, poems, and even "instrumental" sections. This structure clearly involves a mixture of discourses from different disciplines and perspectives, illustrating nicely Bakhtin's argument for the dialogic potential inherent in the novel's ability to incorporate various other genres, including extraliterary ones. Even within a given fragment, the discourse of "The Steel Bird" can be highly dialogic, as when a doctor's report mixes extremely technical medical jargon (Aksyonov was trained as a doctor) with subjective, even poetic observations—the doctor finds his patient's skin "unhappy," his heart "suffering," and his intestines "playful" (117).

"The Steel Bird" depicts the brutal domination of the inhabitants of a Moscow apartment building by this patient, the mysterious Benjamin Popenkov (who later metamorphoses into the steel bird of the title). The steel motif obviously suggests a reading of Popenkov as an emblem of Stalinism and of its possible return within the context of ongoing Soviet oppression. On the other hand, it is also quite possible to read the story as a proSoviet satire of the tendencies of the petty bourgeoisie. Edward Mozejko reviews some of the possible readings of the allegory of the story, noting that in it Popenkov represents "the two most negative aspects of Soviet society: the principle of authoritarian rule, and what is often stigmatized in the

U.S.S.R. as the *petty bourgeoisie* longing for prosperity" (213). Importantly, Mozejko notes that readings of the story as antiSoviet and as antibourgeois are not necessarily contradictory, but that they in fact suggest a "mutually conditioned linkage" between the official Soviet ideology and the bourgeois ideology it so condemned. In short, the story effects a dialogic confrontation between the two ideologies; it criticizes bourgeois tendencies yet undermines the Soviet claim to superiority over those tendencies.

Popenkov, like Stalin, employs language as a central element of his strategies of domination. Popenkov often resorts (especially in moments of stress) to speaking in a strange language that strikes most of those around him as gibberish. For example, mocked by some of his neighbors in a bar, Popenkov leaps to his feet and yells: "Kertl für linker, I knew it, at last! Yes, I am a Steel zhiza, chuiza drong! Aha, we've got . . . fricheki, klocheki kryt, kryt, kryt! In flight—the whistle and claw of a . . . percator!" (*Destruction* 143, Aksyonov's ellipses). Later asked about his strange dialect, Popenkov responds that "I am no ordinary man, and some of my characteristics are even different from those of a bird. That's our language, the language of steel birds" (153). In short, Popenkov's attempts to assert his dominance extend to language itself—not content to use the language of others, he seeks to produce a new and unique language of his own whose structure and meaning he can fully control.

Popenkov's motivation in seeking his own original language becomes especially clear in light of Bakhtin's theories of dialogism. For Bakhtin, no individual or group can maintain a complete domination of language, because meaning in language arises through complex dialogic interactions that go far beyond the intentions of a speaker or author. In particular, all language has been used before and continues to carry the resonances of former use, so that any utterance involves a dialogic mixture of meanings and intentions. For Bakhtin, only the Biblical Adam spoke a language untainted by the speech of others. Henceforth,

Our speech, that is, all our utterances (including creative works), is filled with others' words, varying degrees of otherness or varying degrees of "our-own-ness," varying degrees of awareness and detachment. These words of others carry with them their own expression, their own evaluative tone, which we assimilate, rework, and re-accentuate. (*Speech* 89)

Bakhtin sees language as a powerful political weapon, but it is a weapon that is inherently two-edged—it may serve as a means of oppression, but it functions at the same time as a means of liberation. The dialogic nature of language indicates that there will always be a possibility that opposing voices can arise, even within the most ostensibly authoritarian discourses. Patricia Yaeger emphasizes the importance of Bakhtin for an understanding of the subversive possibilities of language:

Any dominant discourse is inherently flawed, for it can only come into dominance by repressing other discourses . . . Discourse is, then, an arena of permanent struggle in which any language that seems "unitary" is always embattled. (255)

Popenkov's attempt to generate his own original language, then, can be read as an attempt to evade the dialogic nature of all historical languages and to create a discourse within which he can make monological proclamations free of the echoes of the words of others. But his language does indeed remain "embattled," and he is forced continually to resort to Russian to communicate his demands. He speaks strictly in his own language only in the ending monologue after the inhabitants of his building have rebelled against him and moved away, leaving him alone (171). Popenkov thus fails to dominate both his language and his human victims, suggesting a possibility of resistance to the return of Stalinism, especially through language itself.

Popenkov's project recalls Stalin's attempts to manipulate and control language, attempts that are vividly enacted in the "Newspeak" of Orwell's *1984*. Indeed, Popenkov's attempt to dominate language in "The Steel Bird" anticipates the parody of Soviet manipulations of language that underlies much of Aksyonov's later writing. For example, the Soviet penchant for propagandistic sloganeering is a main target of the satire of *The Island of Crimea*. The premise of this book—a sort of "what if" alternative history—is that the Crimea is not a peninsula, but an island, and that its separation from the mainland has allowed the defeated forces of the White Army to retreat there after the Russian Civil War and to maintain their political independence from the Soviet Union. The island of Crimea is a haven for political diversity in which literally dozens of political parties represent a wide variety of ideologies, all of which are tolerated in the island's democratic society. This democratic attitude is shown in the fact that public walls on the island tend to be covered with heteroglossic political graffiti representing the ideas of various factions: "in Crimea every wall was a showcase for democracy" (5). Even Communist slogans are openly permitted, despite the island's antiCommunist stance. But the situation is far different across the way in the Soviet Union. When protagonist Andrei Luchnikov arrives in Moscow he is greeted by a barrage of monological proCommunist signs and banners carrying official Party slogans like *THE SOVIET PEOPLE KNOW – THE PARTY MEANS SUCCESS AND VICTORY* and *GLORY TO OUR COMMUNIST PARTY* (127). Any signs representing opposing ideologies are, of course, strictly prohibited.

Language is, for Aksyonov, one of the central tools with which the Party seeks to enforce its rule and perpetuate its ideology. But, again, language is not so easily dominated. In *Say Cheese!* Aksyonov presents the story (based on his own experiences compiling the literary anthology *Metropol*) of a group of photographers who attempt to assemble and publish an anthology of uncensored and unauthorized photographs. Among other things, *Say Cheese!* achieves dialogic effects through the use of numerous footnotes that comment upon the main text, often in ways that set up interesting dialogues between that text and the notes. One of these notes (while playing with the Soviet penchant for acronyms) includes an homage to the Russian language, which has somehow managed to retain certain subtleties despite decades of Soviet domination:

Truly, Russian can add to its famous acronym GMTF (Great, Mighty, Truthful, and Free) another two letters in parenthesis, GT, that is, Generous and Tolerant. It's incredible how that Cheerful, Casual, and Wandering (CCW) language survives under a regime that bends even photography to its will, won't allow independent publication of one tiny album of pictures. (214)

Similarly, if the Soviets (like Popenkov) have distorted language for their own authoritarian purposes, Aksyonov's work often suggests that marginal groups in society often seek to develop their own distinctive styles of expression as a means of pursuing identities that run counter to those spelled out for them by official authority. Even in his early, less obviously political works, Aksyonov identifies himself with the youth of his generation by reflecting their contemporary language in his work. Thus Lena Karpov compares Aksyonov to Dos Passos in the use of authentic contemporary language in his dialogues: "With the works of Aksyonov the real language of young people walked in the door of Soviet literature. . . . and readers told each other in amazement that at last someone had recorded *the way people of our generation really spoke*" (vii, Karpov's emphasis).

One of Aksyonov's most striking examples of the attempt of a group to forge an identity for themselves through language is embodied in the "Yaki" language of *The Island of Crimea*. Despite the strongly international texture of Aksyonov's fictional Crimean society, most Crimeans of whatever political persuasion think of themselves as Russians, whether they support an attempt to overthrow the Soviet government or whether they seek simply to join the Soviet Union as an additional republic. But one Crimean nationalist group, the "Yakis," refuses to regard themselves as Russian at all. For the Yakis the island is not Russian, but simply Crimean, and they want to pursue political and cultural independence from the Russian past. As part of this project they are developing their own language, a complex patois of "mangled Russian, Tatar, and English with assorted Romance and Hellenic roots" (206). In short, it is a language which reflects the heteroglossia of the fictional Crimean society itself while still allowing the Yakis to express their own distinctive cultural identity.

  The Burn is Aksyonov's most impressive demonstration of dialogic virtuosity, and it is also probably in *The Burn* where the dialects of specific social groups sound most strongly. The richly encyclopedic texture of Aksyonov's most important novel to date is centrally informed by the linguistic peculiarities of specific groups. Perhaps most striking among these is the distinctive American-beat-inspired slang of the book's antiestablishment figures, but *The Burn* as a whole vividly demonstrates Bakhtin's vision of the novel as a locus of interactions and confrontations among the various ideologically motivated languages that make up society as a whole. The book presents a rich evocation of the Moscow cultural scene of the 1960s and 1970s, maintaining precisely the sort of contact with contemporary reality that Bakhtin consistently associates with the novel as a genre. In particular, *The Burn* enacts an ongoing confrontation between the Moscow intelligentsia (represented by the composite figure of the scientist Aristarkh Apollinarievich Kunitser, the saxophonist Samson Apollinarievich Sabler, the surgeon Gennady Apollinarievich Malkolmov, the sculptor Radius Apollinarievich Khvastishchev, and the writer Pantelei Apollinarievich Pantelei) and the forces of official Soviet authority, represented by various incarnations of the Stalinist bully (and sometime cloakroom attendant) Cheptsov. This confrontation is very much a battle of languages, with the free-wheeling jazz-inspired slang of the intelligentsia contrasting sharply with the rigidly authoritative language of Cheptsov. Vishevsky and Pogacar note this linguistic conflict, which they see as central to Aksyonov's entire literary project:

The central historical theme of Aksënov's works is Stalinism, which is the temporal face of intransigent *poshlost'* ("vulgarity"). Stalinism is based on lies, forgetting, and willful ignorance. Aksënov's works present vital ethical questions in vivid cultural and historical terms. The choice between individual freedom and submission to the power of *poshlost'* is offered in the realm of language. Language can be used as a powerful tool against human beings, or as a means of free expression. It is therefore both vehicle and object in the struggle between *poshlost'* and freedom, or art. (145)

This passage well describes the confrontation between Cheptsov and the various Apollonarieviches. However, this contest is not simply a clash of opposing polar opposites, of evil versus good. While Cheptsov represents despotism and the Apollonarieviches represent resistance, there are clear indications that the latter often act in ways that are in complicity with their own oppression. Priscilla Meyer thus notes that in *The Burn*,

members of the intelligentsia, although cast as victims, are shown to be as depraved as their oppressors, and hence unwittingly in collusion with them. Aksenov represents the intelligentsia's problem as a failure to attend to and protect its muse. ("Aksenov" 513)

Meanwhile, Cheptsov is not merely evil but is himself to a certain extent a victim of the dehumanizing and soul-destroying effects of the Stalinist years. He is therefore deemed worthy of forgiveness and is saved from death late in the text when Malkolmov administers to him a dose of "Lymph-D," the "liquid soul" that Malkolmov has spent much of his career developing (425-6).[1]

Compared to the fivefold Apollinarieviches, Cheptsov seems to be a relatively unified character, possibly because the ideology he represents is more monological. Yet he functions more as a generalized embodiment of the ideology of Stalinism than as a realistic human character. As he himself puts it near the end of the book, "I'm now not even a man at all. I'm a philosophical construct" (525). The Stalinist spirit of oppression that Cheptsov represents informs numerous figures of authority in the text, including the mercenary Theodorus in Africa, Colonel Guly in Magadan, the Party "High Priest" Fyodorich in Moscow, and the male nurse in the drying-up station in Yalta. Indeed, at one point the authoritarian energies associated with Cheptsov appear in the guise of three characters at once, representing oppressive forces in both East and West: the writer Tikhonov, chairman of the Soviet Committee for the Defense of Peace, American Vice President Spiro Agnew, and Soviet hockey coach Colonel Tarasov. When Pantelei sees the three approach, he sees them collectively as an image of Cheptsov: "The three of them together, although individually so different, reminded me of my favorite cloakroom attendant" (213).

Meanwhile, as indicated by their common patronymic, the five *intelligents* of *The Burn* are not distinct individuals in the conventional sense but embodiments of different aspects of a single social force.[2] In particular, they represent various facets of the postStalinist Moscow intellectual scene; as a group they thus comprise a more complete representation of the intelligentsia than would be possible through any single character.[3]   But the Apollinarieviches are tied together in complex and subtle ways; they represent not only different aspects of the same social group, but to a certain extent different aspects of the same personality. For example, they share a common background, all having apparently originated in the boyhood experiences of one Tolya von Steinbock in conjunction with his mother's incarceration in the Stalinist-prison-camp town of Magadan, experiences that closely parallel Aksyonov's own.[4]   Indeed, the five Apollonarieviches often seem interchangeable in the text, their identities merging and sliding from one into another in ways that make it nearly impossible to distinguish among them. In certain episodes their character is simply referred to as "the Academician," who could equally well be any of the five. Other episodes are repeated virtually verbatim for different members of the five, indicating the commonality of their experiences.

This inventive mode of multiple characterization may, in fact, be the most memorable aspect of Aksyonov's experimental technique in *The Burn*. Such split characters are not, however, without literary precedent. In Russian literature, for example, they are reminiscent of the doubles of Dostoevsky, or, for that matter, of Nabokov. One also thinks of the five landowners encountered by Gogol's Chichikov in *Dead Souls*, each of whom can be read as an embodiment of one of the principal characteristics of Chichikov himself, who thus becomes a sort of composite of the five.[5]   In a formal sense, however, Aksyonov's Apollonarieviches are even more reminiscent of certain techniques of characterization of Western modernists like Virginia Woolf and James Joyce.

Woolf's work calls traditional notions of the unified subject into question in numerous ways. An obvious example involves the stance that she takes in *A Room of One's Own*, where she notes that the narrating "'I' is only a convenient term for somebody who has no real being" (4). She then assumes a fluid and multiple identity, asking her audience to "call me Mary Beton, Mary Seton, Mary Carmichael or by any name you please—it is not a matter of any importance" (5). Meanwhile, in *The Waves* Woolf employs six different constantly alternating first-person narrators, so that the continual switching from one speaker to another acts to problematize the association of the "I" of the text with any specific speaking subject. These speakers have distinct individual characteristics, but they speak in a common style and can easily be read as different aspects of a single consciousness.[6]

Joyce employs similar techniques for the blurring of character identities. Late in *Ulysses*, for example, the boundaries between different characters become more and more diffuse, and characters begin freely to share thoughts and memories. The splitting, fading, and merging "characters" of *Finnegans Wake* mount an even more radical assault on the very notion of distinct and stable individual identity. These figures are not so much representations of individuals as textual forces, dissolved in the swirl and flow of Wakean language. Joyce himself clearly saw his characters in very much this way, as evidenced by the fact that he referred to them in his working notebooks by abstract symbols, or "sigla," the same sigla being used to represent an entire family of similar characters much in the way that a common patronymic ties together the five Apollonarieviches of *The Burn*.[7] Interestingly, two of Joyce's sigla—corresponding to the twins Shem and Shaun—respectively represent art and authoritarianism, thereby playing very much the same roles as Aksyonov's Apollinarieviches and Cheptsovs.[8]

The complex characterization employed by Aksyonov in *The Burn* can also be usefully illuminated in light of Bakhtin's theories. In particular, the branching characters of *The Burn* echo Bakhtin's vision of self-as-evolving-process, while Bakhtin's dialogic model of subjectivity is clearly consistent with the shared consciousnesses of the various Apollinarieviches or of the various figurations of Cheptsov in *The Burn*. In *The Burn*, then, Aksyonov literalizes the notion of dialogic character, as do Woolf, Joyce, and other creators of split and multiple characters.

Meanwhile, the clash between the linguistic styles of Cheptsov and the intelligentsia is only one aspect of the tremendously rich dialogic texture of *The Burn*, which embodies Bakhtin's argument that the novel is most effective when it can incorporate a complete range of the languages that constitute the heteroglossia of its contemporary society. Such a novel, Bakhtin suggests, would be informed by a "striving for generic, encyclopedic comprehensiveness" as it attempts to "represent all the social and ideological voices of its era, that is, all the era's languages that have any claim to being significant; the novel must be a microcosm of heteroglossia" (*Dialogic* 410-11). *The Burn* is just such a microcosm, and Aksyonov himself has described (in his interview with Lauridsen and Dalgård) the writing of the book as an attempt "to obtain everything, to whirl it around in all possible ways: formal, philosophical, historical, political" (24).

To achieve this encyclopedic scope, Aksyonov has constructed *The Burn* as a rich patchwork of allusions to almost every aspect of human endeavor. The use of the quintuple protagonist directly invokes the languages of physics, medicine, music, sculpture, and literature, while numerous references to politics, history, and religion bring other powerful discourses into play as well. Not surprisingly, some of Aksyonov's most effective allusions are literary ones, and the impact of *The Burn* is greatly enriched by the invocation of a wide range of literary voices. The book serves almost as a catalogue of Russian literature, alluding to nineteenth-century writers like Pushkin, Gogol, Dostoevsky, Tolstoy, Turgenev, Lermontov, Nekrasov, and Chekhov, as well as to more modern figures like Gorky, Bulgakov, Blok, Mayakovsky, Osip Mandelstam, Zoshchenko, Akhmatova, Pasternak, Solzhenitsyn, Yevtushenko, and Aksyonov himself. Importantly, however, Aksyonov also alludes to a wide variety of Western authors, including Homer, Apuleius, Dante, Chaucer, Rabelais, Cervantes, Goethe, Jules Verne, T. S. Eliot, Ezra Pound, Heinrich Böll, Orwell, Hemingway, Sartre, and Allen Ginsberg. Aksyonov's allusions thus actively participate in the dialogue between East and West that is so important to his writing as a whole. Indeed, allusions in Aksyonov's work tend to be extremely active and effective, contributing in important ways to the confrontations between different ideas and attitudes that give his work its dialogic power. For example, in addition to these references to "high" literature *The Burn* (like most of Aksyonov's work) is liberally laced with allusions to Western popular culture, enacting a dialogue between "high" and "low" of the kind that critics like Andreas Huyssen have associated with the democratic and emancipatory energies of postmodernism.

Aksyonov seems equally at home with Dante and Goethe or with Elvis Presley and Frank Sinatra, suggesting an egalitarian impulse that challenges normal political as well as cultural hierarchies. Bakhtin's work suggests a theoretical framework within which to view the significance of such transgressions of conventional hierarchies. Bakhtin himself pays a great deal of attention to canonical authors like Dante, Rabelais, Goethe, Pushkin, Gogol, and Dostoevsky, but at the same time he places a great deal of emphasis on the power of folk culture. This dual emphasis can be read partially as an attempt to challenge conventional literary hierarchies in general. However, within the context of Russian cultural history the distinction between "literature" and "folk culture" carries resonances that are significantly different from the high-low dichotomy of Western culture. In particular, Russian "literature," even when produced by Slavophiles like Gogol and Dostoevsky, is inevitably colored by Western influences, while the rich tradition of Russian folk culture is more closely associated with purely indigenous cultural energies. As a result, what figures in the West as a dialogue between literature and popular culture (as "high" and "low" versions of a single cultural tradition) becomes in a Russian context a dialogue between different, and even diametrically opposed, Western and Eastern cultural influences.

In *The Burn* Aksyonov makes use of both of these dichotomies; the book is informed not only by Western popular culture and by both Western and Russian literature, but by Russian folk culture as well, resulting in a complex and richly polyphonic four-way cultural dialogue. Indeed, if Aksyonov's free intermixing of images from high and low culture undermines the Western high-low hierarchy, his mixture of images from Eastern and Western culture challenges the notion that the two are so dramatically different that no communication or mutual understanding between them is possible. Thus Aksyonov himself has attributed the frequent use of fantastic and grotesque elements in his work to the influence both of Russian folk culture and of the avant-garde reaction against nineteenth-century realism, combining Eastern and Western cultural forces in a single dialogic technique (Lauridsen and Dalgård 24).[9]

A similar East-West dialogue informs Mikhail Bulgakov's *The Master and Margarita*. Written during the 1930s when Bakhtin was doing much of his most important work, Bulgakov's book is widely acknowledged as one of the most important texts of modern Russian literature. Among other things, this complex and enigmatic text is replete with images and motifs of the kind that Bakhtin associates with carnivalesque literature–particularly with the tradition of Menippean satire. In *The Master and Margarita* a mysterious sorcerer named Woland (a figure of Satan and, presumably, the West via his intertextual connection to the German Goethe) steps out of Goethe's *Faust* to visit modern Moscow with his entourage and to wreak havoc on the populace to punish them for their philistine pettiness, greed, and vanity.[10] One of the book's crucial scenes is the "Satan's Ball" episode, a quintessential presentation of many of the images and motifs that Bakhtin associates with the carnival in his reading of Rabelais. Moreover, Woland is a sort of carnivalesque lord of misrule whose overturning of the normal social order reveals the shortcomings of that order. T. R. N. Edwards notes how closely *The Master and Margarita* matches Bakhtin's description of Menippean satire, meeting all fourteen criteria set out by Bakhtin in the Dostoevsky book as characteristic of the genre.[11]

Bulgakov's book resonates with the work of Bakhtin in numerous ways. For example, literature and writing are major subjects of the text. The "master" of the title is a novelist, and another major character is the poet Ivan Nikolayevich Ponyrev (a.k.a. "Homeless"). Much of *The Master and Margarita* involves representations of the work of these writers, recalling Bakhtin's emphasis on "auto-criticism" of discourse in the novel. Allusions to the work of previous Russian writers (like Pushkin and Dostoevsky) and to Western writers (like Goethe) are also prominent in the text. Indeed, Bulgakov's book involves a complex combination of interacting and competing discourses from the realms of science, religion, literature, history, and politics. This dialogic mixture produces a fantastic satire with clear relevance to the social and political situation in the Stalinist Soviet Union of the 1930s. At the same time, the orientation of Bulgakov's satire is extremely complex and ambivalent. His depiction of the Soviet bureaucracy (especially the literary and medical establishments) and his delineation of the impoverished social conditions in Moscow can be taken as severe criticisms of the Stalinist regime, just as the literary mode of the book seems to hark back to the fantastic realism of Gogol and Dostoevsky and radically to reject the principles of socialist realism. Indeed, *The Master and Margarita*—in the traditional (antiWestern) mode of Gogol and Dostoevsky—privileges the spiritual and the irrational over the scientific and the rational, ostensibly opposing the official Stalinist apotheosis of scientific and technological development in a direct way. On the other hand, most of the satire in *The Master and Margarita* seems aimed at lingering bourgeois elements in Soviet society, elements to which Stalin himself expressed firm opposition. Moreover, as Judith Mills has pointed out, Stalin's regime was hardly rational, and it is possible to read Bulgakov's book as a "tribute to Stalin as the significant creative irrational force that could change Russia's and perhaps humanity's vision of reality. The novel could be read as an apologia for Stalin and whatever consequences may flow from his irrational energies" (321). Thus Mills argues that Woland, usually read as an antiStalinist figure, can potentially be interpreted as a figure of Stalin himself—a reading that parallels our suggestion that the carnival for Bakhtin can actually be a Stalinist image. At the same time, Mills complicates her own reading by noting that many of the irrational elements of the text seem to arise from the dreams of Ivan Homeless, which themselves may be induced by injections received in a Stalinist mental hospital—much in the mode of the lobotomies at the end of Zamyatin's *We* (323).

The numerous points of contact between *The Master and Margarita* and the largely contemporaneous work of Bakhtin help to situate Bakhtin in his Russian context and to illustrate that Bakhtin's work was in fact very much of its time and place. Bulgakov's connections to the literary tradition of Gogol and Dostoevsky also help to show that Bakhtin's concerns have a long history in Russian culture. Meanwhile, it is clear that the Russian cultural tradition from which both Bulgakov and Bakhtin significantly draw remained relevant for later Soviet writers as well. Compare, for example, Andrei Sinyavsky's call in his essay "On Socialist Realism" (first published 1959) for a renewed emphasis on "phantasmagoric art" in the work of Russian writers,

an art in which the grotesque will replace realistic descriptions of ordinary life. Such an art would correspond best to the spirit of our time. May the fantastic imagery of Hoffmann and Dostoevski, of Goya, Chagall, and Mayakovski (the most socialist realist of all), and of many other realists and nonrealists teach us how to be truthful with the aid of the absurd and the fantastic. (218-19)

Sinyavsky proposes this return to the fantastic in direct response to decades of official Soviet endorsement of socialist realism, a mode of writing that he sees as being in complicity with the oppressive character of contemporary Soviet life and therefore unable to provide the spiritual enrichment to life that is the true function of literature. Bakhtin's discussion of Rabelais provides a convenient theoretical framework within which to assess Sinyavsky's argument. In particular, Bakhtin argues that fantastic and grotesque imagery in Rabelais is subversive of "official medieval culture." Of course, official Soviet culture is implicated as well, and what Bakhtin describes as "grotesque realism" in Rabelais can clearly be taken as a subversive counter to socialist realism.

The essay on socialist realism, along with Sinyavsky's other writings, eventually led to his notorious arrest and imprisonment along with Yuli Daniel in 1965. Yet Sinyavsky's call for a renewal of the fantastic energies associated with the work of Russian writers like Gogol and Dostoevsky was in large measure heeded. Among other things, *The Master and Margarita* was finally published in the Soviet Union the year after Sinyavsky's arrest, and the coming years saw a resurgence of fantastic energies in the work of writers like Vladimir Voinovoch, Tatyana Tolstaya, Sasha Sokolov, Boris and Arkady Strugatsky, Alexander Zinoviev, Venedikt Erofeev, Anatoly Gladilin, and (perhaps most importantly) Aksyonov.

This new element in Soviet fiction of the 1960s-1980s resonates very powerfully with the work of literary predecessors like Gogol, Dostoevsky, Zamyatin, and Bulgakov. It also responds quite well to readings within the context of Bakhtin's descriptions of the carnival.[12] Such imagery is particularly prominent in the work of Aksyonov. If Bakhtin describes the medieval carnival as a time of festive and exuberant heteroglossia when normal social boundaries collapse and groups from different social classes and backgrounds meet and mingle freely in a mood of celebration and irreverence, one can detect a similar carnivalesque spirit in the emphasis on pleasure, hedonism, and popular culture in Aksyonov's early writing. Olga Matich thus notes that Aksyonov "perceived life as a multicolored, multinational carnival, which became the backdrop of his heroes's adolescent identity crises and later problems of mid-life and aging" ("Aksenov" 642). This spirit carries over into Aksyonov's later work, which is consistently informed by carnivalesque energies and by the kinds of images and motifs associated by Bakhtin with the carnival. Aksyonov makes heavy use of sexual and excremental imagery and of the fantastic, all of which are important elements in Bakhtin's description of the carnival and of Rabelais. Aksyonov also depicts numerous scenes of openly carnivalesque celebration, scenes that typically have strong political intonations. On the other hand, he remains realistic (and skeptical) about the implications of openly subversive conduct in the Soviet Union, and his carnivalesque episodes often take a dark turn when the Soviet authorities react to restore order.

Much of the evocation of youth culture for which Aksyonov is well known has a carnivalesque tone, suggesting that this culture is informed by antiauthoritarian energies that might ultimately pose a serious threat to the Soviet status quo. In particular, much of the alternative culture depicted by Aksyonov is specifically Western in origin. Among the most important of these cultural images are dance and music, especially jazz and rock and roll, which both consistently function in Aksyonov's work as loci of emancipatory energies. In the story "Super-Deluxe," for example, the Russians aboard the liner *Caravan* dance wildly to Western rock tunes in scenes with clearly carnivalesque intonations:

Barriers of age and size were broken down. The seductive sounds of saxophones and guitars drew into the whirling circle huge ladies, falling out of their ruffled dresses, and modest men who, it would seem, should have been more disposed to playing dominoes and, in their turn, out-of-breath captains of our industry who danced alongside asexual longhairs in jeans. Chairs were knocked over and the problems of everyday life were forgotten. (*"Destruction"* 60)

This scene captures quite precisely Bakhtin's vision of the carnival as a time when normal rules and hierarchies are suspended, when boundaries are transgressed, and when the energies of life erupt without regard for conventional decorum.

A similar scene occurs in *The Burn* when young Samson plays his saxophone in 1956 in a dance hall supposedly devoted to patriotic "national" dances and in which "bourgeois" music and dancing are forbidden. But Samson ignores the rules and begins to play an unrestrained jazz that is the embodiment of a "spirit of disobedience, the idea of freedom" (*Burn* 34). This jazz first triggers an outburst of wild dancing but then nearly leads to a riot when forces of authority demand that the music stop. Famous saxophonist Kostya Rogov (a reinscription of real-life Soviet saxophonist A. Kozlov) helps Samson out of the melee, shouting at their antagonists in an outburst of *stilyagi* slang of which both the style and the content are powerfully transgressive:

"Kiss my ass! Your Big Daddy [Stalin] has kicked the bucket, so we're going to play you some jazz! We're going to give you some jitterbugging in a minor key, and our genius Samsik here can play what he likes. As for you, clothears, piss on you!" (35)

Jazz functions as one of the most consistently antiauthoritarian forces throughout Aksyonov's writing, possibly because Soviet authority officially condemned jazz as a bourgeois contamination from the West. Indeed, figures of authority have tended to find the freewheeling lack of structure in jazz threatening in the West as well, a situation indicated by the narrator of *Say Cheese!*: "Why didn't that gang like jazz? Neither Nazis nor Commies could stand it. Because of the improvisations?" (133).

The bulk of *The Burn* evokes a 1960s and early 1970s Moscow in which carnivalesque energies play a powerful role. Indeed, numerous critics have pointed out the carnival atmosphere that pervades the book. Much of this atmosphere seems to arise from that period's hopeful anticipation of emancipatory reforms in Soviet society, though the book ultimately looks back on that period from a perspective from which much of that optimism appears to have been unwarranted. In addition, much of the carnivalesque energy of *The Burn* arises from a sense of the tremendous diversity of cultures in the Soviet Union, a diversity that by its very nature works against the monologism of the

Soviet government.   At the same time, this cultural multiplicity potentially renders it more difficult to galvanize mass resistance to official power, and Aksyonov's work in general shows an ambivalence toward the subversive political power of carnivalism and heteroglossia that rivals Bakhtin's own.

   The Burn contains numerous scenes of carnivalesque revelry, most of which clearly recall Bakhtin's discussions of the carnival in *Rabelais and His World*.   One such scene occurs in Yalta when a band of revelers (including prostitutes and foreigners, but also figures of Soviet authority) bursts into the local police station (189).   This episode, with its irreverent mixture of high and low, of authority and transgression, epitomizes the carnival as described by Bakhtin. Moreover, like much of *The Burn*, these Yalta scenes are based on real events.   In his review of G. S. Smith's *Songs to Seven Strings* Aksyonov describes the 1967-68 establishment of the "Kara Dag Free Republic," an area in the Crimea characterized by "easy-going, unrestrained humor and a certain degree of frivolity" where young Soviet intellectuals gathered in a spirit of emancipation from Soviet oppression ("Back" 338).   This real-world carnivalesque enclave, Aksyonov goes on to point out, was broken up in a raid by Komsomol vigilantes and Soviet military and police authorities on August 21, 1968, the same night as the Soviet invasion of Prague.[13] In a similar way, "night patrols and a squad of select vigilantes" invade the police station of *The Burn* and quickly put an end to the revelry there, arresting the participants with considerable brutality and taking them away to a squalid drying-up tank (190-1).

   The Yalta scenes of *The Burn* thus have clear political implications, but these implications are far more complex than a mere identification of the transgressive power of carnivalesque revelry.   Indeed, Aksyonov specifically suggests in *The Burn* that carnivalesque revelry does not necessarily constitute a powerful subversion of authority.   The scenes in Yalta are later counterpointed by what seems to be a similarly carnivalesque student uprising at the University of Sussex in England, providing a reminder that the spirit of youthful rebellion that informed the "Kara Dag Free Republic" was a worldwide phenomenon.   However, Aksyonov suggests in this episode that the student revolts in the West were often frivolous compared to those in the Soviet Union, where the "oppression" that triggered such revolts was far more real.   In particular, the students at Sussex seem more interested in taking drugs, having sex, and obtaining television coverage for their revolt than in effecting political change, giving their rebellion more the air of a runaway frat party than that of a genuine revolution:

All night long the revolutionaries had been lighting campfires, dancing
the hula, playing cards, smoking grass, working themselves up,
discussing the problem of union with the working class—which for
some reason seemed very undesirous of such a union—and, of course,
fucking one another on all the steps of the vice-chancellor's staircase.
They were waiting for the arrival of the mass media, for who makes
a revolution nowadays without the television cameras? (252)[14]

In a clear comment upon the political irresponsibility of these
students, Aksyonov's inimitable American Professor Patrick
Thunderjet (who had also been present in the earlier Yalta scenes)
proclaims himself the representative of the students of Simferopol and
Yalta—who have far more serious political problems than their English
counterparts. Thunderjet then puts a Rabelaisian end to the Sussex
revolt by climbing atop a pillar and pissing Gargantua-like on the
crowd below, considerably dampening their revolutionary spirits (252-
3).

   Such scenes imply that genuinely transgressive carnivalism requires
a specific authoritarian target and that seemingly carnivalesque
activities might actully work in complicity with official power. These
scenes also suggest that the oppressive policies of the Soviet regime
might paradoxically provide a source of carnivalesque energies.
Indeed, it was the authoritarian monologism of Stalinism that seems to
have provided much of the inspiration for Bakhtin's emphasis on
carnival. Consistent with this motif, some of the most carnivalesque
scenes in *The Burn* occur not in localized areas of release from Soviet
authority but in the prison town of Magadan, a point of concentration
for the oppressive energies of the Stalinist regime. Indeed, the town
itself is the direct result of the monological oppression of Stalinism,
which sought to maintain monological control of the bulk of the Soviet
Union by containing all opposing voices in localized areas like
Magadan. As a result, Magadan itself is a veritable hotbed of
heteroglossia whose population consists of various and sundry groups
thought threatening to Stalin. Many of the inhabitants of Magadan are
already so marginal to Soviet society that they have nothing left to lose
and can thus challenge authority with impunity. As a result, "It may
be that in 1949 Magadan was, in a sense, the freest town in Russia"
(229).

   One of the most carnivalesque areas in Magadan is an underground
tunnel called the "Crimea," where many recently released inmates from
the prison in Magadan await transportation back to the "mainland,"
that is, back to normal Soviet society. The diverse numbers of these
ex-inmates constitute a highly carnivalesque mixture of nationalities,

classes, and professions, all thrust together on a single level that obliterates conventional social distinctions. That this gathering place is underground recalls the central emphasis placed by Bakhtin on images of the underworld in his discussion of carnivalesque motifs in Rabelais (*Rabelais* 381-404). Indeed, there are direct echoes of Rabelais and of other carnivalesque writers in this "Crimea." When Tolya and Sanya Gurchenko go there they encounter a character named "Pantagruel" (engaged in counting his lice) and another character who is reading Apuleius, whose highly carnivalesque *The Golden Ass* is a favorite text of Bakhtin. Sanya and Tolya also overhear torrents of violent profanity and see Valka Pshonka, a preposterous homosexual transvestite who is beaten and insulted by the "Crimean" women. To complete this barrage of carnivalesque motifs, the innocent Tolya drinks *chifir* and then experiences his first sexual encounter while in the midst of a drug-induced fantasy (368-74). As with the revels in Yalta, however, this scene comes to a sudden end when the tunnel is raided by Cheptsov and his troops, though Tolya manages to escape.

This figuration of the prison society of the fictional Magadan as an island separated from the Soviet "mainland" is derived from the perceptions of the town's real-world prison inmates, including Eugenia Ginzburg, Aksyonov's mother. In *Within the Whirlwind*, Ginzburg describes the attitude of the inmates toward the prison province of Kolyma: "We all knew that Kolyma was not an island, but we insisted on calling it one, and on calling the rest the mainland" (185-6). Moreover, as Matich notes, this perception clearly prefigures the imaginative framework of Aksyonov's next novel, *The Island of Crimea* ("Aksenov" 645). Indeed, there are clear links between the island Crimea of the latter book and the underground "Crimea" of *The Burn*. The Crimean island society consists of a richly heteroglossic mixture of different races, cultures, and languages, all of which is informed by a "carnival atmosphere: glamorous international living; glossy, self-indulgent sexual adventure; artistry; western consumerism; and general frolic" (Matich, "Aksenov" 644).

The carnivalesque nature of life on the island of Crimea is well captured in the Crimea Rally, a road race which, with the accompanying festivities, is the society's central cultural event. Huge multinational crowds gather to watch the annual race in an atmosphere of celebration and anticipation that corresponds very closely to Bakhtin's description of the carnival as a time when conventional social barriers break down, but in which difference and diversity still thrive:

The Crimea Rally was an unofficial national holiday. It brought everyone together but at the same time heightened the rivalry among ethnic groups: Tatars backed Tatars, Anglo-Crimeans put their money on the local English, provacuees [descendants of the original White Army troops who fled their at the close of the Civil War] all had Russian favorites, and so on. (272)

Meanwhile, the carnivalesque quality of life on the Crimean island highlights the austerity of life on the mainland, to which it stands in stark contrast. One of the most sought-after prizes in the book's Soviet Union is a vacation, or even a work assignment, on the island. But, as usual in Aksyonov's work, the Soviet authorities are unable to tolerate this reminder of the impoverished quality of Soviet life. Just as the carnivalesque scenes in the Yalta and the "Crimea" of *The Burn* are broken up by force, so too does the festive life of the island of Crimea come to an abrupt end. Even though the island is taking steps to join the Soviet Union of its own accord, the Soviets take the island by force through a massive military invasion. Luchnikov's lover Tanya and his wife Krystyna are killed in the assault, Luchnikov's father is seriously wounded, and Luchnikov himself apparently goes insane. The only remaining ray of hope involves Luchnikov's son Anton, who escapes aboard a small boat with his own wife and daughter—just as Tolya escapes from the "Crimea" of *The Burn* moments before it is routed by Cheptsov and his men.

The implication of these repeated scenes of aborted carnival seems clear: within the oppressive context of the Soviet Union transgressive behavior generally leads not to emancipation but to swift and brutal retribution. On the other hand, one could argue that the dramatic contrast between the spirit of freedom embodied in Aksyonov's various carnivalesque scenes and the spirit of despotism embodied in their repeated violent suppression serves all the better to comment upon the true nature of the Soviet regime. Indeed, Bakhtin's own use of the carnival as am ambivalent metaphor for emancipation gains much of its power from a similar contrast between his figuration of the Rabelaisian carnival and the reality of life in the Stalinist context in which Bakhtin worked. Likewise, the various images of the "grotesque body" (sex, excrement, etc.) cited by Bakhtin in the Rabelais book are powerful largely because of their radical variance from the fastidiousness and prudery of the Stalinist regime, which could not brook such imagery in published literature but which apparently had no problem with the mass torture and execution of Soviet citizens.[15]

Aksyonov's frequent use of sexual and excremental imagery participates in many of the same energies as Rabelais's focus on the bodily lower stratum. As with Bakhtin's figuration of Rabelais, Aksyonov's open use of such motifs in his later work (published, at the time, only in the West) already mounts a political challenge to the Soviet censors, who routinely deleted such passages from his early Soviet-published work (J. J. Johnson 38). On the other hand, as with his various depictions of carnivalesque exuberance, Aksyonov is also well aware that it is not necessarily true that the very notion of sexuality automatically leads to successful subversion. *The Burn*, like much of Aksyonov's work, is filled with episodes of transgressive sexual behavior, but sexuality is also a central locus of oppression in the book. Numerous scenes, in fact, suggest a strong sexual intonation to the oppressive policies of Stalinism, as when Colonel Guly sadistically whips his teenage daughter in Magadan (241) or when Cheptsov beats and rapes his daughter Nina in Moscow (343-4).

Meanwhile, the most ostensibly transgressive sexual activities in *The Burn* involve various incarnations of the prostitutes Klara and Tamara, especially in their relations with the sculptor Khvastishchev. In one carnivalesque scene the two cavort shamelessly in Khvastishchev's studio while he is being visited by Boris Lygher, who appears at the time to be a member of the Executive Committee, but who is apparently nothing more than a chauffeur and (like his friend/rival Cheptsov) cloakroom attendant (272-4). Later, in what is probably the most graphic sexual episode in the book, Khvastishchev and the two young hookers copulate *à trois* (426-7). Such activities certainly violate the strict official moral code of the Soviet regime, but the transgressive significance of these scenes is considerably muted by the fact that both Klara and Tamara are KGB informers whose charge is to engage in sexual relations with intellectuals like Khvastishchev in order to report on their activities.

This suggestion that the Soviet authorities are perfectly willing to use officially proscribed sexual activity for their own purposes (recalling Foucault's comments on official administration of sexuality) recurs several times in Aksyonov's work. In *The Island of Crimea* Luchnikov conducts an adulterous affair with Tanya, but this ostensibly transgressive relationship is officially condoned and even encouraged. Indeed, the Soviet authorities induce Tanya to leave her husband so that she can stay with Luchnikov as a KGB spy. In a similar way, the authorities of *Say Cheese!* keep tabs on photographer Maxim Ogorodnikov by employing the woman Violetta to establish a sexual relationship with him, though he in fact turns the tables by using that relationship to help him escape from Moscow to the West early in the book.

Say Cheese! also includes some of the most Rabelaisian images of human physical processes in all of Aksyonov's work. In *Rabelais and His World* Bakhtin emphasizes that bodily functions like defecation and urination specifically involve a crossing of the boundary between the individual and the external world and therefore provide reminders that human beings are a part of that world. In *Say Cheese!* Ogorodnikov's physical processes play a prominent role. In one scene he urinates on a street in Berlin, producing a stream of Gargantuan proportions:

The urine gushed out of him and then suddenly stopped, his whole body shuddering; then the stream poured out again. Where was this enormous, incomprehensibly enormous amount of moisture coming from? A bladder can't hold more than three liters, but I've pissed all over the street, my urine has been gurgling down the gutter for over fifteen minutes. (136)

Soon afterward Ogorodnikov attends a party at La Coupole in Paris where he suddenly and inexplicably vomits in similarly massive quantities (162-3). Later he engages in sexual intercourse with a secretary in New York City and experiences another massive flow of bodily fluids when he ejaculates voluminously and repeatedly, eventually covering the woman, the bed, and virtually the entire room with semen (222-3). Then, on a flight back to Europe, Ogorodnikov defecates in the onboard lavatory, producing what is by now a predictably immense quantity of excrement that fills the small stainless steel bowl several times over (226).

By this time, Ogorodnikov himself begins to ponder the implications of these episodes, calling specific attention to their echo of Rabelais: "What's happening to me? What do all these Rabelaisian (exactly) effusions and profusions mean?" (227). Meanwhile, changing planes in Copenhagen Ogorodnikov breaks out in a copious sweat in the airport, completing his catalogue of prodigious secretions (230). His question concerning the significance of these secretions goes unanswered, and indeed his bodily functions return to normal once he is safely back in the Soviet Union. Numerous interpretations do, however, suggest themselves. That these Rabelaisian flows occur only in the West suggests that they may involve a cathartic release associated with the lifting of the repression of natural impulses in the Soviet Union, though Ogorodnikov certainly finds these experiences far from unequivocally positive. Or, consistent with Bakhtin's emphasis on secretions as emblems of the crossing of boundaries, these profuse expulsions of bodily fluids might be taken as symbolic of Ogorodnikov's strong sense of having crossed important cultural and political boundaries upon leaving the Soviet Union.[16]

Indeed, Bakhtin's general emphasis on the antiauthoritarian implications of Rabelais's treatment of the "bodily lower stratum" suggests a number of ways Ogorodnikov's Rabelaisian eruptions act as a transgressive counter to the austere political climate that informs his contemporary Moscow. Meanwhile, the fantastic scope of these episodes participates in a complex of fantastic and grotesque motifs that is central to Aksyonov's entire *oeuvre*. Aksyonov himself notes the importance of such images, stating to Lauridsen and Dalgård that "[w]ithout the grotesque, I just can't work" (24). Drawing upon the tradition of fantastic realism of Russian predecessors like Gogol, Dostoevsky, Saltykov-Shchedrin, Bely, Zamyatin, and Bulgakov, Aksyonov fills his texts with devils, angels, dreams, hallucinations, strange transformations, and various other manifestations of magic. To a certain extent such images have a mimetic function, suggesting the strangeness and absurdity of everyday life under the Soviet regime. At the same time, both Sinyavsky's call for a return to the fantastic imagery of Gogol and Dostoevsky and Bakhtin's discussion of fantastic elements in Rabelias identify such imagery as a challenge to the officially prescribed constraints of socialist realism and to the limitations that officially endorsed versions of Soviet reality would place on the imagination in general.

As in the work of many of his contemporaries among Russian dissident and émigré writers, Aksyonov's exploration of the fantastic also resonates with other experimental aspects of his work, aspects that together can be read as a challenge to the dictates of socialist realism or of literary orthodoxy of any kind. Indeed, Aksyonov's career reads almost like an allegory of Bakhtin's vision of the novel as an ever-changing and ever-evolving genre. Mozejko notes that each Aksyonov work tends to differ radically from the ones before it, so much so that Aksyonov "seems to have almost programmatically committed himself to a constant search for new forms of artistic expression, to the revision and renewal of textual constituents of his early realistic prose" (205). Even Aksyonov's earliest writing is already informed by a youthful energy and exuberance that run counter to the socialist norm, but early works like the novel *Colleagues* (1960) are relatively conventional in a formal sense, with linear plots and realistic scenes and characters. By 1965, The "Steel Bird" deviates radically from the socialist realist tradition, featuring fantastic imagery, linguistic innovation, and formal fragmentation. And this trend toward more and more radical experimentation continues at least through *The Burn*, with its wild mixture of languages and discourses, its dramatic departure from linear chronology, and its almost total lack of regard for realistic representation of scenes and characters. If later works like *The Island of Crimea* and *Say Cheese!* seem less radical in form and technique than *The Burn*, they are nonetheless *different* from it–and from each other. Indeed, one of the footnotes of *Say Cheese!* acknowledges the book's relatively conventional chronology, which it claims has been adopted for the convenience of readers despite the fact that a more fragmented chronology would correspond more closely to the sometimes bizarre reality of Soviet life:

Gentlemen, the narrative genre is undergoing metamorphoses left and right that are not subject to the silly theories of our day. While a fragmented, disordered flow of memory would be "much closer to reality," we, however, are using the more conventional horse, even if footnotes are unconventional stirrups, giving up rodeo delights for the sake of the rider's interests, for in this narrative the plot is no less important than the verbal flow. (53)

Thus, even in the midst of what at this point appears to be a relatively conventional narrative, Aksyonov shows a self-consciousness in his literary technique that indicates his awareness of the political implications of narrative form in a way that directly recalls Bakhtin's emphasis on autocriticism in the novel as a principal factor in the genre's capability for ongoing evolution.

This footnote initiates a dialogue with both socialist realism ("the silly theories of the day") and Aksyonov's own *The Burn*, which is centrally informed by the "rodeo delights" he here eschews. Readers are thus asked to consider carefully the implications of the different plot arrangements that can be found in various texts. Indeed, Aksyonov's experimentation with different narrative structures shows a strong awareness that plot is not a purely formal category but a means of reflecting fundamental attitudes about the flow of time and history in the world at large. In short, Aksyonov's treatment of plot can be usefully understood in terms of Bakhtin's notion of the chronotope. Aksyonov also enacts Bakhtin's vision of dialogic interactions among different chronotopes by mixing genres and modes (like fiction and history) in his work. For example, *Love for Electricity* (1971) mixes a fictionalized account of the life of Leonid Krasin (a Bolshevik and close associate of Lenin during the 1905 revolution) with actual historical documents from that period. Other Aksyonov texts ("The Steel Bird," *Surplussed Barrelware*, *The Burn*) seem to have been assembled from diverse fragments from different genres. Such assemblages openly dramatize Bakhtin's continual emphasis on the dialogic power inherent in mixtures of different discourses and genres. *Love for Electricity* is particularly striking for its overt mixture of fiction and history, a technique that was central to the "documentary" or "chronical" novel that was quite popular in the Soviet Union at the time it was written (Johnson, "V. P. Aksënov" 41).

Meanwhile, much of the experimentation with plot structure in Aksyonov's work can clearly be read as a challenge to the rigidly defined chronotope of socialist realism. For one thing, the very fact that different Aksyonov works (like different Bakhtin works) seem to suggest very different chronotopic structures runs counter to the Stalinist project of demanding adherence to an official vision of history. Meanwhile, the complex and radically fragmented chronologies of works like *The Burn* initiate clear dialogic encounters with the distinctive dualistic chronotope of socialist realism, while the romance-like ending of *Say Cheese!* can be taken as a parody of socialist realist happy endings. And Aksyonov's work is truly chronotopic in Bakhtin's sense: it involves not only an intense engagement with time, but also a profound sense of interconnection between space and time. Specific periods and kinds of time tend to be associated in Aksyonov's work with specific places. Thus, *The Destruction of Pompeii* inevitably suggests the ancient Italian city and volcano, though the story appears to be set in the modern Crimea, thus initiating a dialogue between different times and places reminiscent of the combination of ancient Jerusalem and modern Moscow in Bulgakov's *The Master and Margarita.* This comparison indicates that the "destruction" depicted in Aksyonov's story refers to the suppression of the "Kara Dag Free Republic" by Soviet authorities in 1968, especially since Kara Dag itself is a volcano. The link to Pompeii thus emphasizes that this suppression was disastrous and that it involved a defeat for progress and a throwback to the past.

In *The Burn* the Crimea is associated with the recent past of the sixties and with the optimistic sense of exciting new cultural and political possibilities that informed that decade. Moscow, on the other hand, is closely associated with events of the book's present time—the early seventies—and with a sense, following events of 1968, that the optimism of the sixties was premature. Finally, the prison town of Magadan is associated with a Stalinist past that still haunts not only the book's characters but Soviet culture as a whole. Given these correlations between place and time, the fragmented and discontinuous chronology of *The Burn* necessarily leads to rapid changes of place as well. The action shifts quickly back and forth among Moscow, Yalta, and Magadan, adding to the defamiliarizing sense of strangeness that informs the entire book. This kind of spatial dislocation becomes particularly dramatic in the surreal "The Victim's Last Adventure" section that ends the book. This section centers on the 1968 Soviet invasion of Czechoslovakia and makes it clear that this invasion was the single most important contributing factor to the end of the optimism of the sixties.[17] In this section the action shifts rapidly and unpredictably among a variety of settings, including Moscow, Paris, Prague, Italy, England, provincial Russia, and even the moon. These scene shifts (together with a final and radical confusion among the identities of the five Apollonarieviches, who together roughly constitute the "victim" of the section's title)[18] emphasize the sense of unreality associated with the Prague invasion, just as the presence of Cheptsov in all of these settings suggests the difficulty of escaping Soviet power, even outside the borders of the Soviet Union.

There is also a temporal element to Aksyonov's multiple characterization in *The Burn*. The different Apollinarieviches can be taken to represent the different paths that young Tolya might have taken through life, recalling Bakhtin's vision of the open-endedness of history. The book thus becomes a sort of multiple *Bildungsroman*, echoing Bakhtin's emphasis on Goethe's work in that genre as an example of the understanding of historical development embodied in the novel. Moreover, the development of the boy Tolya into multiple adult characters would seem to provide an ideal illustration of Bakhtin's argument that "[r]eality as we have it in the novel is only one of many possible realities; it is not inevitable, not arbitrary, it bears within itself other possibilities" (*Dialogic* 37). Bakhtin's continual emphasis on the multiple possibilities of historical development can be read as an attempt to find a hopeful spark of light amid the darkness of the Stalinist night. Similarly, the multiple development of young Tolya in *The Burn* indicates the multiplicity of life's possibilities, even within the oppressive context of Stalinist Russia. On the other hand, the numerous similarities among the adult Apollinarieviches also suggest that such possibilities are seriously limited in this context.

The confusion and fragmentation of both place and time in *The Burn* are especially striking given that the book is a highly autobiographical account of the events of Aksyonov's own life. The book's structure thus challenges the conventional assumptions of the genre of autobiography, which is presumably intended to provide a coherent account that makes sense of one's life. But Aksyonov's life in the Soviet Union did not, in fact, make sense by any rational standard. The bizarre atmosphere of *The Burn* thus indicates that Soviet history itself is absurd, a judgment that is particularly telling when compared with the official Soviet vision of history as a rational and inexorable movement toward the radiant future of Communism. Indeed, *The Burn* is one of the many reevaluations of the Stalinist past that have been an important of Russian literature in recent years, responding to the blatant fictionalization of history during the Stalinist years and particularly to the perception that the official manipulation of history under Stalin served to efface from the historical record the suffering of the millions of victims of his regime. Solzhenitsyn is perhaps the best known among writers who have sought to give voice to the experiences of these lost souls, though Ginzburg's memoirs are one of the most important documents in this effort as well.

However, unlike Solzhenitsyn, who seems to have made it his project to reveal what he sees as the "real" truth of the Stalinist past, *The Burn*, with its radical ambiguity and fragmentation, suggests that there are in fact many ways of retelling the past, all of which have some validity and none of which are finally authoritative. In Bakhtin's terms, Solzhenitsyn's "truth" of the Stalinist past is monologic, while Aksyonov's is dialogic. This notion of multiple figurations of the past is explicitly enacted in *The Island of Crimea*, where Aksyonov constructs an alternative history in which even the facts of Soviet geography are altered in order to construct a vision of a Russian past that might have been had the revolution not succeeded. Numerous observers have suggested that the reforms set in motion by the February Revolution were already well on their way to modernizing Russian and to improving conditions in Russian society. And one could certainly read Aksyonov's description of his fictional Crimean society as a utopian vision of a Russia in which the bourgeois programs of the Kerensky government were allowed to develop and reach fruition. Indeed, there is a clear utopian element in all of Aksyonov's scenes of carnivalesque celebration, as there is in Bakhtin's discussion of the carnival in *Rabelais and His World*. But the sudden and violent ends experienced by all of these utopian moments indicate that the thrust of Aksyonov's vision, like Bakhtin's, is ultimately antiutopian. Matich thus reads *The Island of Crimea* as a dystopian novel in the tradition of Orwell's *1984*, though acknowledging that Aksyonov's playful tone contrasts sharply with Orwell's more somber vision ("Aksenov" 651).

One can find dystopian elements in *The Burn* as well. For example, in the book's surreal closing scenes, the book's characters continually find themselves being observed by Cheptsov from television screens, recalling the video screens from which Big Brother watches the populace of Orwell's Oceania. Earlier in the book Aksyonov specifically acknowledges Orwell as a predecessor in the depiction of the constant surveillance that informs Soviet life. Aware that anyone he meets might turn out to be a KGB informer, the writer Pantelei proclaims his disgust with the whole situation: "It's pure Orwell. And if that's the case, then it's time to get out of here! If that's so, it's impossible to live her any longer. We've got to get out!" (315).

This suggestion that life might be better outside the Soviet Union anticipates the capitalist utopia of *The Island of Crimea*, though the eventual end of the latter book calls into question the utopian pretensions of capitalism as well. In particular, the material wealth of the island leads to a political naïveté and complacency that make it an easy prey for the Soviet invasion. Indeed, Matich suggests that what she sees as an antiutopian turn in *The Island of Crimea* can be taken as a response to the more strongly utopian orientation of many of Aksyonov's early works. For Matich the book participates in a general critical mood in postStalinist Soviet literature, a mood that critically responds to the tendency toward mythologization with which the Stalinist regime sought to promulgate its authoritarian project. But she argues that, while *The Island of Crimea* is critical of official images of Soviet reality, it is first and foremost self-critical, challenging the utopian elements of its own discourse.

Aksyonov's suspicion of utopianism no doubt derives largely from disappointment associated with the descent of the high hopes of the postStalinist thaw into the dreariness of the Brezhnev retrenchment. At the same time, the echoes of Bakhtin in his critical confrontation with utopianism are strong. Indeed, Aksyonov's work as a whole resonates with so many of Bakhtin's ideas that Aksyonov's *oeuvre* can be read as a kind of introduction to Bakhtin's thoughts on literature, especially as they relate to the political situation in the Soviet Union. That this situation for Aksyonov principally means the Brezhnev years, while Bakhtin's context was principally Stalinist, implies that both Aksyonov and Bakhtin work within the context of broad historical tendencies in Russian history that go beyond the specifics of particular historical events. In addition, the parallels between Bakhtin and Aksyonov suggest important echoes of Stalinism in the Brezhnev regime, thus indicating the lingering shadow that Stalinism cast over the Soviet Union even decades after Stalin's death.

NOTES

1. There is, of course, a Christian intonation to this motif of forgiveness, especially given the status of Aksyonov as a practicing

member of the Russian Orthodox Church. See Clark and Holquist for an argument for the influence of Orthodox thought on Bakhtin as well.

2. Other characters in the book are multiple as well. For example, there appear to be several different figurations of the woman "Alisa" in the book, while the boundaries among the women Inna, Nina, and Marina are sometimes so blurred that they seem to represent a common textual entity.

3. Aksyonov has, however, experimented with such all-encompassing characters. For example, Lyova Malakhitov, the protagonist of *Rendezvous*, is a singer, musician, poet, athlete, and so on, who is "talented in everything, absolutely everything" (*"Destruction"* 89).

4. Aksyonov's mother, Eugenia Ginzburg, has detailed her prison camp experiences in the memoirs *Journey into the Whirlwind* and *Within the Whirlwind*. See Meyer for a discussion of the intertextual dialogue between *The Burn* and Ginzburg's memoirs ("Aksenov").

5. See Fanger for a discussion of the ways these landowners mirror different aspects of Chichikov (170).

6. J. W. Graham discusses the fact that Woolf originally intended to employ a single omniscient narrator in *The Waves* and suggests that the consistent style of the speakers gives the reader the feeling of being inside an omniscient consciousness that "recounts to itself, without comment, the consciousnesses of six speakers, each of whom is talking (or thinking) to himself about his own experiences" (206). To Graham, the individual "characters" are thus to be seen as different aspects of a single narrating consciousness, which is approximated by the character Bernard in a final summation. Woolf herself indicated in a diary entry that the different speakers were not separate characters in any traditional sense. Reacting to a positive review of the book, she wrote: "Odd, that they (*The Times*) should praise my characters when I meant to have none" (*Writer's Diary* 170).

7. Complex and multiple characterization is also a prominent feature of the fiction of Thomas Pynchon, an American contemporary writer whose work bears many resemblances to Aksyonov's. Discussing *The Burn* and *The Island of Crimea*, Ellendea Proffer thus suggests that "[t]he American writer who has the most in common with the Aksyonov of these novels is Thomas Pynchon" (131).

8. See McHugh for a discussion of Joyce's "sigla" technique.

9. There was, of course, a strong avant-garde movement in the early days of the Soviet Union, with artists like the Oberiuty group (Kharms, Vvedensky) exploring much of the same territory as their Western contemporaries. But such avant-garde Russian artists were clearly influenced by Western trends.

10. Numerous critics have discussed the parallels between *Faust* and *The Master and Margarita*. See, for example, Stenbock-Fermor.

11. Edwards further suggests that the historical conditions in which Menippean satire arose in ancient Greece paralleled those in Russia after the Revolution (147). Proffer ("Bulgakov's"), Sharratt, and Wright also link *The Master and Margarita* to the genre of Menippean satire.

12. Bulgakov's influence on Aksyonov seems to have been especially strong, and *The Master and Margarita* has been identified by numerous critics as one of the most important influences on Aksyonov's master work, *The Burn*. See, for example, Meyer, who suggests that the structure of *The Burn* is "based on Bulgakov's novel, both the comic, fantastic dimension and the religious, eternal one" ("Aksenov" 521).

13. For Aksyonov, the fall of Kara Dag was a crucial turning point in Soviet history, marking the end of the post-Stalin "thaw" and the beginning of the "Brezhnev Winter" ("Back" 338).

14. For a strikingly similar depiction of Western student rebellions of the 1960s, see Thomas Pynchon's depiction of the "People's Republic of Rock an' Roll" in *Vineland* (208-17). In Pynchon's case, however, the American authorities put down this revolt with a brutality at least the equal of that exercised by the Soviet authorities in *The Burn*.

15. Bakhtin emphasizes, especially in "Forms of Time and Chronotope in the Novel" that Rabelais's work does not present the processes of the bodily lower stratum as obscene or shocking, but as a natural, and even "lofty" part of human life. It is only to the official ideology of medieval Europe that such natural processes become degraded as "a sad necessity of the sinful flesh" (185). The potential commentary on Stalinist prudery in Bakhtin's suggestions of the devaluation of human life in medieval asceticism is clear.

16. Ogorodnikov's name itself carries connotations of boundaries, deriving from the Russian word for gardener (*ogorodnik*), which is itself etymologically related to the verb *ogorodnit*, meaning to fence or establish boundaries.

17. Ellendea Proffer reads both *The Burn* and *The Island of Crimea* as reactions to the 1968 invasion of Czechoslovakia ("Prague").

18. This confusion of identities can also be taken as an indication that the "victim" in question is the general spirit of the intelligentsia of the sixties rather than any specific individual.

3

"Look Both Ways": Double-Voiced Satire in the Work of Ilf and Petrov

Noting that Stendhal's famous characterization of the novel as "*un miroir qu'on promène le long d'un chemin*" has not generally proved to be a very useful description of the genre, Donald Fanger argues that Gogol's *Dead Souls* may be the only European novel that "might be said to fit and validate" Stendhal's remark (169). Indeed, Gogol's novel is very much a mirror of the whole panoply of Russian life as encountered by Pavel Ivanovich Chichikov in the course of his picaresque journeys. On the other hand, despite Fanger's suggestion that *Dead Souls* stands alone in this respect, roads and traveling have often been popular images in Russian literature. Nevertheless, Gogol's *Dead Souls* is perhaps the outstanding example of the Russian "road" novel. During the late 1920s and early 1930s the popular satirists Ilf and Petrov continued the tradition of the "road" novel, closely following in Gogol's footsteps.[1] In particular, their novels *The Twelve Chairs* and *The Golden Calf* can both claim *Dead Souls* as an important literary progenitor. Through the adventures of their "hero" Ostap Bender and his companions, Ilf and Petrov examine the new Soviet society with a tone and scope that are reminiscent of Gogol's satirical exploration of the society of tsarist Russia.

Like Chichikov, Bender is a marginal figure, a roguish conman who wanders through Russian society in search of easy wealth. Bender's eccentric position enables him to see the weak points of Soviet society and presumably to profit from those weaknesses. His marginal status also allows Ilf and Petrov to present Soviet society from a unique and defamiliarizing perspective. Bender, in short, epitomizes the role of the rogue in literature as described by Bakhtin. According to Bakhtin the status of the rogue as the "other" in a society provides him with a carnivalesque upside-down perspective that destabilizes the accepted order of things: "The rogue continually dons and discards masks so as to expose the falsity of those who presume their roles and institutions are natural" (Morson and Emerson 352). The rogue's function in society thus closely resembles that of a novelist who also uses masks in order to reveal, in a parodic fashion, the various deceptions and illusions that inform official versions of reality.

Especially important for Bakhtin is the picaro, a traveling rogue whose wandering adventures allow the picaresque novel to explore (and criticize) the social tendencies and practices encountered by the hero. Though Bakhtin himself specifically identifies *Dead Souls* as a Menippean satire, it is clear that both *Dead Souls* and the satirical novels of Ilf and Petrov in many ways exemplify Bakhtin's discussion of the picaresque novel as a venue for the presentation of alternative readings of reality. Like Chichikov and Bender, the picaro has a distinct perspective that usually casts a different light on reality and often challenges generally accepted worldviews. Picaros, as outsiders who generally flaunt the accepted rules of the society, serve as parodic reversals of a society's images of authority. Like his literary cousins, the clown and the fool, the picaro "represents a metamorphosis of tsar and god" (*Dialogic* 161). In particular, the picaro provides mirrors that reflect falseness, pretentiousness, and other (generally negative) aspects of a society. The picaresque novel is thus for Bakhtin an exemplary mode of satire and indeed of the genre of the novel, a major function of which is the "laying-bare of any sort of conventionality, the exposure of all that is vulgar and falsely stereotyped in human relationships" (*Dialogic* 162).

The picaro thus serves an inherently negative, critical, and antiauthoritarian role in the novel. In particular his adventures are designed to highlight the way

hypocrisy and falsehood saturate all human relationships. The healthy "natural" functions of human nature are fulfilled, so to speak, only in ways that are contraband and savage, because the reigning ideology will not sanction them. This introduces falsehood and duplicity into all human life. (*Dialogic* 162)

In short, the function of the picaro is precisely the opposite of that of the positive hero of socialist realism, whose adventures are designed to highlight the positive aspects of Soviet society and to provide support for official authority in that society. Indeed, one can read Bakhtin's discussions of outlaw figures like picaros, rogues, clowns, and fools as yet another of his many hidden polemics against the authoritarian ideology of Stalinism.[2]

Given Bakhtin's discussions of the inherently critical nature of the novel (and particularly of the picaresque novel), it comes as no surprise that the rich tradition of Russian satire (going back to Gogol and Saltykov-Shchedrin) suffered mightily during the Stalinist period. Picaresque satirists like Ilf and Petrov were writing under a Stalinist regime in which criticisms of official ideology were severely suppressed. At the same time, such satirists found themselves working in a genre that is by its very nature critical of authority. Understanding that satire is by its nature a negative and critical mode Ilf and Petrov, like other satirists of the same period, ostensibly make their work palatable to the Stalinist regime by directing their criticisms at *enemies* of official authority. In particular, much of their satire seems directed at the residual bourgeois tendencies that Stalin himself was ostensibly so determined to extirpate. As Richard L. Chapple points out, satire was a welcome genre in the Soviet Russia of the twenties and thirties as long as it was confined within the range of permissible targets like

the White, the aristocrat, the bureaucrat, foreign imperialists, capitalists, religious figures, the bourgeois remnants of the past, the philistine, the emigré, the kulak, the intellectual, the embezzler, the drunk, the hooligan, and the corrupt petty official. (6)

However, Bakhtin's deliberations on satire and on the picaresque novel indicate that the project of "limited" proregime satire is inherently unstable and that the genre in which Ilf and Petrov work inevitably tends to be critical of authority. Moreover, Bakhtin's emphasis on the fact that genres themselves embody specific worldviews suggests that individual practitioners of a given genre are not fully in control of the ideological implications of the works they produce in that genre. Thus he suggests that Gogol's attempt to tell a monological story of Christian salvation in the progress of Chichikov was inherently doomed by the fact that such a project was inimical to the genre of *Dead Souls*. "The tragedy of Gogol," concludes Bakhtin, "is to a very real extent the tragedy of a genre" (*Dialogic* 28).

Ilf and Petrov work in this same picaresque genre, which becomes even more inherently subversive within the oppressive context of Stalinism. For example, the peripatetic chronotope of picaresque fiction radically conflicts with the Stalinist vision of history as an inexorable march to the radiant future. Moreover, despite the fact that their satire is ostensibly aimed at bourgeois elements that still permeate the young Soviet society, Ilf and Petrov enhance the inherently antiauthoritarian tendency of the satirical genre via certain specific aspects of their texts that can easily be read as disguised criticisms of the Stalinist regime. The first of their two novels, *The Twelve Chairs* (published 1928), takes place in 1927 and focuses its criticisms on the vestiges of the prerevolutionary aristocracy and on the bourgeois abuses of the NEP period that was by that time on the wane.[3] The second novel of Ilf and Petrov, *The Golden Calf* (published 1931), takes place in 1930 and focuses on the corruption that remains in Soviet society in the early Stalinist years. To a first approximation, both of these novels can be read as thoroughly orthodox Stalinist assaults on the elements of Soviet society that were impeding progress toward Communism. Yet both novels are highly double-voiced in the Bakhtinian sense, offering at the same time highly antiStalinist readings.

The central character of *The Twelve Chairs* is the prewar aristocrat Ippolit Matveyevich Vorobyaninov, now a petty clerk in a government office.   Vorobyaninov's prospects dramatically change when his mother-in-law reveals on her deathbed that she had hidden her jewels (now worth an enormous 150,000 rubles) in one of the chairs from their dining set that was expropriated (along with the rest of their estate) after the Revolution. Vorobyaninov sets out in search of the chairs and along the way strikes a "business deal" with Bender to help him find them. This pursuit takes Vorobyaninov and Bender on a frantic chase across Soviet Russia in the course of which they meet a veritable rogues' gallery of corrupt officials, greedy NEP-style businessmen, and would-be saboteurs, somewhat along the lines of updated versions of the various figures encountered by Gogol's Chichikov in *Dead Souls*.

This first book was a tremendous popular success, and Ilf and Petrov use the same proven formula in *The Golden Calf*. Indeed, Bender was so popular with readers that he reappears as the major character in *The Golden Calf*, despite the fact that he had ostensibly been murdered by Vorobyaninov at the end of the first book. However, the incorrigible Bender has not learned his lesson and is still on the lookout for an easy road to wealth. In *The Golden Calf* he concocts the scheme of finding a corrupt Soviet millionaire whom he can blackmail in order to attain the funds necessary to escape to Rio de Janeiro, which he envisions as a capitalistic paradise where he would feel much more at home than in Soviet Russia. Bender quickly discovers such a millionaire in the person of Alexander Ivanovich Koreiko, now working (in an echo of Vorobyaninov from *The Twelve Chairs*) as a sort of humble Gogolian clerk to hide his ill-gotten wealth. In the course of the book Bender and his companions pursue Koreiko across much of the Soviet Union, once again encountering in the process a variety of colorful personages from various walks of life. This pursuit provides Ilf and Petrov with numerous opportunities to criticize various enemies of the Soviet system, though at the same time their depiction of life in Soviet Russia as a whole is far from flattering.

Central among the vices criticized by Ilf and Petrov in both books are the selfishness and greed that continued to inform various aspects of Soviet life, thereby impeding the movement toward Communism. The primary driving force for the main characters Vorobyaninov and Bender, as well as for numerous others, seems to be their ambition to bypass the rules of the new socialist society and thereby to gain all possible material advantages and luxuries. Vorobyaninov is a survivor of the old tsarist and bourgeois regime who has disguised his aristocratic origins and thus managed to adapt relatively successfully to the new society. At the same time, he has preserved his old bourgeois/aristocratic values and habits, establishing relationships with people only if he expects material benefit from them. Despite his strong dislike for his mother-in-law, he continues to live with her because she cooks and performs domestic chores for him. As she nears death he feels no personal loss, but ponders whether he should hire some helper or whether it would be better for him to marry someone who could assume his mother-in-law's domestic tasks.

In an obvious nod to Gogol, Vorobyaninov lives at the beginning of the book in "the regional center of N.," but when he learns of the jewels he returns to the former home of his family in the city of Stargorod to seek the hidden treasure. There he joins up with Bender, and the two learn that the twelve chairs of the original dining suite have been removed to Moscow. Bender and Vorobyaninov then go to Moscow, but the chairs are auctioned off and dispersed to various locations before they can acquire them. The resultant quest for the scattered chairs then leads the two treasure hunters on a wild goose chase across the vast Russian landscape, in the course of which Vorobyaninov gradually deteriorates both morally and psychologically until finally he murders his partner Bender to avoid sharing the lucre. Not a very positive person to begin with, Vorobyaninov descends to the depths of depravity and degeneration. He is ready to go to any extent to retrieve the jewels, which become an absolute obsession for him. He is, in short, the embodiment of the kind of bourgeois greed that the new Soviet society is supposedly attempting to extirpate.

But Soviet values ostensibly prevail. After finding the first eleven chairs empty, Vorobyaninov finally tracks down the last of the twelve chairs at a club back in Moscow. He then murders Bender and goes to the club to retrieve the loot. There he meets the watchman of the club, who proudly recounts to Vorobyaninov how he had earlier found the jewels in the chair and unselfishly delivered them to the chairman of the club. To his despair, Vorobyaninov further learns that the money has been used to renovate the club, which will now provide services for both its membership and the wider society. The selfless watchman thus serves as a Soviet paragon who has managed to rid himself of the vices of the bourgeois system and to overcome greed and to acknowledge that community needs have priority over his own personal desires and pleasures.

In contrast, the greedy Vorobyaninov represents the remnants of the "rotten" old prerevolutionary system still very much alive in the new society. Meanwhile, the younger Bender (a teenager at the time of the Revolution) serves in both books as a reminder that such bourgeois vices as greed remain a threat even among those who have come of age under the new Soviet system. Anything but a "new Soviet man," Bender openly rejects the socialist system and dreams about Rio de Janeiro, his symbol of a capitalist haven waiting to embrace him and his capitalist ways. Instead of adapting to the Soviet system, he prefers "to work with a legal millionaire in a well-organized bourgeois state with capitalist traditions" (*The Golden Calf* 26). Despite being a conman and a crook Bender has his own moral code, a code which closely resembles the rules of the capitalist economic game: he avoids violence and overt theft, preferring to extract payment from his marks via subtle persuasion and deception: "I wouldn't smother him with a pillow or club him on the head with a pistol. There wouldn't be anything foolish at all" (26). The "plan" Bender develops in *The Golden Calf* is simply to demand that the millionaire Koreiko hand him over one million rubles, in exchange for which Bender will not reveal the details of Koreiko's illegal business activities to the authorities.

In addition to their depiction of Bender and Koreiko, Ilf and Petrov include numerous other obvious satirical swipes at capitalism in *The Golden Calf*. For example, they tell the story of Adam Kozlevich, a petty criminal who realizes while in prison that crime does not pay, so he turns to business instead, with the obvious Brechtian implication that the two activities are not very different. When he is released from prison Kozlevich buys and repairs a decrepit old car in order to open a taxi business and thereby to cash in on NEP and on the movement toward technological modernization that is sweeping across Russia at the time. Unfortunately, he goes into business in the provincial town of Arbatov, whose unsophisticated residents do not realize the virtues of modern transportation. Far from becoming wealthy in his new entrepreneurial role, Kozlevich struggles even to survive. His business activities degenerate into a sort of comedy of errors, and his only customers are various corrupt local officials who use his taxi as a convenient mode of transportation in their illicit activities. Later, in order to escape the unpleasant situation in Arbatov, Kozlevich becomes Bender's driver on the cross-country chase after Koreiko. The complicity between the former Nepman Kozlevich and criminal elements in Soviet society thus serves as a criticism of the shortcomings of NEP itself. The Nepman Kozlevich introduces small business into Soviet society, but this business brings nothing but trouble either to Kozlevich or to the society. Indeed, this NEP entrepreneurship simply creates more opportunities for government officials to commit crime. Ilf and Petrov again support the official Stalinist line: the abandonment of NEP and the return to the creation of a purely socialist society where there is no private ownership of the means of production.

Such criticism of bourgeois greed and corruption in the Soviet population provided relatively safe ground for Ilf and Petrov in the generally risky business of writing satire under the reign of Stalin, though it is clearly possible that an overemphasis on such vices might suggest either that the Soviet system itself was flawed or that these "bourgeois" tendencies were in fact an element of human nature. In similarly orthodox fashion, Ilf and Petrov focus a great deal of their satire on religion, another of the central enemies of the Stalinist revolution from above. The third major character in *The Twelve Chairs* is Father Fyodor Vostrikov, a materialistic Orthodox priest whose role in the book is to demonstrate a complicity between religion and the kind of bourgeois values represented by Vorobyaninov. Father Fyodor's lifelong goal is to become rich, and he spends his time envisioning various outlandish business projects. All his projects, however, comically fail when put into practice. For example, he decides to establish a rabbit farm because he has read somewhere that rabbits reproduce quickly and that their meat is cheap and good. Unfortunately, Father Fyodor's conservative neighbors refuse to introduce rabbit meat into their diets, so he is left without customers. Meanwhile, the entire rabbit population dies after eating some rotten cabbage that a nearby cooperative dumps into the cesspool it shares with the Vostrikovs.

The main goal of all the enterprises that Father Fyodor undertakes is to acquire enough capital for opening his own candle factory in Samara so that he can supply candles to the Church and thereby cash in on his religion. He at last seems to have his chance to obtain the necessary funds when he hears the confession of Vorobyaninov's dying mother-in-law and thereby learns of the existence of the hidden jewels. He then abandons his church and sets out himself in search of the treasure, competing along the way with Vorobyaninov and Bender. After a series of ludicrous misadventures, Father Fyodor loses everything he has in his futile pursuit of the chairs and finally goes insane. In their portrayal of this ridiculous priest Ilf and Petrov suggest (again in line with the official view) the irrelevance of religion to Soviet society and the complicity between the Church and capitalism—those who run the church are just a specific type of businessman who are primarily concerned with the financial success of their business.

In *The Golden Calf* Ilf and Petrov continue their satire of religion, focusing this time on the Catholic Church. Here the role played by the Orthodox Father Fyodor in *The Twelve Chairs* is assumed by the Catholic priests Kuszakowksi and Moroszek. These priests "operate" in the city of Chernomorsk where Bender arrives in pursuit of his millionaire. While Bender is pursuing the millionaire, his driver Kozlevich is approached in a local pub by the two priests, who themselves turn out to be conmen very much in the mold of Bender. They set about attempting to recruit Kozlevich for their church so that they can gain possession of his car. Indeed, the depiction of the priests comes close to caricature that exaggerates their lust for the car almost to slapstick proportions. As in their depiction of the Orthodox priest Father Fyodor, Ilf and Petrov explicitly point out that greed, rather than spirituality, is the motivation of these Catholic priests. The priests are not interested in Kozlevich's soul at all; what they want is free transportation.

These attacks on Catholicism are, of course, perfectly in line with the Communist ideology of the Soviet Union. However, they also match closely the standard Orthodox rhetoric which regarded Catholicism as a perversion of Christianity and one of the world's greatest existing evils. Thus, when Ilf and Petrov make the priests Catholic (and Polish), they also bring resonances of other rather interesting issues into their novel. According to the Russian Orthodox position, the Polish people are Slavs who have chosen the wrong—that is to say Catholic—religion and who, in that sense, have betrayed their Slavic origins. The Poles radically differ from the Russian people, both in their historical development and in their culture with its strong

Western European leanings. Western influences in Russia were often not welcome, especially to the Russophiles, who regarded Western European culture as the source of cultural and religious pollution and contamination of the "pure" Russian soul, as well as the cause of the degeneration of the supposedly great Russian nation, its civilization and tradition. Because Western European influences often entered Russia via Poland, the Polish nation was usually perceived as the source of those evil Westernizing forces bent on destroying Mother Russia. Catholicism, in particular, was seen as the epitome of all that was negative which arrived from the West.

Yet the Orthodox fear of Western contamination of Russian culture itself has much in common with the Stalinist paranoia of outside influences in the new Soviet society. Indeed, the numerous resonances of Russian ideology in Stalin's rule have been noted many times. Despite his violent opposition to the Church, Stalin used many of its techniques and strategies in furthering his own power, to the point that it has by now become something of a cliché to note the extent to which the ex-seminarian Stalin attempted to endow his regime with a religious aura. During his rule, Stalin mercilessly enforced his political position and kept his subjects in terror by using methods of oppression similar to the ones that the Orthodox Church had long used to keep its flocks in submission. Many of Stalin's techniques of political domination are directly reminiscent of various religious rites. For instance, the method of self-criticism that the Communist Party practiced, which was particularly emphasized during the show trials during the thirties, has strong resonances of a religious act: a member of the Party will confess his "sins" and ask his fellow members for forgiveness. Furthermore, the cult of personality that Stalin strongly encouraged—first in regard to Lenin (who was elevated to the status of a socialist saint immediately after his death) and then in regard to himself—also has strong religious overtones.

Thus, when Ilf and Petrov satirize the Orthodox church, their critique can potentially be interpreted as an indirect criticism of Stalin and his techniques of ruling as well. Indeed, a closer look at the "proStalinist" satire of their two novels shows it to be consistently double-voiced: not only is their genre inconsistent with support of authority, but many of their motifs can in fact be read as subtle critiques of the Soviet regime. For example, while the humble watchman in *The Twelve Chairs* appears on the surface to be a positive hero of the kind found in socialist realism, Ilf and Petrov are also careful to point out that he had thought the jewels to be worthless glass beads at the time he handed them over to the chairman. They leave open the possibility that he would not have been so selfless had he realized the true value of the jewels. Similarly, Ilf and Petrov write in a relatively simple style, in accord with the value placed on accessibility in socialist realism. Yet their novels are actually quite literary, employing frequent allusions to other works that tend to generate a complex intertextual network of meaning that goes far beyond the ostensibly proSoviet surface of their own texts.[4]

For example, Gogol (hardly an example of good Soviet ideology) is a constant presence in both of the novels of Ilf and Petrov. Many motifs in Ilf and Petrov also recall Gogol's great literary descendent, Fyodor Dostoevsky. Dostoevsky was a great enemy of Catholicism, regarding it as a perversion of Christianity that furthered its power through violence and brutality.[5] Similarly, Dostoevsky argued (especially in his journalism) that Western European culture was a force bent on corrupting the "pure" Russian soul. In their criticism of the Catholic priests Kuszakowksi and Moroszek, then, Ilf and Petrov appear to be perfectly consistent with the strident Orthodoxy of Dostoevsky. On the other hand, their treatment of the Orthodox priest Father Fyodor serves as a critique of Orthodoxy and thereby of the ideology of Dostoevsky, who after all is Father Fyodor's namesake.

Of course, Dostoevsky's novels are themselves anything but simplistic defenses of Russian Orthodoxy. It is, in fact, the complex and contradictory nature of Dostoevsky's texts that makes him such an important figure for Bakhtin. For example, Bakhtin identifies the "hopeless attempts" of both Dostoevsky and Gogol to express their authoritarian Orthodox ideologies in their fiction as examples of the inherent opposition of the novel form to authoritarian discourse (*Dialogic* 344). Thus any echoes of Dostoevsky that sound in the texts of Ilf and Petrov potentially invest their texts with a dialogic complexity as well. Indeed, though the link with Gogol is more obvious and direct, the texts of Ilf and Petrov—with their crime story plots and their sometimes grotesque satires of greed and corruption—have more in common with the work of Dostoevsky than is immediately obvious.[6] If Vorobyaninov's abject "murder" of Bender might have been taken straight from Dostoevsky, it is also true that scenes like the antics of the innkeeper Trifon Borisovich in *The Brothers Karamazov*, who greedily dismantles his establishment in search of the money supposedly hidden there by Dmitri Karamazov, might have been taken straight from Ilf and Petrov. As Dmitri relates to his brother Alexei,

"Borisich, I mean, has destroyed his whole inn, they say: he's taking up the floorboards, ripping out planks, they say he's broken his 'verander' to bits—looking for treasure all the time, for the money, the fifteen hundred the prosecutor said I'd hidden there." (762)[7]

Reading Ilf and Petrov through Bakhtin's figuration of Dostoevsky as a polyphonic novelist is particularly valuable because it suggests that their texts might not be so monologically orthodox (in a Stalinist sense) as they appear. This is especially true as Dostoevsky himself was a sort of *avant la lettre* critic of Stalinism. A strong opponent of socialism, Dostoevsky often embeds in his texts criticisms of the budding socialist movement in Russia that prophesy the Bolshevik Revolution and the subsequent abuses of Stalinism in striking ways. In his novel *Devils* Dostoevsky portrays a group of young intellectuals led by Peter Verkhovensky who attempt to introduce socialism into Russia by force. Verkhovensky (whose career curiously anticipates that of Lenin in a number of ways) has returned to his homeland from exile in Switzerland in order to further his plan of starting a revolution in Russia. His plan is to infiltrate revolutionary units of five into a small Russian town and thereby to create confusion, fear, and chaos. The resulting disorder will then presumably destabilize the society enough to make the Revolution possible. However, anticipating later writers like Zamyatin, Dostoevsky suggests that this budding revolution may bring not a socialist paradise, but a totalitarian dystopia. In particular, Verkhovensky's summary of the "ideals" of his fellow revolutionary Shigalyov foreshadows the cynicism of Stalinism:

Everyone belongs to all the others and the others belong to each one. They're all slaves and equal in their slavery. In extreme cases there's slander and murder, but for the most part—equality. . . . As soon as a man experiences love or has a family, he wants private property. We'll destroy that want: we'll unleash drunkenness, slander, denunciation; we'll unleash unheard-of corruption; we'll suffocate every genius in its infancy. Everything will be reduced to a common denominator of complete equality. (442-3)

Dostoevsky's satire of the socialist revolutionaries in *Devils* can sometimes be quite funny. For example, a business meeting at which they gather degenerates into comic confusion and miscommunication:

"Verkhovensky, don't you have anything to report to us?" Madame Virginskaya asked directly.
"Absolutely nothing," he replied yawning and stretching on his chair. "I'd really like a glass of brandy, though."

"Stavrogin, what about you?"
"No thank you, I don't drink." (424-5)

Such passages allow Dostoevsky to have fun at the expense of his socialist enemies, though there is a serious element in the way the Beckettian absurdity of such exchanges undermines the supposed rationality of the socialists.

Interestingly, Dostoevsky's socialist revolutionaries bear a number of resemblances to a group of antisocialist revolutionaries Ilf and Petrov depict in *The Twelve Chairs*. In an effort to raise money to finance their quest for the chairs Bender and Vorobyaninov organize a group of malcontents into the "The Alliance of the Sword and Plowshare," a secret society whose goal is the overthrow of the Soviet state. But these revolutionaries are of course no threat to the powers that be. Indeed, they serve simply as dupes from whom Bender can extract financial contributions, supposedly to further his subversive activities. It is hardly surprising, given the presumably proStalinist slant of their text, that Ilf's and Petrov's comically incompetent revolutionaries turn out to be the butts of a considerable amount of satire . On the other hand, the suggestion that certain elements of the Soviet populace would like to see a radical change in the government, while ostensibly calling for vigilance against the enemies of socialism, potentially suggests a widespread discontent that threatens to undermine the myth of Soviet solidarity. Moreover, should one choose to read between the lines it is not difficult to find certain similarities between this small band of subversives and their Bolshevik predecessors on the other end of the ideological spectrum, similarities that are further enhanced if one sees "The Alliance of the Sword and the Plowshare" as an echo of the socialist revolutionaries of Dostoevsky.

In addition to such links with the Russian literary past, Ilf and Petrov also comment extensively on the literary and artistic scene in their contemporary Soviet Union. For example, in *The Golden Calf* Ilf and Petrov quite directly address the difficulties faced by artists under Soviet censorship when they tell the story of the old man Sinitsky, a composer of riddles whose career is ruined because he is unable to make his productions ideologically correct (100-105). Moreover, their description of the products of those who are able to adapt to ideological correctness suggests that the new Soviet society has hardly inspired great art. With the great Communist base in place, the superstructure of the everyday world is responding in kind:

All the inventions of the little antlike world are now based on a solid "Communist" ideology. . . . In the latest hit song a clever mechanic fulfills or even overfulfills his financial norm in three verses in order to win the love of a Young Communist girl. And while the big world heatedly discusses the new way of life, in the little world everything is ready: there is a "Shock-worker's Dream" tie, a plaster statue entitled *The Bathing Collective-Farm Girl*, and cork under-arm pads for ladies sold under the trade name "Worker-Bees' Delight." (101)

Within what is presented as an enthusiastic endorsement of ideological conformity, Ilf and Petrov here combine a Gogolian attack on *poshlost* with implications that are anything but flattering to the Soviet regime. But Dostoevsky here provides an important intertext as well. In particular, the description of Soviet society as "antlike" echoes Dostoevsky's use of the anthill as a symbol for the potential dystopian consequences of rationalist/socialist ideologies.[8]

The story of Sinitsky, especially when read through Dostoevsky, suggests that Russian art (like Russian society in general) has suffered mightily under the Soviet regime. On the other hand, it is true that the Revolution initially inspired revolutionary innovations by numerous artists who supported the Revolution and the changes it brought. Artistic innovation and experimentation were officially supported by many high members of the Communist party, especially by Anatoly Lunacharsky, the head of the new Soviet Commisariat of Enlightenment (in charge of education, culture and art). Various forms of avant-garde art including literature, theater, painting, and sculpture thus flourished during the 1920s. But the situation changed again with the reorganization of the political structure and with the shift in power at the end of that decade. The proponents of socialist realism in literature and other forms of expression emphasized the utilitarian aspect of art and claimed that its purpose was to provide unreserved support for the Bolshevik Revolution and its aims. Avant-garde experimentation and innovation came to be seen as aspects of an antirevolutionary "bourgeois decadence."

One of the important avant-garde artists of the period both before and after the Bolshevik revolution was Vsevolod Meyerhold, who revolutionized Russian theater and greatly influenced the development of world theater as well.[9] By the time of the Bolshevik Revolution Meyerhold was already renowned for his experimentation in theater and for his unorthodox staging and free adaptation of plays. Meyerhold was one of the very few intellectuals and artists who responded to Lunacharsky's invitation to join the forces of the new society and contribute to the development of Soviet art and culture.

Together with the poet Vladimir Mayakovsky and a few other artists, Meyerhold understood what daring perspectives the Revolution potentially opened to Russian society and its artists and saw a parallel between revolution in art and the Bolshevik revolution in Russian society. During the 1920s Meyerhold held a number of prominent official positions, including the directorship of the State Institute for Theater Art and of his own state-sponsored studio, the Theater of Meyerhold. In these positions Meyerhold directed a number of memorable productions that together constituted what was "probably the most remarkable artistic phenomenon of the entire post-revolutionary period" (Thomson 113). Despite his many successes, however, Meyerhold was always a controversial figure, and by the end of the 1920s he had largely fallen out of favor with the increasingly conservative Soviet regime.

Meyerhold's most controversial production was probably his 1926 staging of Gogol's *The Inspector General*. Meyerhold took great liberties with Gogol's text, despite the status of the play as a classic of Russian literature and the status of Gogol himself as a figure of literary authority. In order to emphasize the difference between his own Soviet context and Gogol's tsarist one, Meyerhold transformed the play by emphasizing its satirical aspects and by producing it via a number of avant-garde techniques of stage presentation. Meyerhold's radically unorthodox restaging of Gogol's classic play mirrored similar revisions of the classics by directors like Erwin Piscator and Bertolt Brecht in the West, but it also triggered a storm of protest among many in Meyerhold's Russian audiences, who reacted violently to what they apparently saw as an affront to the nineteenth-century cultural tradition inherited by modern Russia. As Eaton notes, the performance "was so unusual and alien to the expectations of its audiences that it provoked a greater outburst of critical and popular controversy than was customary even for Meyerhold's innovation. Russian audiences resented his tampering with a beloved national property" (209).

Crucial to Meyerhold's new approach to Gogol was, as Eaton points out, his rejection of "the traditional interpretation of the play as sheer farce, by presenting it as a pessimistic vision of public and private vanity, greed and hypocrisy" (209-210). While figures like Lunacharsky and Mayakovsky defended Meyerhold's production, the important German critic Walter Benjamin (who attended public debates organized by Meyerhold himself to discuss the staging of the play) concluded rightfully that the performance of *The Inspector General* and the ensuing uproar marked the beginning of the end for Meyerhold as an officially sanctioned artist (Eaton 210).[10]

By the time of the publication of *The Twelve Chairs* it would have been fashionable to criticize, or even to mock, Meyerhold's avant-garde productions. Ilf and Petrov ostensibly do just that. Several of the chairs that Bender and Vorobyaninov are pursuing are bought by a theater troupe for use as stage props. In order to retrieve the chairs, Bender joins the troupe, currently on a tour in the provinces with its new performance of Gogol's *The Marriage*. The troupe stages this rather conventional play (about a young girl who is courted by several men at the same time) in a highly unconventional manner. In fact, their presentation clearly recalls Meyerhold's production of *The Inspector General*, complete with avant-garde stage effects and contemporary political allusions, horrifying the conservative Vorobyaninov.

Ilf and Petrov apparently present this production as ridiculous, and the implied criticism of Meyerhold seems clear. On the other hand, Vorobyaninov is hardly a reliable critic, and his rejection of the play can almost be taken as a recommendation. The suggestion by Ilf and Petrov of a certain philistinism in Meyerhold's adaptation of Gogol to the contemporary political climate thus rebounds on itself, suggesting in turn a certain philistinism in the rejection of Meyerhold by Vorobyaninov (and by the Soviet literary authorities). Indeed, by having Gogol's play staged according to the principles of Meyerhold's theater, Ilf and Petrov call attention to Meyerhold's approach to Gogol and open up the possibility of reading their work in the way Meyerhold reads Gogol's. *The Twelve Chairs*, like *The Inspector General*, can be read superficially as a "sheer farce." But a slightly different reading reveals a serious undertone that can enable readers to view the book as a serious satire potentially damning to the Soviet authorities, whose own rejection of Meyerhold can be taken as evidence of the narrowmindedness and philistine vulgarity that would increasingly come to characterize Soviet culture during the reign of Stalin.[11]

By this reading Ilf and Petrov ostensibly attack an accepted enemy of the Soviet regime, only subtly to align themselves with that enemy against the regime. The hints of philistinism in modern Soviet culture that sound in this treatment of Meyerhold can be found elsewhere in *The Twelve Chairs* as well. For example, Ilf and Petrov suggest that the vaunted fondness of the Russian people for museums bespeaks not a respect for culture but simply a desire longingly to observe artifacts from the lifestyles of the rich and famous of the tsarist past (156-7). Meanwhile, one of Bender's money-making schemes early in the book involves the renovation of the classics from the Russian cultural past for sale to modern audiences, as when he envisions transforming

Repin's well-known painting *The Zaporozhe Cossacks Answer the Sultan* into *The Bolsheviks Answer Chamberlain* (37). As with the treatment of Meyerhold, such motifs can be read as perfectly conventional Stalinist critiques of the remaining bourgeois elements in Soviet society. In particular, Bender's renovation of Repin clearly echoes Meyerhold's renovation of Gogol. But such episodes can equally well be read as commentaries on the cultural poverty of Stalinism itself, which forced artists to adapt to the demands of current ideological orthodoxy in order to do their work at all. As Zholkovsky notes, "ideological censorship, as a sui generis variant of the adaptation problem, figures prominently" in the writing of Ilf and Petrov (39).

There are numerous ways Ilf and Petrov seem in their writing to be doing Stalin's work, while offering alternative readings that potentially represent biting criticisms of the Stalinist regime. Sprinkled throughout both books, for example, are occasional mentions of the various purges that were already under way in an attempt to eliminate counterrevolutionary forces from the new Soviet society. These purges, which were later to grow into the more overt Stalinist Terror of the mid-1930s, principally took the form in the late 1920s and early 1930s of the removal of individuals from their jobs on the basis of incompetence or corruption. The characters of Ilf and Petrov have good reason to fear such purges, of course, generally being themselves both incompetent and corrupt.

A central example of the purge motif in *The Golden Calf* concerns the story of Berlaga, an employee in the same government office as Koreiko. Concerned by rumors that he is about to be purged, Berlaga feigns madness and manages to have himself committed to an insane asylum to escape punishment. In the asylum, he meets not lunatics but other perfectly sane citizens who have had the same idea and who are rather pleased to be in the asylum. As one of them points out,

"In Soviet Russia," he said, draping himself in his blanket, "the madhouse is the only place where a normal man can live. Everywhere else is a super-bedlam. No, I can't live with the Bolsheviks. I would rather stay here. At least ordinary mad people don't want to build socialism. And, anyway, we're fed here. Outside in that bedlam you have to work. I'm not going to work for their socialism. I have personal freedom here. Freedom of belief, freedom of speech . . ." (*Golden* 188, Ilf's and Petrov's ellipsis)

The patient proves this freedom of speech when an orderly passes by and the patient starts shouting insults as well as "Long live the

Constituent Assembly" and explains to Berlaga that "I can shout what I want. Just try doing that on the street!" (189). Because these words are said by a presumed "raving lunatic" they are largely ignored by the authorities. We know, however, that the speaker is perfectly sane. Moreover, though Ilf and Petrov are careful to depict these fake lunatics as work shirkers and decadent enemies of the people, their criticisms of Soviet society are all too close to the mark. In particular, this episode not only suggests a close parallel between life in a lunatic asylum and life in Russia under Stalin, but also anticipates what would become a standard Stalinist practice of committing political enemies to such asylums.

Another episode that takes on added poignancy in light of later developments in the 1930s concerns the story of the "stand-in" Funt, who makes his living by serving prison sentences in the place of others for a fee. Now ninety years old, Funt has spent most of his life in prison, serving terms under the regimes of the last three tsars, as well as during the Kerensky period and during NEP. When he offers his "services" to Bender, Funt thus indicates his willingness to add Stalin to the list of rulers under whom he has served sentences, a motif that ostensibly shows the recalcitrance of certain reactionary elements of Soviet society, who have failed to learn the lessons of the Revolution. But it is also possible to read the Funt episode as an indication that Stalin can be grouped with Alexander II, Alexander III, Nicholas II, and Kerensky as leaders who maintained their power by fundamentally oppressive means. If nothing else, Funt's appearance in *The Golden Calf* indicates the growing number of Soviet citizens who were being imprisoned under the Stalinist regime, as well as anticipating the massive programs of incarceration that would characterize the coming decade.

Ilf and Petrov can get away with this focus on purges and imprisonment because that focus ostensibly serves the purpose of the Stalinist regime, which sought not to keep the purges secret, but to publicize them and thereby to use them as a warning against their potential enemies. The tone for this use of the threat of purges as official propaganda was set in the famous 1928 trial of fifty engineers for sabotage in the Shakhty mines. Stalin saw to it that this trial (the forerunner of the more spectacular show trials of the 1930s) was widely publicized and took advantage of this event to call for a new vigilance by the Soviet populace in attempting to eradicate reactionary forces from their midst. He also used the engineers involved as scapegoats, making them symbols of the bourgeois menace, whose threat he used as a justification for some of his more oppressive policies. In a speech to the Central Committee of the Communist

Party, Stalin specifically targeted such engineers and other industry
specialists as enemies of the Soviet regime:

Shakhtyites are now ensconced in every branch of our industry . . . By
no means have all been caught.   Wrecking by the bourgeois
intelligentsia is one of the most dangerous forces of opposition to
developing socialism, all the more dangerous in that it is connected
with international capitalism. The capitalists have by no means laid
down their arms; they are massing their forces for new attacks on the
Soviet government. (cited in Bullock 283)

    Ilf and Petrov echo Stalin's warning against engineers and other
bourgeois intellectuals as enemies of the Revolution in their depiction
in *The Golden Calf* of the engineer Talmudovsky, who makes a series
of cameo appearances throughout the book though he is not involved
in the main plot.
While apparently not a member of an organized capitalist conspiracy,
Talmudovsky is clearly a counterrevolutionary. He has no socialist
ideals and is interested only in his own material gain. He is frequently
met in the course of the narrative wandering around the Soviet Union
in search of better paying jobs, a motif that associates him with the
similar peripatetic activities of Bender in his own quest for easy
wealth. Talmudovsky wanders from one job to another regardless of
his contractual obligations.   He is eternally dissatisfied with the
conditions he has to work in, constantly complaining about the lack of
cultural and other activities and the insensitivity and primitivism of
the officials who have to take care of his needs.
    The depiction of Talmudovsky by Ilf and Petrov follows a
perfectly acceptable Stalinist line. At the same time, their enactment
of the Stalinist strategy of scapegoating specific elements of the Soviet
population in order to further his goals suggests certain serious
shortcomings in Stalin's own "communal" spirit, just as the depiction
of private citizens living in perpetual fear of being purged (and in
particular in the fear that their fellow employees might inform against
them) suggests a Soviet society whose true nature is far different from
the worker's utopia envisioned in the official propaganda of Stalinism.
Such scapegoating strategies have, of course, frequently been used in
modern society. For example, in *Civilization and Its Discontents*
(published in 1930 and therefore contemporaneous with Ilf and
Petrov) Sigmund Freud discusses the persecution of the Jews in Nazi
Germany as a general aspect of human aggressivity. It is human
nature, argues Freud, to fight against others rather than to work with
them, so human societies are often held together by focusing natural

aggressive energies on a common enemy, typically a marginal social group. For Freud, through the phenomenon that he refers to as "the narcissism of minor differences," the human instinct for aggression typically finds its outlet in the identification of scapegoats (like Jews) who are in fact only marginally different from the official norm. "It is always possible," he argues, "to bind together a considerable number of people in love, so long as there are other people left over to receive the manifestations of their aggressiveness" (68). Importantly, Freud links this same motif with the attempts of the Stalinist regime to extirpate the remaining bourgeois elements in Russian society. He suggests that the communal energies of Soviet society are generated more through hatred of the bourgeoisie than through love of their own ideals.

Interestingly, Freud damningly compares the "persecution of the bourgeois" in the Soviet Union directly to the persecution of the Jews in Nazi Germany, a suggestion of obvious relevance to the treatment of Talmudovsky by Ilf and Petrov. Talmudovsky is the embodiment of the "bourgeois specialist" so reviled by Stalin. But he is also, as his name indicates, a figure of the Jew, and he is often described in terms of antiSemitic clichés like the repeated mention of his "pendulous bananalike nose" that serves as a sort of leitmotif introducing his appearances in the text. As with their satire of the bourgeoisie, the antiSemitic flavor of the treatment of Talmudovsky by Ilf and Petrov closely echoes Stalin's own antiSemitism. However, read through Freud, the parallel satire in Ilf and Petrov of Jews and of bourgeois elements in Soviet society can be taken as a severe criticism of the hypocrisy of a Stalinist regime that espoused universal Communist brotherhood and then solidified that brotherhood through the persecution of selected segments of Russian society.

In addition to their treatment of Talmudovsky, Ilf and Petrov themselves echo the traditional antiSemitism of Russian society by sprinkling vaguely antiSemitic jokes and stereotypes throughout both their books. Bender himself is rather given to such "humor," as when he gives a speech to a gathering of townspeople in which "he made jokes, recounted some funny motoring stories, and told Jewish jokes, which greatly amused the public" (*Golden* 81). Nowhere in either novel do Ilf and Petrov specifically challenge the antiSemitic proclivities of their characters. On the other hand, the antiSemitic remarks and witticisms that are interspersed throughout *The Twelve Chairs* and *The Golden Calf* take on a special significance in light of the fact that Ilf himself was Jewish. Among other things, the motif of antiSemitism in Ilf and Petrov can thus be taken as a subtle criticism of the antiSemitism that continued to inform the official attitudes of the Soviet regime, despite its professed rejection of such divisive attitudes in favor of Communist universal brotherhood. On the surface it appears that Ilf and Petrov reflect the traditional attitudes toward Jews in Russian society by mocking them in their novels. On the other hand, one could just as well read their treatment of Jews as a subtle parody of the antiSemitic mindset of most Russians of that time, and by implication of Stalin, who played upon the virulent Russian tendency toward antiSemitism by identifying the bourgeois specialists he railed against with Jewishness.[12]

Ilf and Petrov specifically call attention to international rumors of the mistreatment of Jews in the Soviet Union. In *The Golden Calf* the American Zionist journalist Berman interviews the Soviet representative Palamidov about the "Jewish problem," but Palamidov categorically denies that any such problem exists: "No, there are Jews, but no Jewish problem" (294). Berman's desire to find evidence of antiSemitism in the Soviet Union (and his subsequent disappointment at finding no such evidence) can easily be read as a criticism of the foreign bourgeois press who incessantly searched for negative things to report about Soviet society. But the passage can also be interpreted as a subtle criticism of the ways the Soviets dealt with some of the problems that faced them simply by denying that they existed. In addition, Palamidov's insistence that there is no "problem" with antiSemitism in the Soviet Union is clearly double-voiced: he may be indicating that there is no antiSemitism in the Soviet Union, or that the Soviets do not regard antiSemitism as a problem.

Only a few pages after the conversation between Berman and Palamidov, Bender tells a supposedly humorous story whose dark undertones suggest even more clearly the negative treatment of Jews in the Soviet Union. In his "Story of the Wandering Jew" (one of the many inserted genres in the texts of Ilf and Petrov), Bender relates the worldwide travels of his protagonist over a span of 2,000 years. Then, in 1919 the Wandering Jew crosses the Rumanian border into the Soviet Union. There he is captured by Cossacks and executed by a firing squad, simply for being a suspicious "Yid" (309-311). Bender's story is supposedly intended as a slap at certain groups of Cossacks who supported the Germans and Austrians against the Russians in World War I; it is told in direct response to an antiSoviet story that has just been related by the former Austrian army officer Herr Heinrich. But, as with the other "defenses" of the Soviet Union in Ilf and Petrov, the potential for an antiSoviet reading here is clear. The story can easily be read as an allegory of the persecution of Jews by the legal authorities in the Soviet Union.

Bender's story takes on a special significance at the end of the book when Bender himself, having become a millionaire, attempts to escape with his new-found wealth (which has proved useless to him in the Soviet Union) across the border *into* Rumania. In a mirror image of the experience of the Wandering Jew, Bender is captured by Rumanian border guards, who rob him of his wealth and drive him back across the border. On the surface, Bender's treatment in Rumania suggests the cruelty of capitalism, but (when read in conjunction with the earlier story of the Wandering Jew) the experience potentially suggests that there is little difference between the forces of official power inside the Soviet Union and those of capitalist power surrounding Stalin's socialist state.

The suggested parallel between the capitalist Bender and the Wandering Jew contributes to the network of images throughout the work of Ilf and Petrov in which Jews are associated with bourgeois values, or, from another point of view, in which the persecution of the bourgeoisie in the Soviet Union is linked to the persecution of the Jews. The scapegoating phenomenon represented by such antiSemitic and antibourgeois energies again recalls Freud's comments on the "narcissism of minor differences." It can also be usefully illuminated through an appeal to the work of Bakhtin. In his discussions of the carnivalesque, Bakhtin particularly figures the carnival as a place where representatives of different social groups meet and interact on the same level, so that the hierarchies arising from the "minor differences" cited by Freud collapse. Of course, such a collapse of traditional social hierarchies was presumably an integral part of the postrevolutionary society of the Soviet Union. Bakhtin's criticisms of the strictly hierarchical authoritarian society of medieval Europe in *Rabelais and His World* can thus be read as a coded commentary on the continued existence of such hierarchies under Stalin, especially as the book contains so many other veiled parallels between the medieval Catholic Church and the modern Communist Party.

The work of Ilf and Petrov also clearly suggests that such divisive hierarchies continue to exist in their Soviet Union. In addition, Bakhtin's work points toward the way the texts of Ilf and Petrov challenge these hierarchies not only through thematic content, but also through the generic texture of their works. As Peter Stallybrass and Allon White have shown, one can generalize the Bakhtinian "carnival" into a more generalized notion of "transgression," which involves a violation of the rules of hierarchies in any of a number of areas, including the classification of literary works into the categories of "high" and "low" culture. Stallybrass and White suggest that a transgression in any one of these kinds of hierarchies has important

consequences in the others as well.   They also place particular
emphasis on the identification of marginal, excluded groups in
opposition to which those more centrally positioned in a society can
define themselves, using this opposition "to demarcate boundaries, to
unite and purify the social collectivity" (193). In this sense their work
is especially relevant to the motif of antiSemitism that runs through
the texts of Ilf and Petrov. But the emphasis by Stallybrass and White
on the participation of literary genres and conventions in this
phenomenon also suggests a transgressive function in the mixture of
genres that characterizes the work of Ilf and Petrov. The "popular"
fictions of Ilf and Petrov themselves seem to belong to the category of
"low" literature, yet they also manage to open dialogues with classic
writers of Russian "high" culture like Pushkin, Gogol, and Dostoevsky.
Moreover, Ilf and Petrov also manage to incorporate into their texts
bits and pieces of other genres as well, including newspaper stories,
letters, telegrams, how-to manuals, guidebooks, lectures,
encyclopedias, theater performances, and films. The resultant mixture
of genres (and their accompanying ideologies) produces a richly
dialogic texture that in itself is already inimical to the authoritarian
ideology of Stalinism. This mixture of ideologies combines with the
inherent antiauthoritarianism of satire and with a number of specific
motifs in the texts of Ilf and Petrov to generate a potentially powerful
critique of the Stalinist regime, despite the ostensibly proregime stance
of those texts. Indeed, it is this very mixture of proStalinist and
antiStalinist energies that makes the novels of Ilf and Petrov
particularly rich examples of double-voiced discourse. Moreover, Ilf
and Petrov themselves suggest such readings with the seemingly
innocent epigraph to *The Golden Chairs*: "Look both ways before
crossing the street."

     If Ilf and Petrov often seem to repeat the standard rhetoric of
Stalinism, they do so in a way that allows for that repetition to be read
as subtle parody, regardless of whether or not Ilf and Petrov
themselves anticipated such readings. One could argue, then, that the
central informing technique of the two satirists is what Bakhtin calls
"gay deception," the process through which rogues, fools, and picaros
in the novel repeat bogus discourses of authority and rob them of their
power. Such characters thus "turn what was a lie into gay deception.
Falsehood is illuminated by ironic consciousness and in the mouth of
the happy rogue parodies itself" (*Dialogic* 402). Ostap Bender is
obviously just such a gay deceiver, but Ilf and Petrov may be as well.
In their ostensibly simple texts the rhetoric of Stalinism turns into a
self-parody so subtle that it escaped the Stalinist censors. But this
parody contains potentially powerful subversive energies because it

illuminates the falsehoods of Stalinism in the most damning voice of all–Stalin's own.

NOTES

1. "Ilf and Petrov" is the joint pen name used by Ilya Arnoldovich Fainzilberg (1897-1937) and Yevgeny Petrovich Katayev (1903-1942).

2. It is interesting to note that, although their books are firmly set in the reality of the Soviet system of the late 1920s and early 1930s when Stalin was a major political force in the society, Ilf and Petrov never explicitly mention Stalin.

3. NEP (New Economic Policy) was the economic policy adopted by Lenin in 1921 to allow limited free enterprise in the Soviet economy, especially in small industry and agriculture. The purpose of NEP was to provide a respite from the economic hardships associated with the Revolution and Civil War. However, the new policy caused considerable resentment among many ordinary citizens because it was perceived as a cynical betrayal of the Revolution and its socialist ideals. NEP lasted until 1929 when Stalin declared a return to the road to socialism and embarked upon a program of merciless extirpation of all remaining bourgeois elements in Soviet society.

4. In their two novels, Ilf and Petrov refer to a wide range of both Russian and Western authors, including Tolstoy, Lermontov, Pushkin, Esenin, Leonid Andreev, Shakespeare, Homer, Milton, and d'Annunzio.

5. For a discussion of Dostoevsky's virulent antiCatholicism see Dirscherl.

6. Dostoevsky has often been perceived in the West as a dark and brooding writer driven by metaphysical angst. However, his work has a strong comic and satirical element, as Bakhtin was one of the first to emphasize.

7. Ilf and Petrov specifically signal the relevance of *The Brothers Karamazov* to *The Golden Calf* by having Bender send to Koreiko an enigmatic telegram signed as coming from "The Brothers Karamazov" (114). While this passing reference does not at first seem significant, it does plant a seed that potentially asks readers to compare Ilf and Petrov to Dostoevsky. Indeed, many aspects of the work of Ilf and Petrov can be read as subtle evasions of the Soviet censors, in the Russian tradition of Aesopian language.

8. In addition to his warning in *Notes from Underground* that a Chernyshevskyan rationalist utopia would reduce human civilization to the status of an anthill (37), Dostoevsky has the Grand Inquisitor use the same image in his description of the desire of humanity for "a

means for uniting everyone at last into a common, concordant, and incontestible anthill" (*Brothers* 257).

9. For example, Meyerhold's radical innovations in staging and dramatic presentation influenced the epic theater of Brecht. See Eaton.

10. The decline in Meyerhold's fortunes continued through the 1930s. After publicly denouncing Soviet policies toward the arts in June 1939, he was arrested and presumably executed.

11. Ilf and Petrov directly satirize the vulgarity and *poshlost* of Soviet culture in a variety of ways. In *The Twelve Chairs*, for example, they present some of the compositions of the hack poet Nikifor Lapis, whose doggerel "epic" verse the "Gavriliad" depicts its "hero" Gavrila in a variety of utterly banal activities. While the *Gavriliada* of Pushkin is not one of the poet's most respected works, the implied contrast between Lapis and Pushkin nevertheless makes a powerful commentary on the fate of Russian culture under Soviet rule. In particular, Pushkin's poem is a wildly irreverent and antiauthoritarian parody of the Christian Annunciation, while Lapis's poem is thoroughly without antiauthoritarian (or any other) energies.

12. Robert Conquest remarks that Stalin's antiSemitic feeling goes back to as early as 1907, when he was remarking, in the small underground paper he then controlled at Baku, "Somebody among the Bolsheviks remarked jokingly that since the Mensheviks were the faction of the Jews and the Bolsheviks that of the native Russians, it would be a good thing to have a pogrom in the Party" (65).

4

Language, Genre, and Satire in the Works of Mikhail Zoshchenko

In his short story "Poverty" (1925) Mikhail Zoshchenko tells a tale that might serve as a mini-allegory of his entire literary career. The story deals with the electrification of a large communal apartment building in postrevolutionary Moscow. But the replacement of outmoded kerosene lamps by bright new electric bulbs turns out to be a mixed blessing—the increased illumination serves mainly to bring to light the squalid conditions inside the building. As the nameless narrator exclaims, "We put in the light, lit up the place, and—ye gods!—what dirt, what filth all around!" (*Nervous* 142) The narrator sets out to renovate his flat to improve the squalid conditions revealed by the new lights, but his landlady Elizaveta Ignatyevna Prohkorova cuts the wires in her own room because the new light forces her to spend too much time cleaning and straightening up. Elizaveta Ignatyevna, of course, is immediately denounced as a "degenerate petty-bourgeois" by the building director, while the narrator dutifully declares that he will keep the electricity in his own flat: "I think the light will sweep out all our trash and rubbish" (143).

This narrator's high hopes for electrification echo Lenin's own, as can be seen from Lenin's famous 1920 slogan: "Communism equals Soviet power plus the electrification of the countryside." "Poverty" is thus not only amusing, but extremely topical. It is also highly ambiguous. The story ostensibly praises Lenin's electrification project and condemns the bourgeois tendencies of the landlady, while the narrator adheres to a strictly orthodox Party line. Yet the suggestion of squalor in contemporary Moscow hardly represents an unqualified endorsement of the new socialist system. Furthermore, the story offers a number of alternative interpretations. One might, for example, relate the illumination of squalor by the new electric bulbs to the light shed on conditions in the Soviet Union by Zoshchenko's satirical writings. Those who would criticize Zoshchenko for not focusing on the positive aspects of Communism would then be cast in the ostrichlike role of the landlady, preferring to ignore problems rather than attempting to solve them.

The ambiguity of this and other early Zoshchenko stories is enriched by the dialogic texture of his language. Indeed, language itself is the principal subject of the early stories, very much in the spirit of Bakhtin's emphasis on language as an object of representation in the novel. Vera Alexandrova notes the central importance of language in these stories, describing Zoshchenko's "hilariously absurd mixture of popular idiom and hastily acquired and undigested literary turns of phrase" (113). Among other things, the complexity of Zoshchenko's language creates subtle instabilities that make the exact meaning of his stories highly ambiguous. In particular, his language tends to undermine the authority of his narrators by making it very difficult to tell whether those narrators are the objects of praise or of ridicule. Any number of commentators have suggested that the effect of the early stories depends upon the complex relationship between Zoshchenko and his narrators. McLean notes that this relationship contributes to Zoshchenko's "artistic camouflage," relating such techniques to attempts of earlier Russian writers like Gogol and Leskov to evade censorship through ambiguity. "The basic ruse is to create uncertainty in the reader's mind about the author's relation to his work and in particular about his emotional attitude toward the events and characters presented" (McLean xi).

The "ruse" to which McLean is closely related to the *skaz* technique used by numerous Russian writers in the postrevolutionary years. The *skaz* technique has its roots in the tradition of Russian folk tales and was prominently used by contemporaries and immediate predecessors of Zoshchenko like Remizov, Babel, Zamyatin, and (to some extent) Bely. The technique was prominently discussed by the Russian Formalists (especially Eichenbaum), and in both *Problems of Dostoevsky's Poetics* and *The Dialogic Imagination* Bakhtin identifies *skaz* as one of the most effective ways in which a novel can import folk energies and "extraliterary" materials, adding to the richness of voices in the text. In particular, *skaz* narration typically features a well-defined narrator whose voice is clearly distinguishable from that of the author, thus effecting an inherently double-voiced narration.

Gleb Struve notes Zoshchenko's deft use of the *skaz* technique, identifying Leskov, Remizov, and Zamyatin as important predecessors, but also suggesting that Zoshchenko made important modifications and innovations in the use of the technique. Zamyatin himself enthusiastically praised Zoshchenko's early work. Discussing Zoshchenko in the context of the latter's compatriots among the "Serapion Brethren," Zamyatin argues that "[a]mong the entire literary youth of Petersburg, Zoshchenko alone has an unerring command of popular dialogue and the *skaz* form" (*Soviet* 96). In another essay Zamyatin describes the *skaz* technique of Zoshchenko's early stories as a sort of linguistic defamiliarization:

Zoshchenko makes excellent use of the syntax of popular speech; there is not a single mistake in the order of the words, the verb forms, the choice of synonyms. He knows how to lend amusing novelty to the most worn, most hackneyed words by a (seemingly) wrong choice of synonyms, by intentional pleonasms. (78)

I. R. Titunik notes the importance of *skaz* in Zoshchenko's writing, and indeed suggests that "[i]f there is one Russian writer to be singled out as the *auctoritas et exemplum* of skaz technique, one Russian literary master whose credentials are based predominantly, if not, in fact, exclusively, on expertise in skaz, it is Zoshchenko" (84). Titunik goes on to note, specifically citing the work of Bakhtin, that Zoshchenko's use of *skaz* is primarily designed to introduce conflicts among competing voices into his texts (95). Indeed, the mixture of styles and ideolects in Zoshchenko's early stories recalls Bakhtin's work in a number of ways, especially as the subject matter of these stories typically deals with such politically charged issues. Thus, in stories like "Poverty," "Nervous People," and "Dog Scent" Zoshchenko's narrators ostensibly condemn the remnants of bourgeois tendencies among the Soviet populace, which would place Zoshchenko very much in the mainstream of socialist thought in the new regime. Yet one can also easily read these stories as suggesting that these "bourgeois" tendencies are not the product of a specific ideological system but merely of human nature, so that the Communist project of extirpating these tendencies is doomed to failure. The double-voicedness of Zoshchenko's stories is such that, depending on how one interprets subtle intonations in his language, the stories may be interpreted as anywhere from highly orthodox to extremely subversive.

It is not surprising, given the ambiguities inherent in Zoshchenko's early satires, that he soon found it necessary to seek other modes of expression given conditions in the Soviet state under Stalin. It is conventional in descriptions of Zoshchenko's literary career to suggest that he later drifted away from the satirical emphasis of his early stories and made a sincere attempt to write the kind of "positive" literature demanded by the Soviet regime.   Yet ambiguity and potential satire remain in the later works as well.   For example, Zoshchenko's series of twelve "Stories about Lenin" (1939-1940) can be read as iconographic apotheoses of Lenin intended to instill good socialist values in Soviet children. But is also quite possible to read the Lenin stories as a sly satirical assault on the Soviet "cult of personality" that tended to deify leaders like Lenin and Stalin.[1]

In the same way, Zoshchenko's 1933 text *Youth Restored* is susceptible to multiple interpretations. *Youth Restored* begins with a series of no fewer than seventeen introductory sections in which the narrator repeatedly apologizes for his ignorance and lack of qualifications adequately to deal with the medical and scientific matters that are the subject of the book. Zoshchenko then follows with the story of Vasily Petrovich Volosatov, an aging physicist who attempts by various means to restore his lost youth. Finally, the book ends with a series of ostensibly serious scholarly notes (occupying slightly more space than the story itself) that presumably illuminate the topics dealt with in the story. Not surprisingly, this heterogeneous textuality has led to numerous critical disagreements. A. B. Murphy argues that the use of science in *Youth Restored* is basically serious, concluding that "most of the notes are written in the style of popular science, and the theories presented therein are clearly intended to be taken at their face value" (98). Similarly, Gary Kern acknowledges that the form of *Youth Restored* is "ludicrous," but nevertheless places the book in what he calls Zoshchenko's "post-humorist phase," calling it a "quasi-medical, quasi-psychological literary attempt to deal with profound depression" (*Youth* 3). On the other hand, Slonim believes that the use of science in *Youth Restored* is parodic (96). In this vein Domar calls the notes at the end of *Youth Restored* "wickedly ingenuous" (220). She grants that it is conceivable that Zoshchenko was attempting to follow the Party line in *Youth Restored*, but argues that he did not succeed in doing so: "as in the case of his beloved literary predecessor, Gogol, he intended one thing and produced another; he went into his work for edification and came out with mischief" (221). Meanwhile, Struve disagrees with Kern's suggestion of "pre-humorist," "humorist," and "post-humorist" phases in Zoshchenko's career, arguing that "Zoshchenko's work is all more or less of a piece" (151). He thus suggests that *Youth Restored* is in fact written in very much the same satirical *skaz* vein as the earlier stories. He notes that the book was written at a time when Soviet writers were being pressured to bring science and literature together, but suggests that, far from participating in this project, Zoshchenko is in fact mocking it. For Struve *Youth Restored* "reads like a sort of synthetic parody of many Soviet works, with their stock situations and ready-made themes" (152). Indeed, he suggests that "[t]he most amazing thing about Zoshchenko's novel is that it was taken seriously as an attempt to introduce science into literature and bring the two together" (153).

As with the Lenin stories, the interpretation of *Youth Restored* depends upon subtle nuances of intonation that can radically alter the relationship between the text and issues outside the text. But the interpretation of *Youth Restored* also hinges on the way one reads the relationship between different parts of the text. Kern reads the scientific ruminations in the text as serious, largely because he sees little interaction between the different parts of the text. He suggests that the combination of fiction and nonfiction genres in the book is "bewildering" because of the disjunction between these genres. He argues that "*Youth Restored* is an extremely unusual, engrossing work, but one that does not admit of an easy interpretation. The ironic story and the serious commentaries do not mix, or even mock each other" ("After" 354).

Indeed, genre is clearly a crucial category for the reading of a text like *Youth Restored*, with the genre in which a reader views the text greatly affecting the impressions that reader derives from the text. From the point of view of Bakhtin, however, one need not choose a single genre within which to envision a given text. For Bakhtin different styles or genres within a single work not only can, but inevitably do mix, creating important dialogic interactions: "When there is a deliberate (conscious) multiplicity of styles, there are always dialogic relations among the styles" (*Speech* 112). These relations occur because for Bakhtin language is always interested, always invested with ideological force, and any work that seeks to explore the workings of language inevitably investigates the ideological climate of its world: "In the novel formal markers of languages, manners and styles are symbols for sets of social beliefs" (*Dialogic* 357). *Youth Restored*, then, includes many of the same kinds of dialogic relations that inform Zoshchenko's earlier satirical stories, except that now those relations are made even more overt by being displaced from the micro level of dialect to the macro level of genre.

Indeed, perhaps the genre with which *Youth Restored* has the most characteristics in common is Menippean satire, which is inherently multigeneric, though it is also true that for Bakhtin the ability to absorb and include aspects of multiple genres is a crucial characteristic of the novel as a whole. For Bakhtin the novel is an ever-evolving genre that remains capable of change and innovation largely because it remains in close contact with contemporary reality and does not calcify into a fixed set of generic assumptions but remains open to different influences. In particular, the novel is unconcerned with generic purity and can thus absorb a variety of other genres: "In principle, any genre could be included in the construction of the novel, and in fact it is difficult to find any genres that have not at some point been incorporated into a novel by someone" (*Dialogic* 320-21). Importantly, these genres need not be literary, or even fictional. In fact, the relationship between fiction and nonfiction, so central to *Youth Restored*, is also crucial to Bakhtin's vision of literary history. Bakhtin notes that the novel often crosses the boundary between what is traditionally considered fiction and what is traditionally considered nonfiction. Indeed, he argues that

These phenomena are precisely what characterize the novel as a developing genre. After all, the boundaries between fiction and nonfiction, between literature and nonliterature and so forth are not laid up in heaven. Every specific situation is historical. And the growth of literature is not merely development and change within the fixed boundaries of any given definition; the boundaries themselves are constantly changing. (*Dialogic* 33)

Genres are especially crucial to Bakhtin because he sees a genre as the embodiment of a specific worldview, a particular conception of reality. As a result, when different genres meet in the novel, different worldviews meet as well, leading to potentially productive dialogues that keep the worldview of the novel itself dynamic and fresh. From the point of view of Bakhtin's theories of the novel *Youth Restored* is not an aberrant text but a paradigm of the spirit Bakhtin refers to as "novelness." It is not a bewildering and enigmatic collage of incompatible and noncommunicating genres but a locus of dynamic interactions among worldviews of the kind that can restore the youth of the novel as genre, even if the youth of Zoshchenko's protagonist Volosatov is lost forever.

In point of fact, the complex generic mixture of *Youth Restored* has much in common with the texts of a number of modern Soviet writers, ranging from Olesha, Shklovsky, Pilnyak, and Zamyatin to contemporary authors like Aksyonov and Zinoviev. For example, Zinoviev's massive *The Yawning Heights* is composed of more than eight hundred pages of bits and pieces of various simulated documents ranging from scholarly treatises to latrine wall graffiti. The specific form of *Youth Restored* (a literary text followed by exhaustive and not entirely relevant commentaries) strongly anticipates Nabokov's *Pale Fire*, and the link to Nabokov's openly parodic text suggests parodic readings of Zoshchenko as well. As with the poem and appended commentaries of *Pale Fire*, the primary generic conflict in *Youth Restored* occurs between the ironic story of Volosatov and the ostensibly scholarly notes to that story. Moreover, this conflict generates a highly dialogic exchange between these two principal genres.

The Volosatov story is very much in the mode of Zoshchenko's early short stories, and its characters are the object of considerable satire. At first glance, Volosatov's profession is not particularly germane to the plot of the story, but it is in fact important that Volosatov is a scientist, a respected astronomer who regularly lectures in Leningrad. On the other hand, Volosatov turns out to be a vain and somewhat ridiculous figure, and the exposure of his follies in the story initiates a challenge to the authority of science. As the story begins, the fifty-three-year-old Volosatov resolves to attempt to restore his lost youth. Scientist that he is, he first turns to doctors for help, only to discover that the treatments they prescribe reduce him to the status of a near-invalid. So he decides to take matters into his own hands, embarking on a program of physical exercise that nearly causes his death. Finally, after considerable study, he concludes that the secret lies in a change of his daily routine, and indeed he does begin to feel his strength return after modifying and regularizing his habits. But his vigor really returns only after he resorts to the thoroughly banal step of leaving his fifty-year-old wife in favor of the nineteen-year-old Tulya, a woman of great physical beauty but questionable character who at her young age has already been through five husbands and seven or eight abortions.

Tulya represents another of Zoshchenko's ostensible attacks on the bourgeoisie: she is an inveterate opportunist who employs her considerable sexual charms for the sole purpose of obtaining a well-to-do husband. The narrator describes her bourgeois leanings:

She was born for the capitalist system. She needed carriages and motorcars, chambermaids and girls with hatboxes. She needed foppish men with riding-crops and monocles. Lapdogs with blue wool sweaters. Doormen courteously opening doors for her. (38)

Tulya, however, was born in 1914, so that she has lived most of her life under the socialist system. That she is still such a bourgeois thus suggests that the system is failing in its project of creating a new breed of socialist citizens. Indeed, the suggestion that she is the product of "mysterious and complex processes of life" indicates that her bourgeois greed is an element of human nature that no new socialist system can eradicate.

Tulya's foil in the book is Volosatov's twenty-three-year-old daughter Lidia, a loyal Communist who "devoted all the thoughts of her life to work and social commitments. She was an activist, shock worker, and enthusiast" (36). On the surface, the narrator has nothing but praise for Lidia, labeling her "exceptionally nice" and ostensibly endorsing her socialist views. But she is clearly depicted as a fanatic whose political fervor leaves little room for personal affection or compassion. At one point, her political commitment is even directly attributed to the fact that she, in contrast to Tulya, is sexually unattractive.[2] Lidia continually rails against her father for the political naiveté of his lukewarm support for the socialist system, yet in their exchanges it is consistently Volosatov who comes off as the voice of reason. Lidia, with the tunnel vision of a true believer, is unable to see how anyone could possibly be less than a wholehearted supporter of Communism: "Everything is so clear," she tells her father. "Distinct. Such a grandiose, majestic vista of the new life is unfolding, where classes, slavery, exploitation do not exist" (47). Volosatov, meanwhile, responds by agreeing that socialism is preferable to capitalism. But he reasonably suggests that even socialism has its problems. In particular, he is skeptical of the ability of socialism radically to change the human race, suggesting that "the improvement of a race doesn't come of itself and no tendency towards this could be seen for hundreds of years" (47-8). In particular, he wonders about the impact of "the instinct peculiar to every animal, the instinct of accumulation and concern for a rainy day" (48).

Volosatov's suspicion that the socialist narrative of a coming utopia may be slow to develop is mirrored in the plot of the story. Not surprisingly, Volosatov's relationship with Tulya leads not to paradise but to disaster. Finding his new wife in the arms of another man, the physicist has a stroke that nearly claims his life. Gradually, though, he recovers, after which he goes back to his original wife, who welcomes him. He seems to adjust well; his wife now seems less boring, and he no longer argues with Lidia. And his youth does indeed appear restored: "He walks around tanned and invigorated, works a great deal and with zest, and no longer complains of headaches and humming in his ears." Yet he has learned little. In the story's last lines we learn that whenever he talks of the pleasures of his new life "he sighs softly and casts a furtive glance in the direction of Tulya's house" (77).

This ending thoroughly undermines the plot resolution typically associated with socialist realism in which a positive hero triumphs over adversity. Indeed, plot development in general is a complex issue in *Youth Restored*. The book begins with the almost interminable series of introductions, which serve only to call attention to potential flaws in the book's scientific formulations. Then the plot progresses in a relatively linear fashion once it gets started, except for occasional digressions when the narrator provides information like descriptions of Volosatov's family or neighbors. But the eighteen commentaries at the end of the text are keyed to specific points in the text, and the reader who turns to these endnotes when they are called out will find the story continually interrupted by the commentaries, which are only marginally related to the story. Zoshchenko himself, in a note added to a later edition of the novel, suggests that the reader read the entire story first before turning to the notes. But even the reader who follows this advice still finds that the commentaries disrupt the normal time flow of the narrative, because the process of reading is only half over when the story ends.

The unusual temporal movement of *Youth Restored* can be usefully described via Bakhtin's notion of the chronotope. In the case of *Youth Restored*, the mixture of genres involves a very clear mixture of different chronotopes; in the story time moves forward in a relatively conventional fashion, while in the commentaries time stands still—they have no narrative element at all, nor do they appear sequentially related in any fashion. To assess the significance of this complex chronotopic mixture, one needs to compare the structure of *Youth Restored* to assumptions about time in Soviet society. For example, *Youth Restored* was first published in 1933, a year after socialist realism had been officially endorsed by the Stalinist regime. At first glance, *Youth Restored*, with its combination of narrative movement and documentary stasis, is informed by the same dual chronotopic structure as socialist realism (and Stalinism) with its apotheosis of the radiant future and concomitant support for the status quo. However, Volosatov is hardly a typical positive hero, and (though his story ostensibly ends on an optimistic note) the narrative in fact concludes not with an anticipation of Communism but with a look backward at Tulya, that embodiment of capitalism. Meanwhile, the ostensibly scholarly tone of the static commentaries might lend them an authority analogous to the authority of Stalin, but their own frequent invocation of figures from the past involves not heroic Communist figures like Lenin but figures from the tsarist past (like Gogol and Tolstoy) or from the bourgeois West (like Kant and Nietzsche). The chronotope of *Youth Restored* can, in fact, be read as a parody of the dual chronotopic structure of socialist realism, one that reveals the internal contradiction between Stalin's conservatism and his call for movement toward the fulfillment of Communism.

This interpretation is reinforced by the fact that *Youth Restored* initiates a number of potentially subversive dialogues with socialist realism. Socialist realism typically involved not only formulaic plots but fixed and sometimes crude systems of symbols that leave little room for ambiguity in interpretation. For example, Clark notes that placing a mustache on a positive character was enough to establish that character as a representative of Stalinism ("Political" 232). *Youth Restored* employs several such symbols, but in ways that are ambiguous or even openly subversive. Thus Tulya accepts Volosatov's marriage proposal only on the condition that he shave off his mustache: "She said men didn't wear such moustaches nowadays, that this was funny, and she'd simply be ashamed and mortified to go on walks with him" (63). Even if one accepts the symbolic link "mustache equals Stalin," there is nothing overtly antiStalinist in this passage; it merely sets Stalin up as an enemy of Tulya's bourgeois values, a role he himself cherished. But the suggestion, even coming from Tulya, that men with mustaches are funny or even ridiculous has clearly subversive undertones.[3]   And these undertones are reinforced by other motifs in the text. When Volosatov informs the crude neighbor Kashkin that one earth year lasts 165 years on Saturn, Kashkin responds by calculating (somewhat inaccurately) that on Saturn "their Five Year Plan in Four Years goes on for 500 years" (45). Like Tulya, Kashkin is hardly an admirable or authoritative character. Nevertheless, this passage, especially when combined with Volosatov's own doubts about the speed with which the goals of Communism can be reached, inevitably suggests that Stalin's plans for the industrialization of the Soviet Union may not be realized ahead of schedule, as Stalin urged, but in the far distant future—if at all.

In the fifth commentary, Zoshchenko continues his subtle assault on socialist realism by focusing on writers like Tolstoy and Gogol who gave up literature for religion, arguing that it would not have been a simple matter for these writers to return to literature (97). First, Zoshchenko argues, they would have had to overhaul their entire psyches. In short, writers are not machines who can crank out literary works on demand. Real literature must be consonant with the writer's own beliefs and personality and not simply a response to some social imperative. Moreover, Zoshchenko leaves no doubt that socialist realism is implicated in this commentary. As a specific example he chooses the ill-fated second part of *Dead Souls*, arguing that Gogol sought in that work to create a "positive hero," indicating a clear parallel between Gogol's late project and socialist realism. But what Gogol really sought to do in the second part of *Dead Souls* was to create a literary form for his late religious fervor that would convert readers to religion and save their souls. Zoshchenko's commentary thus clearly points toward a kinship between socialist realism and religious propaganda. Moreover, if Zoshchenko's "beloved predecessor" Gogol failed in his attempt at didactic literature, perhaps the implication is that Zoshchenko was likewise unable to rein in his literary talent for utilitarian purposes.

At other times Zoshchenko's attacks on socialist realism are more direct. In the long ninth commentary he points out the value of rest and suggests that successful rest must differ from work in order to renew the energies that work dissipates. The implication, of course, is that art and literature, to be effective, should maintain a certain independence of politics. Zoshchenko states this implication quite bluntly at the end of the commentary in a Bakhtinian attack on the monological view that all literature should be of a single type:

Fortunately it is changing now, but a year or two ago these mistakes were very much felt. A situation developed in which absolutely everything—the theater, magazines, movies, and even the circus—was all given from the same perspective. Everything dealt with two or three revolutionary themes. Such singlemindedness, undoubtedly correct, led in practice to certain distortions. Time-serving works appeared which concentrated all their fire on one target, so to speak, not touching on anything else and not providing diversion. (122)

Despite the obligatory disclaimers (like the suggestion that the described abuses lie in the past and that their basic philosophy is "undoubtedly correct"), Zoshchenko's criticism of socialist realism here is quite clear. In the last commentary of *Youth Restored* Zoshchenko openly acknowledges that his work is not consistent with the project of socialist realism. He admits that he writes about the bourgeoisie, but states that the bourgeois tendencies he describes are not the properties of a particular social class or ideology, but universal human characteristics: "Each of us has these or those traits of the bourgeois, the property owner, and the moneygrubber." Then, in a direct reference to the Stalinist demand that socialist literature be accessible to the masses, Zoshchenko describes his own efforts to achieve that accessibility. In particular, he claims that he has now simplified the complex linguistic texture of his earlier stories, making his work more straightforward. However, he also suggests (somewhat sarcastically) that the new simplicity of his work involves a somewhat infantile attempt to make his work attractive to readers who have no real interest in literature (153-4). In point of fact, *Youth Restored* is not less complex than Zoshchenko's earlier stories but considerably more so, and through this very complexity Zoshchenko is able to include a remarkable amount of criticism of the Stalinist regime in the work. For example, Zoshchenko draws (in good Bakhtinian fashion) not only on the folk traditions of "minor literature," but also on the authoritative tradition of science to enact complex cultural dialogues in his text.

This dialogic complexity continues in the later *Before Sunrise*, an ostensibly straightforward autobiographical account of Zoshchenko's attempts to deal with personal depression. As such, *Before Sunrise* can be read as a sort of sequel to *Youth Restored*: both consist largely of apparently serious advice for dealing with one's personal problems, yet both contain ambiguities and subtle ironies that make possible a wide range of intepretations. *Before Sunrise* was reviled by Soviet critics, and indeed its publication in the Soviet Union was suspended after the first two parts appeared in the journal *October* in 1943. However, Soviet critics did not object to the book because they recognized its subtly subversive dialogic complexity. On the contrary, they read it entirely literally and rejected it because of what they saw as Zoshchenko's egocentric and even pathological focus on his own psychological difficulties. Western critics have also tended to take Zoshchenko's project in *Before Sunrise* at face value. McLean, for example, suggests that *Before Sunrise* lacks the "irony and banter" of *Youth Restored* (xxiii). Similarly, Murphy notes that certain incidents related in the book are patently absurd but nevertheless concludes that "*skaz* and other ironic devices are absent from the book as a whole" (134). Domar calls *Before Sunrise* "cryptic," but reads it straight: "The story is told in a completely serious tone and in standard literary language" (236). Only Struve—consistently on the look-out for antiSoviet themes—seems to suspect that *Before Sunrise* might be more than it seems. Writing at a time when he had access only to the portions of the book published in 1943, Struve notes that *Before Sunrise* seems to be a serious introspective examination of Zoshchenko's personal problems, an examination that leads him to reject Freud and to elevate Pavlov as a source of solutions to such problems. Struve concludes that the book fails to achieve this goal. On the other hand, recognizing Zoshchenko's previous subtle strategies, he openly wonders whether "like *Youth Restored*, it was not meant to be a gigantic hoax" (322).

A look at *Before Sunrise* through the optic of Bakhtin shows that Struve's suspicions may be well founded. Like *Youth Restored*, the later book sets up a number of dialogues between science and literature as Zoshchenko employs a basically literary mode of writing to explore ostensibly serious scientific issues. As Zoshchenko explains in a prologue to the book, "It will be a literary work. Science will enter into it, just as in other cases history enters into a novel" (5). Again, then, the book might be interpreted as a thoroughly orthodox response to the official call for an integration of science and art under Stalin. But the kinds of psychological issues explored by the book were inherently controversial in a Soviet context, as the Soviet critical reaction shows. Moreover, there are subtle instabilities in Zoshchenko's treatment of these issues. Zoshchenko consistently cites the Soviet scientific hero Pavlov as his main resource in solving his psychological problems. At the same time, he openly rejects the Soviet anathema Freud, and even attempts (absurdly) to link Freud to fascism and to the privileging of irrationality. On the other hand, Zoshchenko goes about finding a solution to his depression by delving back into his childhood and infancy, seeking in a rather Freudian vein a key that will unlock the secret to his neuroses. As Murphy notes, "The terminology used by Zoshchenko may be based on Pavlov's work on conditioned reflexes, but the method he eventually used to conquer his fears was close to the systems of psychoanalysis which have been widely practised in the West" (133). And the results of Zoshchenko's researches are highly Freudian as well. For example, he locates a major source of his difficulties in a long-forgotten early-childhood emergency surgery that had been performed without anesthesia. Then, even as he explicitly describes this operation as a case of Pavlovian conditioning, he directly calls attention to the relation between the trauma of this surgery and that Freudian commonplace, castration anxiety: "What a confirmation of trauma! What a psychic castration! What a violent response might be made in the future to the conditioned stimulus!" (221).

Before Sunrise is also similar to *Youth Restored* in its Menippean generic complexity. Zoshchenko notes near the end of *Before Sunrise* that, despite his scientific message, the book is still a work of art: "It is written in many genres. And the genre of an artist, I dare to hope, is not the weakest among them" (327). Indeed, some of the richest dialogues in the book have to do with generic intertextual connections. Kern, for example, notes that the form of the book is reminiscent of Tolstoy's *Confession*, except that the religious "Tolstoi uses reason to extinguish itself and ignite faith, whereas Zoshchenko (to his own mind) remains steadfastly with reason" (355). Indeed, Zoshchenko questions the usefulness of Tolstoy's thought early in *Before Sunrise* by arguing that "Tolstoi's philosophy was a religion, and not science"

(7). Zoshchenko, meanwhile, consistently apotheosizes reason in *Before Sunrise*, but it is certainly possible to find a great deal of complexity in the book's treatment of reason. Reason itself was a central official value of Soviet society, yet life in the Soviet Union under Stalin often seemed patently absurd, and the ex-seminarian Stalin consistently sought to build a religious aura around his reign. The link suggested by Kern between Zoshchenko and Tolstoy thus sets up a dialogue between reason and religion that is potentially quite subversive.

Of course, the Ur-text of religious confessions is the one by St. Augustine, and Zoshchenko's book parallels Augustine's in many ways. In particular, Augustine explains in his *Confessions* that he can openly and honestly discuss the follies of his former life because that life is now over. Having completed the process of religious conversion at age twenty-eight, Augustine has been reborn a totally new person and thus has the kind of objective and authoritative perspective that allows him to assess his earlier life as a completed narrative. In the same way, Zoshchenko claims that his problems with depression were completely solved by the age of thirty, so that speaking of his problems before "about thirty" is like "speaking of the dead" (5). Indeed, his description of his "cure" is highly reminiscent of Augustine's conversion experience: "I became an entirely different man. . . . An entirely different life began, completely unlike what had been before" (*Before* 6).

Augustine begins the story of his past in the dim days of his infancy, even though he admits that he has no actual memory of this period. Instead, he pieces together the story of his infancy through the accounts of his elders and his later observations of other infants—on the assumption that all infants undergo basically the same experiences (Augustine 5-6). This suggestion of a universal narrative of infant experience obviously anticipates Freud, and Augustine's attempt to delve into the prememory of infancy clearly parallels the project of psychoanalysis. Zoshchenko undertakes a similar project in *Before Sunrise*. At first, he rejects an investigation of his infancy on the basis of the fact that infantile experiences are necessarily banal and that in any case he has no memory of that period. But, having failed to find the key to his troubles in later experiences, he is eventually forced to delve further and further into the past and to piece together a narrative of his infantile experiences that eventually includes key episodes like the surgery at age two and a trauma experienced when a violent storm erupted while he was nursing at his mother's breast.

Zoshchenko's cure at thirty parallels Augustine's conversion at twenty-eight in an obvious way. But it also parallels the "conversion" undergone by Russian society as a result of the Revolution of 1917. Indeed, the suggestion that both Zoshchenko and Augustine could be completely different individuals after their conversions is directly analogous to the claim that the new Soviet society could produce a new breed of "Soviet man." *Before Sunrise* thus suggests not only a parallel between Augustine and Freud but also one between Augustine and the Revolution, resulting in a complex three-way dialogue among religion, psychoanalysis, and Communism that indicates suspicious similarities among the Soviet state and two of its central ideological bugbears.

Zoshchenko goes out of his way to argue that the Pavlovian keys to happiness adduced in his book apply only to himself with no implication that they would work for others. Yet he spends a great deal of the latter part of the book presenting examples of others whose cases parallel his own. These parallels are, in fact, suspiciously exact—no matter what ailment the characters invoked in these passages have, they all turn out to be due precisely to the same sort of conditioning that caused Zoshchenko's own problems. Once this conditioning is pointed out to them they are instantly cured. A young woman is unable to have a baby; arch-physician Zoshchenko comes to the rescue by showing her that her inability to carry a pregnancy to term is a conditioned reflex caused by the trauma of a stillbirth in her teenage years. A young man has serious difficulties with digestion; Zoshchenko cures them by demonstrating that his problems stem from an infantile episode in which the man's mother fell asleep while nursing him and nearly smothered him with her breasts. A vain and beautiful woman who has had many lovers suddenly loses all interest in romance; Zoshchenko is about to explain the cause of her torpor (it is, of course, a conditioned reflex), but he decides not to do so because he decides she is better off the way she is as her lack of interest in romance will keep her out of trouble. Several other cases proceed similarly, though one wonders exactly why it is that these troubled personages come to Zoshchenko for the cure to their woes. In fact, there are subtle hints that these illustrations may be less than fully ingenuous, as when Zoshchenko admits in one case that "I would not have remembered this story either had my conclusions not matched it so closely" (257). Moreover, Zoshchenko's interpretation of Pavlov seems seriously flawed—he himself acknowledges that conditioning requires repeated exposure, yet the examples he presents in his case history are usually isolated one-time events.

Marxist critics have often condemned psychoanalysis (especially in its simplistic "vulgar" Freudian version) for its inflexibility in

imposing a single narrative on human experience that does not allow
for variations due to changes in social and historical conditions.
Further, the psychoanalytic Oedipal narrative is seen as impoverishing
in that it reduces individuals to stereotypes. Theodor Adorno thus
argues that psychoanalysis and other "depth psychologies" contribute
to a general alienation between people and experience in modern
culture, routinizing individual experience into standardized case
histories (65). Zoshchenko in *Before Sunrise* is a sort of vulgar
Pavlovian, and his presentation of his own case histories suggests that
theories of human behavior endorsed by the Soviet state can be at least
as mechanical and impoverishing as those produced by bourgeois
thinkers like Freud.

Zoshchenko also adduces the cases of several writers whose
illnesses he claims to have been due to conditioning similar to his own,
including Edgar Allan Poe, Balzac, Saltykov-Shchedrin, and (most
extensively) Gogol. In fact, one begins to suspect by this point that
Zoshchenko can explain any and all ailments of any and all personages
by recourse to the same prefabricated interpretation. On the other
hand, the particular examples that Zoshchenko chooses as analogues
to his own may be significant. Saltykov-Shchedrin, for example,
coined the term "Aesopian language" and was one of its earliest
practitioners, suggesting that one might look for instances of Aesopian
language in Zoshchenko's text. The connection to Gogol also suggests
numerous dialogues, reinforcing the connection between Zoshchenko's
scientific cure and the tradition of religious conversion. Indeed, the
parallel between Zoshchenko's case and that of Gogol is especially
close, perhaps too close to be coincidental. According to *Before
Sunrise* both Zoshchenko and Gogol turn out to have phobias
connected with food; beds have negative associations for both, so that
both prefer to sleep in chairs or sofas; both have a fear of women.

Given the recognized influence of Gogol on Zoshchenko's work,
one might consider the close similarities listed in *Before Sunrise*
between Gogol's case and Zoshchenko's a signal to look in Gogol's
work for parallels to *Before Sunrise*. And a parallel can quickly be
found. Indeed, in many ways the text that *Before Sunrise* resembles
most is not Augustine's *Confessions* or Tolstoy's *Confession*, but
Gogol's "Diary of a Madman." As Michael Holquist points out,
Gogol's story is clearly related to the genre of autobiography and
counts Augustine's *Confessions* as one of its predecessors. However,
"Diary of a Madman" gains much of its effect from its violations of
the generic expectations normally associated with autobiography. In
particular, as Holquist shows, Gogol's story employs a complex
combination of chronotopes which demonstrates that the sequential

structure usually associated with autobiography arises from conventional assumptions about the nature of time and of the temporal functioning of individuals in society. The madman of the title narrates the story in the form of a diary, but—because of the narrator's madness—this form does not give the story a coherent temporal flow. Instead, the narrator gradually loses any rational sense of time as the story progresses.

At first glance the irrational "Diary of a Madman" would seem an unlikely intertext for *Before Sunrise*, as Zoshchenko's book seems to be largely a paean to rationality. On the other hand, the chronotopic structure of *Before Sunrise*, like that of Gogol's story, is complex and highly unconventional for an autobiography. As with *Youth Restored*, the narrative of *Before Sunrise* ends midway through the book; only the first half is taken up with Zoshchenko's autobiography, while the second half consists of the series of case histories paralleling his own and of quasi-scientific ruminations on psychology. And even the first half of the book employs a complex combination of chronotopes. Zoshchenko's reminiscences of his past are given in several groups, including sixty-three episodes from young adulthood (approximately ages 16 to 30), thirty-eight episodes from childhood (ages 5 to 15), twelve episodes from early childhood (ages 2 to 5), and finally the lengthy attempt to recover the prememory phase of infancy. Within a given group, the different episodes appear to be given in a plausible chronological order, but the groups of episodes are themselves in reverse chronological order as Zoshchenko delves more and more deeply into his past. Even more significantly, the episodes within each group are merely snapshots, flashes of memory frozen in time with no narrative connection between them. The individual episodes are related almost exclusively in present tense, as if to emphasize the lack of narrative development. *Before Sunrise* thus encompasses a variety of models of temporal movement, ranging from forward progression to stasis to backward regression, all complexly intertwined.

The identity of Gogol's madman disintegrates as his sense of temporal connection breaks down. Yet Zoshchenko's text, which purports to relate his success in stabilizing and solidifying his own sense of identity, shows very much the same temporal confusion as Gogol's. As with "Diary of a Madman," the chronotopic structure of *Before Sunrise* deviates strongly from what would be conventionally expected of autobiography. It also contrasts sharply with the well-defined structure associated with socialist realism. Indeed, Zoshchenko acknowledges that his book is in danger of going beyond the acceptable range of Soviet literature. Thus, just before a

digression on the death of Gogol, Zoshchenko attempts to justify his
emphasis on the topic of death:

It seems to me that a discussion of this subject does not contradict the
principles of socialist realism. With all its great optimism, socialist
realism certainly does not close its eyes to everything that goes on in
the world. And it does not hypocritically put off decisions to
questions which need to be decided. (292)

The challenge here to those who would condemn Zoshchenko's
book is clear, and the call for socialists not to be blind to "everything
that goes on in the world" recalls the illumination metaphor of the
early story "Poverty." Indeed, Zoshchenko winds up *Before Sunrise*
with a similar metaphor, arguing that those would attack his book are
probably people who are afraid to see their true selves, "people seized
by fears, seized by the lower forces which do not permit them to raise
their head and see the world illumined by the blinding sun. . . . These
people are content to spend their life by the light of the lamp, so long
as their fears are not disturbed" (328). But Zoshchenko claims to be
confident that his view will triumph, ending the book (except for a
brief Afterword) with a confident declaration: "There can be no
question of the lower forces getting the upper hand. Reason must
conquer" (329).

This ending, of course, is the same as that of Zamyatin's *We*. Kern
notes this connection, but explains that Zamyatin is obviously being
ironic, whereas Zoshchenko seriously means his tribute to reason as a
signal of "a triumph over the forces of darkness" ("After" 357). Yet
the intertextual dialogue between *We* and *Before Sunrise* inevitably
calls Zoshchenko's apotheosis of reason into question. Granted,
Zoshchenko explicitly holds up reason in his text as the key weapon
in his own battle against psychological problems. Yet Zamyatin's D-
503 does the same, concluding his text with a similar homage to reason
on precisely the same grounds—his social maladjustment has been
"cured" by a lobotomy that removes his imagination and renders him
incapable of anything but completely "reasonable" thought. In *Before
Sunrise* Zoshchenko supposedly sets out to demonstrate the value and
superiority of reason, but the same can be said for D-503 in *We*. In
the case of Zamyatin's book, it is clear that the narrator fails in this
task, and the obvious disjunction between D-503's project and
Zamyatin's places *We* clearly in the Russian *skaz* tradition. In the case
of *Before Sunrise* Zoshchenko himself is ostensibly the narrator, so
that the gap between author and narrator that traditionally informs
skaz narratives seems nonexistent. Yet surely one is not required to

believe that anything said in the name of "Zoshchenko" in a fictional narrative must be a sincere statement of the historical Zoshchenko's real beliefs, especially given Zoshchenko's own demonstrated facility with the *skaz* technique. Numerous oddities and instabilities in *Before Sunrise* point toward ironic readings of the text, and it is quite possible to read the book not as a paean to reason and to Soviet science but as a particularly subtle example of Aesopian language in which an overemphasis on reason (as with the treatment of Pavlov) is shown to be impoverishing to human life.[4]

Zamyatin, like Gogol, was an important influence on Zoshchenko's work. And the texts of Zamyatin and Gogol that *Before Sunrise* seems to draw from most are stories not of the triumph of reason, but of its failure. In point of fact, regardless of Zoshchenko's own intention, the dialogue between reason and irrationality in *Before Sunrise* is highly unstable and open to a range of interpretations, especially in the light of the intertextual connections to Zamyatin and Gogol. Bakhtin consistently emphasizes the importance of such connections, arguing that a literary work takes its meaning not merely from authorial intention but from its participation in a whole range of dialogues with other texts and with society at large, where "society" includes both the world of the writer and that of the reader. In *Before Sunrise* many of these dialogues are explicitly triggered through reference to the works or lives of other writers, including such diverse figures as Byron, Chopin, Gogol, Nekrasov, Poe, Flaubert, Saltykov-Shchedrin, Andreyev, Maupassant, Bryusov, Balzac, Goncharov, Chernyshevsky, Blok, Gorky, and Tolstoy. In addition, Zoshchenko's real-life acquaintances like Zamyatin, Blok, Esenin, Remizov, Mayakovsky, Shklovsky, Fedin, and Gorky appear directly as characters in the text. Other connections are more subtle, as in the parallel to Augustine or in the numerous similarities between Zoshchenko's persona in the text and Dostoevsky's Underground Man.

Such intertextual dialogues combine with the intratextual complexity of *Before Sunrise* to produce a rich dialogic mixture of genres and voices that stands in stark contrast to the monologism of the Stalinist regime under which it was written. In particular, *Before Sunrise* is a combination of scientific and literary genres, and as such it incorporates both scientific and literary worldviews. Of these, the literary perspective is given a weight at least equal to that of the scientific one, so it is not surprising that Zoshchenko's explicit arguments for the primacy of reason and of science are undermined by the text. Of course, the obvious importance of generic mixtures in works like *Youth Restored* and *Before Sunrise* calls attention to phenomena that, for Bakhtin, are at work in less overt ways in all novels. *Before Sunrise* was rejected by Soviet critics as a "filthy, repulsive, and disgusting" exploration of Zoshchenko's personal psychological eccentricities. But from the point of view of Bakhtin's theories of genre it may be, as *Tristram Shandy* was for the Russian Formalists, one of the most typical novels in world literature.

NOTES

1. Scatton presents for a reading of the Lenin stories as a non-ironic (and unsuccessful) celebration of Lenin in the Russian hagiographic tradition. Loseff, on the other hand, sees the stories as a prime example of the use of "Aesopian language" in modern Russian literature, suggesting that they are written with the same parodic *skaz* techniques as Zoshchenko's early satirical stories and that the varying locutions in the stories set up subversive internal dialogues (202-204).

2. In the commentaries (especially Note IV) Zoshchenko espouses a quasi-Freudian model of artistic creativity as arising from a sublimation of frustrated sexual energies. He does not link this model to Lidia's commitment to Communism, but the parallel is obvious. *Youth Restored* thus subtly suggests a sexual motivation behind political fanaticism, which resonates with Freud's suggestion of strong erotic elements in the fascination that totalitarian dictators exercise on their followers.

3. Mustaches, in fact, loomed large in Zoshchenko's career. There is a story that Zoshchenko's political censure in 1946 was influenced by one of the Lenin stories in which a bearded character played a negative role. Warned that this character bore too close a resemblance to Kalinin, Zoshchenko removed the beard. Unfortunately, this left the character with a mustache that inevitably linked him to Stalin.

4. One might also compare Zoshchenko's narrator in this respect to Dostoevsky's Underground Man, a link that further complicates Zoshchenko's complex figuration of the opposition between rationality and irrationality in *Before Sunrise*. The Underground Man supposedly attacks the tyranny of reason and apotheosizes passion and irrationality. But he is such an abject figure that he inadvertently makes points *for* reason as well. "Zoshchenko" is similarly abject before being "cured" by reason, but even as he apotheosizes reason he dialogically makes points on both sides of the debate.

5

Good and Evil, Truth and Lie: Dualism and Dialogism in the Fiction of Yuz Aleshkovsky

Always sensitive to the social aspects of language, the narrator of Gogol's *Dead Souls* suggests that language functions quite differently in different social contexts. He notes that world culture is extremely diverse and that this diversity is directly reflected in the world's languages. Each of the world's many peoples, he argues, "has distinguished itself in its own original fashion by its own word, which, whatever the subject it describes, reflects in its description a part of its own character." Moreover, according to this narrator the Russian language carries a power that is unmatched by any other:

A knowledge of the heart and a wise comprehension of life will find expression in the sayings of a Briton; the Frenchman's short-lived phrase will flash like a gay dandy and then be lost for ever; the German will invent his involved, thinly intellectual sayings which are not understood by everyone; but there is not a word that is so sweeping, so vivid, none that bursts from the very heart, that bubbles and is tremulous with life, as a neatly uttered Russian word. (118)

This figuration of language as a living thing is distinctively Russian and can be related directly to cultural influences like the kenotic tradition of Russian Orthodoxy, for which the relationship of material written signs to their meaning is somewhat analogous to the

relationship between the body and spirit of Christ. Moreover, this
apotheosis of the Russian language resonates with the narrator's
ongoing rejection of foreign linguistic contamination of Russian
culture, as when he complains that the pretentious members of
Russian high society have a tendency to be "over-generous with
French, German, and English words, so that you get sick and tired of
them" (175).

There is every reason to believe that Gogol personally sympathized
with his narrator's rejection of such foreign linguistic influences. But
in point of fact the above description of the vitality of the Russian
language is reinforced by the richly energetic language of Gogol's own
texts, which is anything but pure, sometimes seeming to take on a life
of its own and to escape the control of its author almost entirely.
Indeed, both Gogol's recognition that language is shot through with
social and ideological resonances and the complex voicing of Gogol's
own *skaz*-like narratives provide clear anticipations of the work of
Bakhtin on the dialogic properties of language. Bakhtin himself
recognized this link, often citing Gogol's work. Moreover, Bakhtin's
affinities with Gogol's treatment of language as a living and vital force
and his consistent emphasis on the materiality of the sign are
distinctively Russian, providing evidence that Bakhtin was importantly
influenced by Russian Orthodoxy, regardless of his actual religious
beliefs, which remain unclear.[1]

On the other hand, Bakhtin's emphasis on language as a potential
locus of subversive challenge to authority—and especially his
privileging of the energies associated with linguistic representations of
bodily functions like sex and excrement—seems to run directly counter
to the kinds of monological authority represented by the Russian
Orthodox Church and supported by the political and religious
reactionary Gogol. But Bakhtin's Stalinist historical context is not
Gogol's nineteenth-century Russia, and Bakhtin's distinctive
figuration of language as potentially subversive of official authority
is closely related to his own contemporary context. Similarly, his
focus on images of the "material bodily lower stratum" responds quite
directly to the notorious prudery of the Stalinist regime.

Yuz Aleshkovsky is a contemporary Russian satirist whose work
not only clearly participates in the tradition set by predecessors like
Gogol and Saltykov-Shchedrin but that also resonates with the work
of Bakhtin in remarkable ways. In works like *The Hand* and *Kangaroo*
Aleshkovsky launches an overt assault on the ideology of Stalinism
that differs dramatically in tone from Bakhtin's more subtle hidden
polemics. But many of Aleshkovsky's techniques are remarkably
reminiscent of Bakhtin's work, and it is certainly clear that

Aleshkovsky's writing can be usefully viewed within the context of Menippean satire, a genre on which Bakhtin placed considerable emphasis.[2] The complex and highly nonlinear plot structures of Aleshkovsky's books are informed by frequent digressions, extensive forays into the fantastic, and numerous insertions of texts from a variety of genres. Aleshkovsky's heroes are typically rogues and scoundrels, recalling not only Gogol's Chichikov but also Bakhtin's emphasis on the subversive energies to be found in the literary depiction of such marginal figures. Aleshkovsky also places language itself at the very center of his work, in much the same way that Bakhtin identifies language itself as the main object of representation in the novel. And, echoing Bakhtin's emphasis on the chronotope as a crucial distinguishing feature of the novel, Aleshkovsky treats time and history as crucial not only to his novels but to the ideology of Stalinism.

The entire text of *The Hand* consists of an extended monologue by KGB colonel Vasily Vasilievich Bashov (nicknamed "The Hand" because of his methods of torturing prisoners with his powerful hands) who is in the process of interrogating high-ranking Soviet official Vasily Vasilievich Gurov. The arrest and interrogation of Gurov recall the way many once-important Party and government officials were purged during Stalin's regime, but they also represent the culmination of the long personal vendetta on the part of Bashov. Bashov has spent his entire life seeking revenge upon those who attacked and destroyed his childhood village, killing his father and other family members and injuring Bashov's own genitals in such a way as to render him impotent for life. The orphaned Bashov then grew up in the "Anti-Fascist Children's Home," where he was already plotting the career that would lead him into the KGB and therefore into a position from which he could avenge himself on the killers of his father. Gurov, a youth at the time of the attack and apparently the son of its leader, is the last on Bashov's list of designated victims.

The fictional attack on Bashov's village, which had resisted collectivization, was part of Stalin's historical 1929 campaign to force collectivization and to destroy the kulaks as a social class. Bashov's fictional personal story thus resonates with real Soviet political history, and many aspects of *The Hand* comment directly on that history. Indeed, history is central to Bashov's hatred of the Soviet regime, which he sees as an attempt to destroy Russia's rich cultural past, creating a new Soviet man who, far from being superior to his predecessors, was utterly devoid of any moral character because of his lack of connection to any meaningful cultural or moral tradition. Indeed, the Russian characters in *The Hand* in general are almost completely ignorant of history, as when Stalin himself attempts to refer to the Eighteenth Brumaire of Louis Napoleon Bonaparte so important to Marx, but gets it wrong, referring instead to "Louis Bonaparte's 18th Humidor" (98).[3]

History is also central to *Kangaroo*, whose protagonist/narrator Fan Fanych is a career criminal whose picaresque adventures bring him into contact with a number of important historical personages and who claims inadvertently to have effected important changes in the flow of history in the course of his criminal activities.[4] Early in the book, for example, Fan relates the story of how he and an accomplice were hired to murder the husband of a woman with whom Fan was having an affair. Rather than actually commit the murder, however, they "prove" to the woman that the murder has been committed by presenting her with a severed hand they have bought from the morgue, after which they dispose of the hand by tossing it into the tiger's cage at the Moscow Zoo. The remainder of the hand is found by the zookeeper the next morning, after which it is declared by Stalin's security chief Yezhov to be evidence of a bourgeois plot. Stalin then uses this plot as an excuse to end the New Economic Policy and to begin radical efforts at both industrial and agricultural collectivization. Thus, says Fan, "our little act of generosity was the end of officially sanctioned private enterprise in the Soviet Union" (13).

Later Fan tells the story of a trip to Germany on which among other things he is examined by Sigmund Freud, "a nice guy, but unbelievably nosy" (164). Even more importantly, Fan goes to a bar where he meets Hitler and Goering and discusses with them his attitude (or lack thereof) toward politics. "I'm just an international crook on tour from country to country," he tells them, "a gangster, if you like. And I don't want to get involved, on principle" (169). Significantly, Hitler and Goering express the same attitude, suggesting that National Socialism is simply a more organized version of Fan's own individual criminal activities and recalling Bertolt Brecht's figuration of Hitler as a gangster in *The Resistible Rise of Arturo Ui*. Meanwhile, later in the evening Fan makes off with Hitler's wallet, so enraging the future Führer that he immediately goes off to burn the Reichstag. And the rest, as they say, is history. Fan thus turns out to be directly (if inadvertently) responsible for both Stalinism and Fascism, the two great political evils of the twentieth century:

I've heard some people say it's Hitler, and Stalin even more, who's to blame. That's total crap. It's Fan Fanych who's to blame for

everything, Fan Fanych alone and nobody else. And he alone has got
to atone for it, too. (173)

This motif not only conflates Stalinism and fascism, but suggests
that both were motivated by impulses that were fundamentally more
criminal than political. Meanwhile, Fan Fanych does, in fact, atone
for his sins, and most of the text relates the story of his arrest,
interrogation, and incarceration by the Soviet authorities.
Significantly, however, he is charged not with one of his many real
crimes but with a totally fictional one. Aleshkovsky comments on the
falsification of charges that informed such events as the famous show
trials of the 1930s as well as Stalinism in general by having Fan
convicted on entirely fabricated charges. Fan is finally arrested in
1949 after a long life of crime simply because his old antagonist the
KGB Colonel Kidalla is about to retire and wants to end his career
with a spectacular case. And Kidalla makes no attempt to hide the
purely fictional nature of the charges against Fan. Indeed, he offers
Fan a menu of computer-generated crimes from which he can choose
the crime to which he is to confess. Fan being Fan, he chooses the
most outrageous of the crimes, which involves the "case of the vicious
rape and murder of an aged kangaroo in the Moscow Zoo on a night
between July 14, 1789, and January 9, 1905" (23).[5] The subsequent
prosecution of Fan for this crime thus presents Aleshkovsky with a
number of opportunities to comment upon the absurdity of the
Stalinist legal system and indeed of Stalinism in general.

This motif of falsified crimes lies at the heart of *The Hand* as well,
and is indeed the principal means by which Bashov gains revenge
against his enemies. Bashov himself is a highly placed KGB official
whose early career is boosted when he personally saves Stalin from an
attack by a mad dog.[6] Bashov then becomes a member of Stalin's
inner circle, often serving as Stalin's personal bodyguard and generally
enjoying his direct support. As in *Kangaroo* the historical events
related in *The Hand* appear rather unlikely, if not fantastic. In both
cases the narrators are rather unreliable, and it is often quite clear that
the histories they relate have been fabricated. But then history was
constantly revised and falsified under Stalin, and Russian historians
still joke that their occupation was particularly hazardous in those
years because it was so difficult to predict the past.[7] Aleshkovsky's
work thus very much participates in the attempts of much postStalinist
literature to counter the fictionalization of history under Stalin by
recovering the truth, showing what Boris Shragin has called a
"nostalgia for history." One might compare, for example, the works
of writers like Solzhenitsyn, who have been centrally concerned with

the recovery of the experiences of individuals who lived and suffered under Stalin but who were effaced from history under his regime. Indeed, Aleshkovsky himself speaks approvingly of the work of Solzhenitsyn and characterizes it as a "passionate, sympathetic attempt to bring the West to an understanding of the suffering, the instructive experience of the peoples enslaved in Soviet camps" (Phillips 512).

Of course, Aleshkovsky's work differs quite markedly from Solzhenitsyn's in that it seeks to capture the "instructive experience" of the Soviet past in a fantastic and symbolic (and often comic) style, rather than in the self-serious, semi-documentary mode favored by Solzhenitsyn. Moreover, while Aleshkovsky's work does evoke some of the pathos of individual suffering that so informs Solzhenitsyn's work, it seems less concerned with concrete individuals and more concerned with ideas, even if those ideas themselves emphasize the importance of individual experience. Aleshkovsky's work acknowledges that Stalin's constant revision of the past tended to rob the suffering of his victims of historical meaning. But in Aleshkovsky's work the most direct victim of Stalinist violence is in a sense history itself rather than specific individuals. In particular, Stalin's rewriting of history is figured in Aleshkovsky's work as a debasement of the past that destroys any real sense of cultural tradition and deprives individuals of any sense of cultural identity.

Various forms of such cultural debasement are for Aleshkovsky the most serious negative consequence of Stalinism. In *The Hand* a central aspect of this debasement involves language, and the text suggests in a number of ways that one of Stalin's greatest outrages was to convert the vital Russian language cited by Gogol into a deadened collection of bureaucratic slogans and clichés.[8] Bashov, of course, is an insider in the Stalinist regime, but he is a sort of virus who uses his position to attack the system from within, much as the Stalinist regime was itself self-destructive, devouring and destroying many of its own most loyal members. Importantly, Bashov's opposition to the ideology of Stalinism is largely linguistic. His own discourse is anything but the mechanical officialese of Stalinism, consisting of a barrage of obscenities and nonstandard idioms and expressions that lend to his speech a tremendous energy and a powerful antiofficial force, despite his own authoritarian position relative to his interlocutor Gurov.

The English translator of *The Hand* acknowledges in a note at the end of the text his debt to Kirill Kostov's *Dictionary of Nonstandard Russian* in translating Aleshkovsky's text, and indeed Bashov's colorful language is anything but standard. It can, in fact, be seen as a sort of carnivalesque inversion of the sterile discourse of Stalinism, and its tendency to Rabelaisian excess is highly reminiscent of Bakhtin's emphasis on the subversive power of marginal and unofficial language use. Indeed, Bashov specifically calls attention to his language quite early in the text:

I gather you're wondering why I use thieves' jargon and obscenities so often? At one time I did have an assignment working with criminals. As for the obscenities, I use them because dirty words, Russian mother-oaths, are my personal salvation in the foetid prison cell that is now the home of our mighty, free, great, etcetera, etcetera language. (4)

Of course, one could interpret Bashov's unending stream of invective and obscenity as simply an attempt to intimidate his prisoner Gurov. But this use of obscene language and imagery is in fact a common strategy of Soviet émigré writers, who have used the technique both to proclaim their newfound linguistic freedom and to highlight the lack of that freedom in the Soviet Union.[9] Bashov himself immediately goes on to contrast his use of unofficial language with the abuses suffered by the once-great Russian language at the hands of the powers that be under Stalin. Indeed, he suggests that his own speaking style results precisely from an attempt to inject new life into a language that Stalinism has left deadened and impoverished:

Poor sucker, it gets chased under the bunks by every thug in the cell: propagandists from the Central Committee, stinking newsmen, scabby literati, pulp-writers, censors, even our proud technocrats. They chase it into editorials, resolutions, interrogation reports, the lifeless speeches at meetings, congresses, rallies, and conferences, where it has gradually lost its dignity and health. (4)

Elsewhere, Bashov makes it clear that his distaste for the language of Stalinism goes far beyond its stylistic banality or its fastidious avoidance of the obscene. The problem with language under Stalin, he argues, is that it has been used to tell so many lies that it no longer has any real meaning. Far from containing the almost mystical force of meaning described by Gogol in relation to the Russian language, the "dead word" of Stalinism has no connection to reality at all: it represents nothing but the fictional constructions of official power, amounting to nothing but "a dead reality existing solely in the skulls of our leaders and those western idiots, great friends of the Soviet Union, who know our life from advertisements and extravagant displays at exhibitions" (93).

Bashov directly attacks many of the empty clichés of Stalinism, which he finds offensive not only because of the ideology they serve but also because of the violence they do to the Russian language and to any conception of truth. Moreover, he does so in terms that make clear his desire for a more spiritual view of language of the kind associated with the Orthodox kenotic tradition.[10] He describes the slogans and keywords of Stalinism as "word graves" in which lie buried the former semantic richness of the Russian language (121). And, providing a long catalog of Soviet clichés to illustrate his point, he argues that words, like men, have souls and can have their spirits destroyed by totalitarian domination (92-3).

The authoritarian slogans of Stalinism, imported into Bashov's text, lose their authority and become objects of inquiry, even mockery. In this sense, Aleshkovsky's treatment of the language of Stalinism provides an especially vivid example of Bakhtin's notion that "authoritative" language cannot survive within the dialogic linguistic climate of the novel. Bakhtin describes authoritative language as that language which "demands that we acknowledge it, that we make it our own; it binds us, quite independent of any power it might have to persuade us internally" (*Dialogic* 342). This language, of which the official language of Stalinism is obviously a prime example, does not seek dialogue or agreement; it seeks only obedience and "demands our unconditional allegiance" (*Dialogic* 343). But all language in the novel is open to challenge and to dialogic exchange, so that authoritative language collapses when imported into the novel, either entering into dialogue with other competing languages or simply becoming an inert linguistic object devoid of all power. Bakhtin notes the failed attempts of writers like Gogol, Dostoevsky, and Tolstoy to make authoritarian statements within their novels and argues that "the authoritative text always remains, in the novel, a dead quotation, something that falls out of the artistic context" (*Dialogic* 344).

The Hand presents a particularly rich exploration of the relationship between authoritative language and the novel. It is easy, for example, to see that Bashov's narration undermines the authority of the language of Stalinism, because that is an intentional project. Indeed, Bashov's treatment of the slogans of Stalinism effects a combination of the two fates predicted by Bakhtin for authoritative language when brought into the novel—Bashov explicitly declares the language of Stalinism inert, but in doing so he challenges its authority and therefore dialogizes it. Of course, at first glance Bashov's language itself might be taken as a form of authoritative discourse. Despite his hatred of Stalinism, he is in fact a powerful Stalinist official. Moreover, he is the book's only speaker, and his discourse is directed at a prisoner who is entirely in his power. Actually, though, Bashov's language is highly dialogic. For one thing, his Rabelaisian excess and his highly distinctive idiolect clash powerfully with the official language of Stalinism and with Bashov's role as Stalinist enforcer, calling attention to the fact that he is a violent enemy of the Stalinist system despite his official position within it. Moreover, the very fact that Bashov's speech is directed at a specific interlocutor and with the anticipation of a response from that interlocutor gives it a dialogic quality of the kind so frequently discussed by Bakhtin.

In his essay "The Problem of Speech Genres" Bakhtin emphasizes that the nature of any given conversation is heavily conditioned by the context in which that conversation occurs. Bashov's interrogation of Gurov obviously occurs in a highly specific context, making Bakhtin's notion of speech genres clearly relevant. Bakhtin notes in this essay that certain forms of conversation (like military commands) are strictly standardized by their genre and present little opportunity for individual stylistic variation or dialogic interaction. But most utterances are for Bakhtin highly dialogic, constituted as much by their listeners as by their speakers, who must speak in a certain way in order to achieve the response they desire. Bashov's interrogation of Gurov clearly does not obey any rigid rules of Stalinist police procedure. And though Bashov does not generally pose direct questions to his prisoner, he clearly does construct his speech in order to achieve a particular impact on Gurov. Indeed, in the end Bashov induces Gurov to shoot *him*, ending not only Aleshkovsky's text but Bashov's long life of abjection and *ressentiment*.

That it is Gurov who executes Bashov rather than the other way around seems a surprising reversal. But Bashov's hatred of his enemies consistently involves an element of self-hatred, and much of his invective is directed at himself throughout the text. Among other things this self-hatred indicates the complicity of Bashov in the Stalinist system that he so despises. "I'm an executioner," he proclaims at one point. "I'm a monster. I'm a flunky for the regime that I curse. I'm shit!" (47). But it also participates in what is perhaps the most powerful dialogization of Bashov's narration, which is its *skaz*-like tendency to undermine itself, perhaps making points very different from those he intends.[11] For example, Bashov's Orthodox vision of language is only part of his intensely religious worldview, and he consistently opposes the spiritually bankrupt ideology of Stalinism with his own Christian perspective. In Aleshkovsky's texts (as in Gogol's) the devil is a real and present danger, and for Bashov the world's evil is directly attributable to the machinations of Satan, though for him Satan and Stalin are virtually synonymous.[12] Thus one of Bashov's own favorite slogans declares that "Satan thirsts to destroy All, but the Creator wants to save Each." But the hate-filled and mentally unstable Bashov is hardly an appropriate missionary of Christian ideals, and his citations of religion tend to sound more like the ravings of a lunatic than the sincere beliefs of a truly religious man.

Aleshkovsky himself is apparently a believing Christian. Echoing Solzhenitsyn's famous 1978 Harvard speech prophesying doom for the West, Aleshkovsky decries at a 1982 symposium of exiled Soviet writers the decay of morals in the modern world and declares that the West will not be able to stand up to the expanding power of the Soviet Union because the people of Soviet bloc nations understand the difference between good and evil in a more profound way than do their Western counterparts. Aleshkovsky's apotheosis of the moral power of Russian culture (despite the contamination of Communism) is reminiscent of the ideas of nineteenth-century Russophiles like Gogol and Dostoevsky, two of his most important literary predecessors. But his belief that the power of Soviet morality would overwhelm the West appears severely misplaced after the collapse of the Soviet system within a decade after his tirade against evil. In retrospect, then, Aleshkovsky's own speech is self-undermining, much in the manner of his character Bashov.

But if Aleshkovsky's own religious perspective is similar to that of Bashov, then the text of *The Hand* would seem to undermine the intentions of Aleshkovsky as well as those of Bashov. In a phenomenon that is highly reminiscent of the texts of Dostoevsky (and especially of Bakhtin's readings of those texts as "polyphonic" novels), the narration of *The Hand* allows opposing viewpoints to sound with at least as much force as does Aleshkovsky's own authorial perspective. Structurally, the entire novel is highly reminiscent of the "Grand Inquisitor" section of *The Brothers Karamazov*, in which Ivan Karamazov's poem depicts a fictional Grand Inquisitor's interrogation of Christ. This interrogation is in fact a monologue, but Ivan's attempt to make an argument against Christianity with his poem apparently backfires. Ivan's brother Alyosha thus responds that the poem "praises Jesus, it doesn't revile him" (260). The complexities of this chapter are immense, however, and one could equally well argue that Ivan's poem undermines Dostoevsky's *pro*Christian project.

As the similarity in names indicates, Gurov is in many ways an ideal "other" for Bashov, so much so that their relationship becomes almost that of doubles, though Bashov's bitter and mocking diatribes declare his desire to be independent of the other for his own subjectivity. In this sense, the symbiotic relationship between Bashov and Gurov recalls the dynamics of the relationship between Golyadkin and his double in Dostoevsky's *The Double*. Meanwhile, the conflicts and contradictions embedded in Bashov's monologue recall Bakhtin's suggestion that the various voices that sound in *The Double* can all be seen as arising from within "the bounds of Golyadkin's self-consciousness . . . [as] part of his interior dialogue with himself or his dialogue with his double" (*Problems* 217).

However, the Dostoevsky work that provides the best illumination of *The Hand* is probably *Notes from Underground*. Despite the carnivalesque energy embedded in his language, Bashov is anything but a Rabelaisian apostle of freedom and life. He is a dark figure of bitterness and despair––one might even think of him as what would occur if Dostoevsky's Underground Man somehow gained the power of a KGB colonel. In this sense, it is instructive to recall Michael André Bernstein's discussions of the dark side of dialogism and carnival. In particular, Bernstein suggests that dialogism, rather than providing an emancipating vision of communal bliss, can actually lead to an oppressive domination by the other. He argues that "what Bakhtin understands by the 'dialogical imagination' is uncomfortably similar to Nietzsche's account of the slave's reactive, dependent, and fettered consciousness" (201). To support his point, Bernstein turns to *Notes from Underground*, which he sees as "a pastiche of countless prior texts, in part because that is all the Underground Man himself really consists of, except for his additional burden of finding this existence-as-pastiche intolerable" (215). Indeed, the Underground Man is perfectly aware that his consciousness has been largely conditioned by his reading, that even his most intensely felt emotions have been "picked up from books" (*Notes* 52).

But, as Bernstein notes, the intolerability of finding himself always already defined by preexisting discourses leads the Underground Man to a feeling of Nietzschean *ressentiment*:

As long as one desires an original, authentic consciousness and voice–as long, that is, as the fact of living a belated and already scripted existence is seen as the ultimate wound, making any claim to personal dignity derisory–*ressentiment* must remain consciousness's dominant emotion, structuring the narratives one lives, the narratives one tells, and ultimately the narratives in which one figures as one more increasingly sorry character. (Bernstein 219)[13]

Bernstein's (accurate) description of the Underground Man's sense of belatedness at first seems to contrast quite starkly with Bashov's yearning for a cultural and moral tradition in which to participate.

However, Bashov—as much as the Underground Man—has a strong sense of being constituted by others. In particular, he is vividly self-conscious (and resentful) of his status as a product of a Stalinist system that he abhors. But he also resembles Dostoevsky's character in being formed largely by his readings of literature. Indeed, as he grows up in the Anti-Fascist Children's Home he spends most of his time reading anything he can get his hands on, apparently sublimating (because of his physical impotence) normal adolescent sexual desires into a desire to read: "I wanted to read, passionately and uninterruptedly, the way Sasha and the other kids wanted to masturbate" (93). And in this process of reading he stumbles upon *The Count of Monte Cristo*, the romanticized revenge theme of which becomes the inspiration for his lifelong quest for vengeance.

Bashov's entire life, then, is informed by a bovarystic reading of literary texts, a motif that shows his own belatedness but that also serves as a commentary on the fictionalization of reality in the Soviet Union under Stalin. Indeed, Bashov consistently figures his professional activities in the KGB as a process of authorship, of constructing fictionalized cases to destroy not only his own personal enemies but also the presumed enemies of the state. He thus describes KGB investigators as "playwrights and prose stylists" and suggests that the cases put together by the KGB are the "truly most elaborate works of Socialist Realism." Further, he notes that the blatantly fictional nature of the charges leveled in these cases contributes to the "fusion of literature and life" that for him centrally characterizes life under the Stalinist regime (25).

Bashov's bovarysme and his characterization of the Stalinist strategy of deliberately confusing fiction with reality both resonate directly with some of Bakhtin's comments on the novel as genre in his essay "Epic and Novel." Here Bakhtin suggests that the novel differs principally from the epic in that the epic takes place in an absolute past time that has no real connection to the present, while the novel is characterized by an intense contemporaneity. This zone of temporal contact between the novel and reality makes the novel as a genre more able both to respond to historical changes in society and to comment upon real historical experience in a meaningful way. A novel like *The Hand*, with its heavy use of real historical personages and events, vividly illustrates Bakhtin's notion of the permeability of the boundary between fiction and reality in the novel. On the other hand, Bakhtin also emphasizes the importance of maintaining a distinction between fiction and reality, despite the close communication between the two zones that is effected by the novel. Indeed, he warns that the contact between the novel and historical reality might lead naive readers to confuse the two: "And here we encounter the specific danger inherent in the novelistic zone of contact: we ourselves may actually enter the novel. . . . It follows that we might substitute for our own life an obsessive reading of novels, or dreams based on novelistic models" (*Dialogic* 32).

Bakhtin's comments illuminate Aleshkovsky's novel here, but Aleshkovsky's novel also adds specific resonances to Bakhtin's commentary. In particular, Aleshkovsky's association of bovarysme with Stalinism suggests that Bakhtin's warnings against confusing fiction with reality may constitute an element of his ongoing guerrilla campaign against Stalinism. This motif of blatant fictionalization also provides a clear link between *The Hand* and *Kangaroo*, which both deal with the motif in prominent ways. Thus Fan's scripted trial in the latter book is described as "the greatest moment in legal history, when life and Socialist Realism art converge" (103). However, Aleshkovsky's two books approach their subject matter in very different ways. Indeed, these two books deal with almost identical themes throughout, but they treat those themes in very different ways and from quite different perspectives. In particular, *The Hand* critiques the Stalinist system from within through its focus on the KGB officer Bashov, while *Kangaroo* critiques the same system from without, through its focus on Fan Fanych, a marginal figure who is very much outside official circles of power. Moreover, if the former book is reminiscent of the abjection often encountered in Dostoevsky's *Notes from Underground* the latter is informed by the kind of exuberance found in Rabelais's *Gargantua and Pantagruel*.[14]

The preposterous and comical nature of the crime with which Fan Fanych is charged in *Kangaroo* highlights the Rabelaisian nature of that text, the language of which still challenges the sterility of Stalinism, but in a mode more of mockery than of bitterness. The difference between *The Hand* and *Kangaroo* can also be seen in their basic rhetorical structures. Both books have a single narrator who addresses his discourse to a single listener. But, where Bashov bitterly rails against his prisoner and enemy Gurov, Fan addresses his narration to his friend "Kolya." And, while *The Hand* ends with the death of Bashov at the hands of Gurov, *Kangaroo* ends in a moment of celebration and community. Fan Fanych, having been released from prison after the death of Stalin, drinks a toast with his friend: "Let's drink to Freedom, old buddy!" (278).

Both *The Hand* and *Kangaroo* take their material primarily from Soviet history (especially from the Stalinist era), and both can be regarded principally as reinscriptions of that history. Thus Bashov's campaign against highly-placed members of the Party and the *nomenklatura* recalls the way so many high officials did indeed fall victim to Stalinist purges of the 1930s, suggesting in addition that their fates were appropriate retribution. Fan Fanych's adventures also directly comment on the Stalinist purges of loyal Communists. When he is at last convicted and sent away to a camp for political prisoners, he finds that the inmates there are all loyal Communists, mostly former associates of Lenin during the days of the revolution who have been purged by Stalin as an effort to solidify his power. In *Kangaroo*, however, these purged Party members appear not so much as evil doers for whom turnabout is fair play as comically misguided and unrealistic idealists who are simply unable to deal with political reality.

Fan's stay in the prison camp is depicted in a surprisingly comic tone, despite the dark resonances of such camps in Soviet history. For example, the idealists met by Fan in the camp are anachronistically led by Dostoevsky's old antagonist, the nineteenth-century Russian radical Nikolai Chernyshevsky.[15] Besides adding a merely humorous element, this use of Chernyshevsky makes several important commentaries on the prisoners who follow them. For one thing, these prisoners remain loyal Communists who are intensely devoted to the revolution despite the dark turn that it has taken under Stalin. Thus, by having them led by a radical hero from the past Aleshkovsky is able to suggest their inability to learn from history and to change their ideas in the face of ongoing historical developments. Moreover, the association of Communism with the past utopian thinker Chernyshevsky highlights the utopianism of Communism and suggests that it (like much utopian thought) is informed by nostalgic visions of a lost great past—that it is informed, in short, by what Bakhtin calls "historical inversion" as part of his own frequent attacks on utopianism.

Aleshkovsky's criticism of Communism as unable to change with the times adds a new antiCommunist resonance to Bakhtin's continual emphasis on "unfinalizability" and on the importance of an ability to change with history. Of course, this suggestion that the ostensibly futurist rhetoric of the Revolution actually concealed an inability to deal with the future also recalls Clark's suggestion that both Stalinism and its pet genre socialist realism were informed by complex and contradictory attitudes toward the future. As Clark notes in her essay on the subject, Bakhtin's concept of the chronotope helps to illuminate the attitude toward time and history that was central to Stalinism. This concept is also extremely useful to describe *Kangaroo*, in which the critique of the Stalinist fictionalization of reality focuses on the fictionalization of time itself, suggesting that the chronotope of

Stalinism was fundamentally meretricious. This motif is to a certain extent reinforced by Fan's own fictionalizations of history, but it is treated more specifically in the book as well. For example, the Stalinist prosecutors at Fan's trial openly conflate the present with the future. Seeking the death penalty despite the fact that this penalty had been outlawed at the time of his 1949 trial, the prosecutors argue that this is in fact a "trial of the future" and that the death penalty is therefore allowable because that penalty will probably be reinstated in the future (112).[16]

But the chronotopic fictionalizations of Fan's captors are most spectacularly illustrated in the process of his interrogation, when they seek to confuse him by "scrambling the time" (119). While Fan is being held in a special cell, they try to destabilize his sense of time by convincing him that it is evening when it is in fact morning, and so on. And this attempt is figured specifically as an attack of the Soviet authorities on Fan's human nature. In particular, Fan's captors are attempting to prove a theory (which they attribute to Stalin) that "the human organism's biological clock is also relative" and can be reset according to the will of the Party. In short, this experiment is part of the overall effort of the Soviet system to create a fundamentally new race of humans informed by Communist principles, an effort that the religious conservative Aleshkovsky clearly sees as a crime against nature and as an outrageous attempt to undo the nature of humanity as created by God.

Fan's captors next attempt to convince him that his cell is in fact a spaceship and that he has been launched into space. An electronic calendar in his cell/spaceship shows that hundreds of earth years are passing but that, due to the time dilation effect of relativity, essentially no time is passing for Fan. In a satirical move that recalls the time-travel motifs in earlier works like Bulgakov's *Bliss* and Mayakovsky's *Bedbug*, Fan wonders whether so much time has passed on earth that the long-promised Communist utopia has in fact at last been attained; that this passing of time is in fact faked then suggests a falsity in the utopian vision itself. Meanwhile, Kidalla and Fan's other captors go to great lengths to gain complete control over Fan's sense of time. In particular, they attempt to convince him that he is traveling so rapidly that time is not passing for him at all. They even shave him and trim his hair and nails during his sleep so that his body will show no physical signs of the passing of time. But the agent charged with this duty fails to trim Fan's little toenail, the growth of which assures the prisoner that time is in fact passing and restores his sense of temporal sanity.

For Aleshkovsky the biological clock is the most important clock of all, and natural biological processes like the growth of hair and nails serve as guarantors that time does go on despite the efforts of oppressive systems like Stalinism to manipulate the movement of time to their own advantage. That Fan's body saves him from the manipulations of his Stalinist captors emphasizes that Stalinism itself was counter to nature and that natural biological functions provide a locus of basic truth that can provide stability amid the blatant prevarications of Stalinism. For Aleshkovsky, as Meyer puts it, "all normal bodily functions are a measure of one's humble and Godly humanity" ("*Skaz*" 458). This confrontation between history and bodily physicality also directly recalls Bakhtin's interpretation of the emphasis on physical functions in Rabelais. As in Rabelais, then, biological functions in Aleshkovsky help to connect humanity to history and to oppose artificial attempts to deny the historicity of human life. In Bakhtin's discussion of Rabelais, this use of the physical counters the medieval Catholic tendency to reject the temporal world and to focus on an idealized eternity. But Bakhtin's figurations of medieval Catholicism tend to comment upon Stalinism as much as on the Church, and Aleshkovsky's work reinforces this link, suggesting that Stalin's regime was similarly involved in a denial of physical and temporal reality. In particular, the treatment of time in *Kangaroo* suggests that Stalinism involved a denial of true historicity in its efforts to shore up the status quo through emphases on both an idealized past (the revolutionary times of Lenin) and an idealized future (the promised Communist utopia). *Kangaroo*, however, debunks both of these idealized times. Representatives of the revolutionary past like Chernyshevsky and the other prisoners encountered by Fan in prison are treated as comically inept and hopelessly naive to historical reality, while the promised Communist march into the future (symbolized by Fan's simulated spaceflight) turns out to be nothing but illusion.

For Aleshkovsky both the glorious past and the glorious future of Communism are fictions; what is real is the ongoing natural rhythm of human and animal life. The physical—for Aleshkovsky as for Bakhtin's Rabelais—is a source of authenticity. Aleshkovsky makes this motif clear late in *Kangaroo* when Fan (who has a knack for being on the scene at important historical events) witnesses the momentous Yalta conference at which the allied leaders planned the post-World War II future of Europe. At this conference, Stalin's own body rebels in an Aesopian episode whose implications are quite clear. In particular, his right foot begins to denounce him in the most contemptuous terms: "You're a dope!" cries the rebellious appendage.

"Asshole of all time! Shit of all peoples!" (192). Stalin, of course, responds with his usual paranoia. Just as he had liquidated so many of his own former aides and supporters, so too does he consider cutting off the foot. But then he begins to wonder whether he can trust the left foot, or his hands, or any of the other parts of his body. His response is to declare his own body an enemy and to attack it through the power of Soviet science: "Mr. Brain, Messrs. Ass, Heart, Liver-and-Spleen, your attempts are doomed to total failure. The great might of our national medicine—maybe even supplemented with foreign assistance—will be unleashed on you!" (194). Stalin's physical body becomes a locus of truth and a source of opposition to his duplicitous policies. He responds by suppressing that truth and attempting to efface the physical reality of his own body, just as his policies have sought to impose an artificial social and ideological system on the human reality of the Russian people.

Aleshkovsky continually figures Stalinism as duplicity, while opposing that duplicity to the truth to be gained by both biological reality and spiritual faith. His strategies in this effort again parallel the attempts of émigré writers like Solzhenitsyn to oppose the official (false) history of Stalinism, with its emphasis on ideas and institutions, to an unofficial (true) counter-history based on the day-to-day experiences of common, ordinary people. To a certain extent this project also echoes Bakhtin's continuing opposition to theoretism and continual focus on the prosaic details of everyday life and language. Moreover, as Morson and Emerson point out, Bakhtin's own emphasis in this regard follows a long Russian tradition of "antiideological" thinkers like Alexander Herzen, Leo Tolstoy, and Anton Chekhov (23).

However, Aleshkovsky's comments outside his fiction suggest that his opposition between truth and lie relies on a monological conception of truth that lacks the subtlety of Bakhtin's dialogical approach. Aleshkovsky differs markedly from Bakhtin in that the latter generally argues for a dialogic mediation of dual oppositions while the former tends strongly toward dualistic thinking, seeing the world in rather Manichean terms. For Aleshkovsky the contest between truth and lie is part of the larger one between good and evil that seems central to his thinking. And the difference between good and evil is absolute; Aleshkovsky argues forcefully that what he sees as the moral decay of the West is largely attributable to an inability to distinguish good from evil, to the fact that "enlightened awareness and fearless confrontation of world evil are repeatedly hindered today by the marvelous facility of evil to pass itself off as good" (Phillips 511). In short, Aleshkovsky seems to accept the kind of "ready-made truth" that Bakhtin associates with monological thinking (*Problems* 110).

Of course, Bakhtin's readings of Dostoevsky should provide an ample reminder that an author of fiction can personally hold strong and even one-sided opinions without necessarily producing works that reflect those opinions in a monological way. Indeed, using Bakhtin to read Aleshkovsky's work calls attention to complexities in that work that escape simple good-evil oppositions. In *The Hand* the principal antiStalinist voice is a member of Stalin's inner circle, and the line between victims and victimizers is ambiguous at best. *Kangaroo* is somewhat more dualistic in that its protagonist operates outside the system, but Fan Fanych is a notorious criminal who is far from a pillar of morality, even if he does effectively represent individual liberty.[17] To a first approximation, Aleshkovsky's flawed heroes can be read as answers to the prescribed positive heroes of socialist realism, but in the final analysis the moral ambiguities of Aleshkovsky's work probably escape any specific strategic intentions he might have had. Indeed, Aleshkovsky's own fiction may provide the best rebuttal to their author's personal belief that the world's conflicts can be figured as a simple and unambiguous contest between good and evil.

NOTES

1. Though Clark and Holquist consistently depict Bakhtin as a thinker in the Russian Orthodox tradition, they present no direct evidence of Bakhtin's religious beliefs. Instead, they deduce these beliefs, largely on the basis of Bakhtin's association with other thinkers whose religious beliefs are known. See also Patterson for an extensive treatment of Bakhtin as a religious thinker.

2. Edward J. Brown discusses *The Hand* in this context, comparing Aleshkovsky to his Soviet contemporary Alexander Zinoviev as well as to Menippean predecessors like Rabelais, Laurence Sterne, and James Joyce.

3. Bashov makes sure to emphasize the point of this passage, assuring Gurov that "those were Stalin's very words: '18th Humidor'." Stories of Stalin's ignorance are, of course, legion, as when Milovan Djilas reports in his *Conversations with Stalin* that Stalin was unaware that Holland and the Netherlands were the same country (cited in Sinyavsky, *Soviet* 81).

4. This protagonist is generally referred to in the text as "Fan Fanych," though he uses any number of aliases in his criminal career. Aleshkovsky employs this motif of uncertain names in *The Hand* as

well. Bashov's real patronymic is Ivanovich, but he had taken on the new one in childhood order to conceal his true origins. Meanwhile, Bashov is convinced that Gurov's true surname is Conceptiev. The variable names of Aleshkovsky's characters may suggest the difficulty of establishing a firm and stable identity under the conditions of Stalinism.

5. These calendar dates refer to Bastille Day and to "Bloody Sunday," the beginnings of the French Revolution and the 1905 Russian Revolution respectively. Elsewhere in *The Hand* Aleshkovsky provides additional connections between the French Revolution and the 1917 Russian Revolution, as when Bashov notes that "my feeble little mind could not help correlating the glaring reality of the Soviet hell, or the hell of the French Revolution, with its ideological and moral sources" (94). Of course, many participants in and observers of the Russian Revolutions of both 1905 and 1917 compared contemporary events to their French predecessors.

6. Dogs seem to act almost as judges of moral character in *The Hand*. Not only does this dog attempt to kill Stalin, but Gurov's own dogs later abandon him when his crimes are revealed. Priscilla Meyer notes that Aleshkovsky often "takes animals as touchstones of appropriate instinctual behavior" because they are immune to propaganda ("*Skaz*" 458).

7. This anecdote was related to us by Professor David Edwards of the Department of History at the University of Arkansas.

8. Such parody of the Soviet penchant for cliché has by now become a literary tradition in its own right. Beginning with satirists like Zoshchenko and like Ilf and Petrov, the tradition has been revived in recent years by writers like Iskander, Zinoviev, and Aksyonov, in addition to Aleshkovsky.

9. Writers like Aksyonov, Miloslavsky, and Tertz/Sinyavsky have all challenged the puritanical taboos of official Soviet literature, though Edward Limonov is probably the most spectacular example of this phenomenon.

10. Aleshkovsky's own outlaw vocabulary would at first glance itself appear to do violence to any Christian conception of language. However, as Meyer notes, Aleshkovsky's vocabulary serves an almost "holy purpose." For example, she notes a Russian tradition of viewing such language as a protection against evil spirits, especially the devil ("*Skaz*" 460).

11. See Meyer for a (somewhat sketchy) discussion of *skaz* elements in Aleshkovsky's work.

12. This connection is not, of course, unique in modern Russian literature. Most readers of Bulgakov's *The Master and Margarita* see his Satanic Woland at least partially as a figure of Stalin.

13. That the Underground Man provides a striking illustration of Nietzsche's notion of *ressentiment* has been noted before. For example, Walter Kaufmann makes this connection in one of his editor's notes to *The Genealogy of Morals* (564, III.15). And of course Nietzsche's great admiration for Dostoevsky's work is well known.

14. There is, of course, humor in Dostoevsky (and in *The Hand*), though it is often of the muted and sometimes dark type associated by Bakhtin with "reduced laughter." Similarly, Rabelais and *Kangaroo* have their dark elements. The difference is one of emphasis, not strict polar opposition.

15. Chernyshevsky maintains his antipathy toward Dostoevsky in *Kangaroo*, claiming that an epidemic of epilepsy among the prisoners was caught from Dostoevsky.

16. The death penalty was, in fact reinstated on January 13, 1950.

17. If *Kangaroo* is more dualistic than *The Hand*, one might also argue that Bakhtin's book on Rabelais, with its strict opposition between subversion and authority, is far more dualistic than his book on Dostoevsky, with its emphasis on polyphony and attacks on either-or monologism. See Morson and Emerson for a discussion of binary thought in *Rabelais and His World* (445-7).

6

The House that Bitov Built: Postmodernism and Stalinism in *Pushkin House*

The narrator of Flann O'Brien's *At Swim-Two-Birds* declares that as a genre "the novel should be a self-evident sham to which the reader could regulate at will the degree of his credulity" (33). Further, this narrator offers the following advice to would-be authors of modern literary works:

The entire corpus of existing literature should be regarded as a limbo from which discerning authors could draw their characters as required, creating only when they failed to find a suitable existing puppet. The modern novel should be largely a work of reference. Most authors spend their time saying what has been said before—usually said much better. A wealth of references to existing works would acquaint the reader instantaneously with the nature of each character, would obviate tiresome explanations and would effectively preclude mountebanks, upstarts, thimbleriggers and persons of inferior education from an understanding of contemporary literature. (33)

This passage stands as a striking summation of the kind of allusiveness that has characterized many of the works of Western modernism, including O'Brien's text itself. However, O'Brien's particular ironic and self-parodic tone is probably more typical of postmodernist texts, and his notion of the novelist as an assembler of previously existing bits and pieces has a rather postmodern tone. In particular, the authorial role described by O'Brien clearly recalls the decentered models of authorship espoused by Western theorists like Roland Barthes and Michel Foucault.

O'Brien's description of the novel as a self-conscious patchwork of borrowings from previous texts also closely resembles Bakhtin's vision of the novel. In an important essay that centrally contributed to the growth of Bakhtin's popularity among Western critics, Julia Kristeva attributes her concept of intertextuality to Bakhtin, suggesting that for Bakhtin "any text is constructed as a mosaic of quotations; any text is the absorption and transformation of another" (64). As the link to Bakhtin would suggest, allusivity and reflexivity are properties not just of modern Western texts but of many Russian texts as well, from the early fiction of Pushkin and Gogol to the recent experimental novels of Aksyonov, Voinovich, Sokolov, and others. Indeed, works of Russian literature are quite often formally similar to the works of Western postmodernism, though the ultimate implications of the same formal techniques can differ substantially between Western and Russian texts. One of the most interesting demonstrations of this phenomenon in recent Russian literature is Andrei Bitov's *Pushkin House*, a sophisticated exercise in postmodern reflexive fiction that nevertheless manages to make a number of important social and political statements within its Soviet context.

As Rolf Hellebust notes, Bitov has used in the writing of *Pushkin House* myriad stylistic and formal literary devices not often associated with Soviet literature:

The first impression of an informed Western reader exposed to *Pushkin House* is that the author seems to have used the subversive literary devices of every postmodern writer he has read as well as some he has not. These include the essayism of Musil (340-344), the paratextual apparatus of Borges (345), Nabokov's exposure of fictional artifice (284), Eco's concern with intertextuality (129-131), and the repetition and narrative multiplicity of Robbe-Grillet. (267)

Indeed, translator Susan Brownsberger argues in her afterword to *Pushkin House* that the book is "as much a response to Joyce and Nabokov as it is to the traditional Russian classics" (360). However, Hellebust goes on to argue that it would be a serious mistake to read Bitov's book simply as a work of Western postmodernism and that its real significance can only be understood by an appreciation of its place in the tradition of Russian literature. Actually, Hellebust and

Brownsberger are both right. Bitov does draw upon both Western and Russian literary traditions in his search for techniques with which to build his *Pushkin House,* as Brownsberger suggests. But the real significance of Bitov's book can only be appreciated within a Russian context, both in terms of Russian *literature* (especially of the nineteenth century) and in terms of the social and political context of Bitov's contemporary Soviet Union.

The most distinctive feature of *Pushkin House* involves its extensive array of quotations, allusions, and epigraphs taken from other literary works. Brownsberger notes the importance of Pushkin for Russian literature and points out that Russian literature "has been called the house that Pushkin built" and that Bitov's novel is "a parodic 'double' of the house that Pushkin built—wittily ornamented, in the postmodern manner, with architectural motifs from the past" (359). However, Bitov does not restrict himself to the Russian literary tradition. In addition to Russian sources like Pushkin, Bitov also appropriates material from Western writers like Sterne, Joyce, Proust, Dante, Cervantes, A. Dumas, and Shakespeare. Indeed, the title of *Pushkin House* may identify Pushkin as Bitov's most important resource, but Bitov suggests in a footnote near the end of the book that he had considered titling it either "*A la recherche du destin perdu* or *Hooligan's Wake,*" suggesting (though partly in jest) a strong influence of both Proust and Joyce (345). In good postmodernist fashion, Bitov draws upon many sources of the past for his *Pushkin House,* creating an impressively complex and eclectic literary mansion.

Eschewing any concept of the Romantic artist-creator, Bitov constructs his novel through a series of self-conscious literary devices that recall Western postmodernism but that are also very much in the Russian Formalist tradition of the "baring of the device." The title of Bitov's book refers to a Soviet literary institute in what was then Leningrad, but it also suggests a metaphoric link between the construction of his text and the building of a house.[1] Bitov acknowledges this link near the book's end when he writes that "The building is finished, roof and all, people are living in it" (340). But Bitov's title also indicates his heavy use of material from Pushkin and other great writers of the Russian literary past. Indeed, very much in the vein of Nabokov's *The Gift, Pushkin House* contains a series of chapters, each of which acknowledges its debt to a specific predecessor (or predecessors) in Russian literature. It begins with a prologue whose title and epigraph are derived from Chernyshevsky's *What Is to Be Done?* Subsequent chapters then similarly acknowledge their debts to Turgenev's *Fathers and Sons,* Lermontov's *A Hero of Our Time,* and (finally) a combination of Pushkin's *The Bronze*

Horseman and Dostoevsky's *Poor Folk*.[2]   However, the most important predecessor of *Pushkin House* is probably *Evgeny Onegin*, itself constructed from a patchwork of "individual parodic stylizations of the languages associated with various literary schools and genres of the time" (Bakhtin, *Dialogic* 47).   In short, if Bitov's novel is like a house, it is a house constructed from used materials which still carry the nail holes from their former use.

Bakhtin's work points toward readings of *Pushkin House* that reveal powerful political implications both in Bitov's dialogue with the literary past and in his sophisticated self-conscious use of form and technique. *Pushkin House* exemplifies Bakhtin's vision of the novel as a powerfully political genre in numerous ways. For example, Bitov's book resembles *Evgeny Onegin* (and *The Gift*) in its incorporation of numerous genres, both literary and nonliterary. The text includes a number of inserted genres, including short stories written by characters in the novel, an extensive discussion of an essay in literary criticism written by the protagonist, poems, and even a literal copy of a fragment of newsprint. The principal narrative line involves a fictionalized biography of the protagonist, Lev (Lyova) Odoevtsev. This biography includes most of the elements typical of the genre, including a description of Lyova's family background, childhood experiences, personal relationships, education, and professional development. The text even includes a great deal of the textual apparatus (like footnotes and appendices) normally associated with the scholarly biography. However, both the footnotes and the appendices act principally to call attention to the fictionality of the narrative by making metafictional comments on the construction of the text. Similarly, Bitov's narrator (who is ostensibly Bitov himself) undermines the illusion that he is presenting a genuine biography by frequently intruding in the narrative to make reflexive commentaries that call attention to the artificial construction of his text. Actually, *Pushkin House* employs a sort of dual narrative voice, somewhat in the mold of Gogol's *Dead Souls*.[3]   The main narrative (in normal typeface) is related by a "storyteller" (albeit a rather self-conscious one), while the text is frequently punctuated with italicized sections related by an author figure who makes metafictional comments on the techniques employed in main sections. These sections of Bakhtinian autocriticism are introduced with "*(Italics mine—A.B.)*," identifying this author-narrator with Bitov himself.[4]

Unlike the works of dissident and émigré writers like Aksyonov or Aleshkovsky, *Pushkin House* includes very little overt criticism of the Soviet regime—or very little explicitly political material of any kind.   But Bitov's reflexive concern with the techniques used to construct his own text hardly represents a turning away from the world of social and political reality. Indeed, Bakhtin's work implies that no such turning away is possible, as there can be no strict separation between literature (especially the novel) and reality. True to Bakhtin's emphasis on autocriticism in the novel, *Pushkin House* seems largely to be about itself and its own language and structure. From a Bakhtinian perspective, however, the inherently ideological nature of language and of literary form implies that self-referential fiction is not only relevant to the real world, but perhaps considerably more so than realistic fiction, which on the surface appears to engage that world more directly.

In this same vein recent critics like Robert Siegle have argued that reflexive fiction has an inherent political potential in the way it "suggests that narrative derives its authority not from the 'reality' it imitates, but from the cultural conventions that define both narrative and the construct we call 'reality'" (125). In short, by calling attention to the conventions and artifices that go into its own construction, a reflexive text can at the same time call attention to the similarly conventional artificial basis of social and political systems. Siegle notes that

any code system divides up an expression continuum (from sounds and marks to phonemes and graphemes) by an arbitrary act that parallels the equally arbitrary way culture segments the content continuum (of things and experiences) and elaborates rules for the combination of these units (grammar and syntax for language, clothing and mores for behavior, politics and economics for group behavior, genres and conventions for art, concepts and theoretical systems for philosophy or theology or poetics). (10)

Siegle's argument that literary texts are constructed according to much the same principles as social habits and political institutions suggests a clear relevance of reflexive fiction to real-world issues. On the other hand, numerous critics have pointed out that the exposures and subversions of literary conventions in reflexive fiction are not necessarily subversive in a social and political sense, especially in the context of a Western bourgeois society that itself requires constant challenges and subversion in order to preserve its status quo. Dana B. Polan points out that an element of reflexivity resides in all art and that in bourgeois society even works of popular culture like Disney cartoons are often highly reflexive, without offering the slightest challenge to social or political orthodoxy. Polan offers Bertolt Brecht as an example of an artist whose reflexive works *are* subversive because they address their formal transgressions to specific social and political targets. However, for Polan experimental technique itself does not guarantee revolutionary impact, because if

art does not connect its formal subversion to an analysis of social situations, it becomes little more than a further example of the disturbances that go on as we live through a day. And a work of art that defeats formal expectations does not lead to protest against a culture that itself deals continually in defeating expectations. (351)

Polan's point is well taken. However, Bitov is not writing in a bourgeois society in which transgression and individualism are central cultural stereotypes. Instead, he is writing within the context of an authoritarian society where even the slightest transgression is viewed by the authorities as potentially dangerous. In this context, any sort of challenge to authority or accepted practice is potentially subversive, and it is thus no surprise that the Soviet authorities suppressed publication of Bitov's "nonpolitical" book.

Bitov's use of reflexive literary techniques is in fact subversive in a number of ways. For one thing, the overt fictionality of *Pushkin House* has special implications in the light of the blatant fictionalization of reality that so long characterized the Soviet regime. For another, in his Soviet context the mere association with Western literature or Western literary techniques is enough to cast suspicion on the offending author. And Bitov's overt exposure of his authorial work in constructing *Pushkin House* offers a challenge to the traditional notion of the author as an invisible godlike power in a Soviet context in which *any* challenge to *any* authority is potentially disruptive. Bitov ends the book with an appendix subtitled "The Relationship Between Hero and Author" in which the narrator discusses *in extenso* this relationship and offers his view of it. Among other things, this appendix suggests that the relationship between an author and his characters is fundamentally a matter of power. *Pushkin House*, the narrator claims, is not concerned with the political power exercised by governments, nor is it concerned with the social power gained by authors in their quest for recognition and success. It is, however, centrally concerned with the element of power in the relationship between authors and their characters.

In particular, Bitov's characters sometimes seem to escape his control. In the appendix the narrator goes on to suggest that, as novels near their conclusions, characters often begin to rebel against their authors. Then, presumably, the characters simply cease to exist when the novel ends. Wondering whether Lyova might in fact be living on in the real world, Bitov's narrator collapses the usual ontological separation between author and character by going to visit the "real" Pushkin House to see whether Lyova is still there. The narrator goes to Pushkin House, looks around with curiosity, and is pleased because what he sees is quite compatible with what he has described in his book. He then does indeed meet Lyova, who turns out to be "just about as I had imagined him, only considerably taller and blonder, which astonished me" (345).

The narrator admits that he has "violated literary etiquette" by entering his own novel and conversing with his character, thus enacting a sort of postmodern literalization of Bakhtin's notion that in the polyphonic novels of Dostoevsky the author gives up his normal control over his characters and descends to their level to engage them in dialogue. In Dostoevsky's novels, according to Bakhtin, "the author speaks not *about* a character, but *with* him (*Problems* 63). This violation of etiquette also participates in what has by now become a postmodernist commonplace—Brian McHale notes that the appearances of authors of their own texts is one of the standard techniques through which postmodernist authors challenge our conventional assumptions about reality. However, McHale notes that these appearances represent not an attempt to seize control of their texts, but to disavow such control, in the mode of the demystifications of authorship by recent theorists like Barthes and Foucault (199-202). In particular, if the author can appear within his own fiction, he thereby cedes his usual position of godlike authority over the text.

In one of his italicized authorial intrusions Bitov specifically challenges the omniscient stances taken by the authors of traditional realism:

God alone, if it is first agreed that He exists, can see from above. But only Lev Tolstoy has permitted himself to write from God's standpoint, and we won't even discuss here the extent of his competence for his efforts. (56-57)

Bitov's identification of Tolstoy as a figure of the kind of godlike artist he is seeking to undermine is particularly interesting when read in the context of Bakhtin's frequent criticisms of Tolstoy as a writer who misrepresented reality in his ostensibly "realist" works. In this sense Bakhtin echoes the conventional Stalinist view of Tolstoy's writing. However, in his 1930 preface to *Resurrection* in Tolstoy's *Collected Literary Works* Bakhtin takes a somewhat different tack and praises Tolstoy as an important predecessor of socialist realism: "As a model for the socioideological novel, *Resurrection* can be of great use to the literary aspirations of the present day" (257). As Clark and Holquist note, this sudden change in attitude toward Tolstoy, especially when read in the context of Bakhtin's earlier criticisms, suggests another of Bakhtin's sly attacks on the Soviet regime in which he subtly equates the quest for a responsible socialist literature with the religious fanaticism of Tolstoy (155).

Bitov's dialogue with Tolstoy and other realist writers may suggest a subtle critique of socialist realism as well. Bitov's ostentatious use of literary artifice already stands in direct defiance of one of the central tenets of socialist realism—that texts should be simple, straightforward, and easily accessible to the masses. Moreover, Bitov's characterization flagrantly violates the socialist realist requirement that the protagonist of a text should be a "positive" hero (preferably from the working class) with good socialist ideals. But the characters of *Pushkin House* hardly fit this mold. Most are exconvicts or former exiles, women of questionable morals, drunken Petersburgers ready to cheat or steal, or, like Mitishatyev or Lyova's father, persons with dubious ethical standards. Lyova's character is itself somewhat dubious.[5] In addition, Lyova is a nobleman, a descendant of a famous aristocratic family, and thus already has the wrong pedigree for a "positive" hero. And where the hero of socialist realism is supposed to work for and believe in the coming "radiant future" of Communism, Lyova is fascinated by and preoccupied with the past. Finally, where the positive hero is expected to eschew individualism and to place the good of the community above his own interests, Lyova is obsessed with his own subjective concerns. He is, in fact, intensely self-conscious, much like the heroes of Dostoevsky.

By the time Bitov wrote *Pushkin House*, the stranglehold of socialist realism on Soviet literature had already been significantly loosened. However, the mode was still the official doctrine in Russian literature, giving Bitov's subversive dialogue with the traditions of socialist realism clear political implications. Similarly, there is far more at stake in Bitov's dialogues with nineteenth-century Russian literature than mere textual play. *Pushkin House* begins on the day of the annual celebration of the Revolution, sometime in "196-," already suggesting a political dimension to the book. Similar subtle political resonances sound throughout the text.

Lyova works in Pushkin House, a literary institute and museum associated with the Academy of Sciences in Leningrad. In this particular year it is his turn to keep watch over the institute for the three days during which the other employees are celebrating the anniversary of the Revolution. However, the first time we meet Lyova in the book's prologue he is already (ostensibly, at least) dead—we see his body lying on the floor of Pushkin House amid a heap of scattered papers. The reader is thus led to expect that she will be reading the story of events leading up to this death, that the book will be a sort of murder mystery. Bitov's prologue, entitled "What Is to Be Done," thus resembles the beginning of Chernyshevsky's *What Is to Be Done?*, which opens with an apparent suicide and with the suggestion that the book will tell a story of frustrated love leading to that suicide. But these expectations are not to be realized: both Bitov and Chernyshevsky proceed to tell far different stories than their beginnings imply.

By beginning with the aftermath of Lyova's death, *Pushkin House* echoes the classic detective story opening. However, by starting with the end of its story, Bitov's book also resembles Nabokov works like *Lolita*, in which readers learn of the deaths of Humbert Humbert and Lolita in a foreword that precedes their story, or *Laughter in the Dark*, in which Nabokov outlines the entire plot of the novel in the first paragraph. There is a great deal of parodic textual play in these openings, which thoroughly undermine the conventions of plot-driven fiction. However, Bakhtin's notion of the chronotope suggests that the plot structures of novels have implications that go beyond mere formalism. In particular, they are related to specific chronotopes, which are themselves related to particular worldviews. In a postmodernist work like *Pushkin House*, however, one might expect to find parodies of worldviews as much as embodiments of them. Among other things, Bitov's technique of fixing the ending before beginning the narrative parallels the Marxist model of history, in which the eventual outcome is presumably foreordained and in which only the details leading up to the eventual triumph of Communism are to be determined.

This Marxist model of history is directly reflected in the socialist realist convention of happy endings and complete closure. Bitov thus parodies both the literary conventions of socialist realism and the Marxist teleological narrative of history in his radically inconclusive book. In the first section of the novel, entitled "Fathers and Sons" (à la Turgenev), Bitov introduces the Odoevtsevs, a formerly aristocratic family who chose to stay in Russia after the Revolution coping with and adapting to the Soviet regime. Lyova's father and paternal grandfather (Modest Platonovich Odoevtsev) are both famous scholars, although Modest Platonovich "disappeared" during the Stalinist terror and Lyova only learns of his grandfather's continuing existence after Modest Platonovich's return from exile to Leningrad in the postStalin fifties. This section relates the story of Lyova's childhood and adolescence, the events of which allow him casually to comment on the evils of the Stalinist past. For example, both Modest Platonovich and the family friend "Uncle Dickens" served time in Stalinist prison camps, and Lyova himself is born in Siberia where his parents were exiled at the height of the Stalinist terror. Moreover, the central fact of the entire "Fathers and Sons" section of the narrative concerns the revelation that Modest Platonovich had apparently been arrested after being denounced by his own son, Lyova's father.

After telling this poignant story, however, the narrator decides that he is not pleased with it. He then introduces the first of the book's several "Version and Variant" sections in which he retells previously narrated material with modifications. In this case, he envisions for Lyova a completely different family background and a new set of early experiences. But the narrator then concludes that, despite these changes, Lyova would probably still turn out the same. Despite changing all the earlier details, the narrator concludes that he will inevitably arrive "back at the same point in the novel," which will then presumably continue as before (96). So he decides that he might as well stick with the first version of his story: "Quite frankly, we like the first variant of Lyova's family better. It's more to our taste" (100). Besides calling attention to the fictionality of his narrative, Bitov thus somewhat pessimistically suggests that regardless of environment and circumstances one's life turns out the same—at least within the restrictive confines of the Soviet Union. At the same time, he offers a subtle parody of socialist realism, whose heroes always reach predefined (and entirely predictable) ends.

These attempts to construct a suitable narrative of Lyova's past (and thus suitably to construct Lyova himself) identify *Pushkin House* as what Bakhtin calls a "novel of development," albeit a rather strange and eccentric one. The novel is principally the story of the life and growth of Lyova Odoevtsev: it starts with his birth and ends with his (apparent) death. In the course of the novel, Lyova physically and psychologically matures and at the end he is not the same as at the beginning of the novel. Bakhtin suggests that such development, or changeability, in a character is typical of the novel as a genre. Comparing the novel with the epic, he concludes that the epic has static heroes who do not change in the course of the narrative in which they participate. Despite any adventures that might befall him, Odysseus is the same at the end of the *Odyssey* as at its beginning. He does not question his identity and is never uncertain about it. His adventures are only elements of the plot, devised in order to teach Homer's readers particular lessons.

Actually, the epic hero (as described by Bakhtin) is in many ways curiously similar to the positive heroes of socialist realism, who also do not change in meaningful ways, being limited to strictly prescribed courses of development leading to their successful integration into socialist society. Bakhtin's novelistic heroes, on the other hand, are much more fluid and unformed. Their experiences do influence their personalities and throughout the novel we watch them change in unpredictable ways as they interact with the ongoing flow of history. *Pushkin House* is in a sense the story of Lyova's development as an individual and of his search for an identity through attempts to recover the truth about his past. And this development is certainly highly contingent, especially when Bitov's intrudes in the narrative, retracting or modifying accounts that have gone before. In keeping with the book's metafictional mode, *Pushkin House* is not only the story of Lyova's "development" but also the story of the development of *Pushkin House* itself.

The close relationship between the evolution of Lyova as a character and the unfolding of the narrative in which he participates suggests a conception of subjectivity very much like that put forth by Bakhtin. Bakhtin's notion of the dynamic and ongoing development of characters in the novel seems to suggest that individuals in the real world develop similarly; it is also part of his incessant effort to suggest the possibility of genuine change amid the monologic stasis of Stalinism. Moreover, by using novelistic characters as his central metaphor for human subjectivity, Bakhtin indicates a central role for narrative in the development of human identity. Indeed, throughout his career Bakhtin was fond of drawing metaphorical parallels between literary texts and human subjects, and he often talks about texts and individuals in interchangeable terms. In this he anticipates a number of recent theorists who have emphasized the importance of aesthetic concepts to human identity. Michel Foucault, for example, argues in *The Use of Pleasure* that individuals (or at least free male individuals) in ancient Greece sought to constitute themselves as ethically admirable subjects after the model of aesthetically admirable works of art. For Foucault, the Greeks practice several "technologies of the self" through which individuals can exercise a creative freedom in constituting themselves as individuals, "by offering oneself as an example, or by seeking to give one's personal life a form that answers to criteria of brilliance, beauty, nobility, or perfection" (*Use* 27). In short, Foucault sees the principal goal of Greek life as the making of one's life into a masterful work of art for appreciation, admiration, and potential emulation by others.

Foucault's identification of works of art as important models for human subjectivity directly recalls much of Bakhtin's work, especially the early meditations on authorship in his "Architectonics of

Answerability" project.[6] Indeed, Holquist has argued that the parallel
between the authorship of literary texts and the constitution of the
human subject is perhaps the most important metaphor of Bakhtin's
entire career: "The suggestion of Bakhtin's total *ouevre*, conceived as
a single utterance, is that our ultimate act of authorship results in the
text which we call our self" ("Answering" 66). Bakhtin's particular
emphasis on narrative also brings to mind the recent work of Paul
Ricouer, who concludes that narrative is the principal means by which
we make sense of the flow of events that we encounter in life. It is
therefore through constituting one's experiences in the form of
narratives that one is able to establish and maintain a sense of identity
as an individual who is continuous over time:

What justifies our taking the subject of an action, so designated by
his, her, or its proper name, as the same throughout a life that
stretches from birth to death? The answer has to be narrative. To
answer the question "Who?" as Hannah Arendt has so forcefully put it,
is to tell the story of a life. The story told tells about the action of the
"who." And the identity of this "who" therefore itself must be a
narrative identity. (246)[7]

It is important to recognize that the "identity" cited by Ricoeur here
does not imply a sameness over time, but merely a narrative
connectedness. Thus, narrative identity "can include change,
mutability, within the cohesion of a lifetime" (246). The narrative
subject, then, is constantly in the process of being constituted through
the dynamic unfolding of the narrative in which she participates. The
resultant interactive nature of the narrative identity so produced has
important social consequences. For example, as Ricoeur notes, the
concept of narrative identity can be applied to communities as well as
to individuals.
    Foucault, of course, is one of the leading thinkers of Western
postmodernism, while Ricoeur's concept of narrative identity has been
suggested by Richard Kearney as a model for the development of a
postmodernist conception of human subjectivity (32). Bitov's
explorations of the development of Lyova Odoevtsev through narrative
thus represent another of the ways *Pushkin House* recalls the central
issues of postmodernism. Indeed, the starts and stops that inform the
fragmented narrative of Bitov's novel are almost reminiscent of the
texts of Samuel Beckett, which enact "not only the loss of the narrative
ability to order the past, present, and future of a sentence, or more
generally of a text, but also the loss of our ability to unify the past,
present and future of our own psychic or biographical experience"

(Kearney 313).[8] Beckett's texts, in short, are paradigms of what Jameson sees as the "schizophrenia" of postmodernism, the loss of any sense of continuity in time brought about by the radical alienation of individual subjects in late consumer capitalism.[9]

But Jameson's identification of postmodernism as the "apotheosis of capitalism" suggests that his comments may not be strictly relevant to the texts of Soviet writers like Bitov ("Cultural Logic" 77). Whether or not Jameson's analysis of postmodernism and of later consumer capitalism is correct, any sense of temporal discontinuity that one might find in Russian texts is probably related to historically specific events (like the breaks in Russian history effected by Peter the Great and by the Bolsheviks) that give the phenomenon a different intonation than it would have in the texts of Beckett or other Western writers. In the same way, Bakhtin's figurations of literary models of human subjectivity, however similar they may sound to the post modern, posthumanist mediations of Foucault, have a poignancy and a pathos within the context of Russian history that are unavailable to Foucault's Western perspective. One could argue, in fact, that Bakhtin is seeking to recover precisely the conventional humanist sense of self that Foucault is attempting to surmount. In Russia the problem is not to overcome overly rigid conceptions of the self, but to be able to conceive of a self to all.

Ricoeur's notion of narrative identity indicates that a stable sense of self requires the ability to conceive continuous narratives, which in turn suggests that any instabilities in the Russian subject might be related to the lack of continuity in Russian history. By violating the expectations of smooth narrative development and by implicating those violations in the development of his main character, Bitov similarly suggests a relationship between narrative and subjectivity. Much of *Pushkin House* might recall the work of Western thinkers like Foucault or Ricoeur, but it is again Bakhtin, with his Russian background, who probably provides the best key to Bitov's novel.

Similarly, from a Western point of view Bitov's play with historical determinism in *Pushkin House* might be read as a parody of nineteenth-century realism or of the Hegelian teleological history that so strongly informed the structure of Western narratives in that century. But if Bitov's book parodies a philosophy of history, it is not Hegel's, but Marx's. In particular, the narrative structure of *Pushkin House* directly parodies the Marxist concept of the inevitability of Communism. Despite the suggestions of determinism that run through the book, Bitov's plot is far from deterministic. In fact, it involves a number of surprising and unpredictable twists and turns (reminiscent of Bakhtin's discussions of Dostoevsky's plots) that thoroughly undermine any notion of a predetermined outcome. Even Lyova's death is not final. Having read the entire book with the expectation of finding Lyova dead in the end, the reader finally arrives at the last section, which tells the story of the last three days of Lyova's life, culminating in his apparent death in a Pushkinesque duel with his old friend Mitishatyev. However, the narrator again steps in at this point, granting a *deus ex machina* reprieve in which Lyova turns out merely to be unconscious. As if that weren't enough, the narrator then also resurrects Uncle Dickens (whose death and burial have been described earlier in the novel) to help Lyova clean up the mess left by his altercation with Mitishatyev. Indeed, even the narrator himself lends a hand, helping to replace some broken windowpanes: "But in actual fact it was I, *I*, who put in the glass for him! By night, like a fairy, I finished weaving the magic canvas" (327).

Thus, *Pushkin House* does not reach its foreordained conclusion after all—just as the radiant future of Soviet Communism was never to be. Bitov suggests that even though we might think we know what comes at the end of the novel (or of history, per Marx) we might well be wrong: both novels and history are far too complex to be so easily predicted. In short, the narrative structure of *Pushkin House* is ultimately subversive of the official Soviet model of history. It is, however, quite consistent with Bakhtin's view of history as an ongoing, dynamic process in which there is no "last word."

As Morson and Emerson point out, Bakhtin viewed history as "a matter of multiple potentials"; Bitov's "Versions and Variants" sections are clearly reminiscent of this emphasis on the multiplicity of history (46). In addition, *Pushkin House* displays an overt yet complex unfinalizability. Not only is the final resolution of the plot unpredictable from what has come earlier, but the book literally refuses to end, even after the plot has been resolved. By page 327 Lyova has been safely resurrected and order has been restored in Pushkin House. Bitov then presents an epilogue that relates the aftermath of the book's earlier events, including the return of the regular staff to Pushkin House and Lyova's subsequent confrontation with his boss, who Lyova is convinced will detect evidence of the recent events at the institute. This confrontation, we are led to believe, will finally bring the culmination of the novel: "And here at last is the sum, peak, crescendo-mescendo, apogeee, climax, denouement" (334). But no such decisive conclusion occurs: in fact the boss notices nothing and even gives Lyova the day off as a reward for minding the shop during the holidays, asking only that he take time to escort a visiting American writer on a tour of Leningrad. The tour itself is then anticlimactic: the museums of Leningrad are closed for the day, and Lyova is unable even to locate the site of Pushkin's fatal duel.

One conventionally expects that an epilogue will neatly wrap up and summarize the events of a book, but Bitov's epilogue ends inconclusively. It is in fact a mock epilogue that challenges the very notion that any sequence of events *can* be terminated in such a neat way. In this sense Bitov's epilogue resembles Western postmodernist works like Thomas Pynchon's *V.*, which similarly ends with an inconclusive epilogue.[10] Again, however, Bitov's parody of neat endings has special resonances within his Soviet context. Moreover, Bitov goes beyond even Pynchon, recalling the complex textual apparatus of Zoshchenko by following the epilogue with an appendix in which he meditates on the relationship between an author and his fictional characters. This appendix does finally "conclude" the book, except that it remains inconclusive, ending with an ellipsis that emphasizes the unfinalizability of the text. Moreover, the book's table of contents lists an additional section which does not in fact appear in the novel. This section is to be a commentary on the book by Lyova himself, written to commemorate the 1999 edition of the novel. But, as 1999 was still more than twenty years in the future at first publication of the book, this section has yet to be written and cannot even be approximated. The historical vision embodied in the chronotopic structure of *Pushkin House* suggests the impossibility of predicting what might occur between 1978 and 1999, a suggestion that would in fact be borne out by the dramatic historical changes beginning in 1991. In *Pushkin House*, as in history, there is literally no last word.

The interminable termination of *Pushkin House* is a highly successful enactment of Bakhtin's concept of unfinalizability in the novel. Describing the novels of Dostoevsky, Bakhtin argues that much of their power derives from the way they avoid any sense of finality or inevitability:

Nothing conclusive has yet taken place in the world, the ultimate word of the world and about the world has not yet been spoken, the world is open and free, everything is still in the future and will always be in the future. (*Problems* 166)

In Dostoevsky's novels, this radical unfinalizability results from the unpredictability of the outcomes of the various dialogic confrontations that occur as the novels proceed, though Bakhtin also notes that (with the exception of *The Brothers Karamazov*) Dostoevsky tends to impose "conventionally literary, conventionally monologic" endings on his novels in an attempt to achieve final resolution (*Problems* 39). In this sense, then, Bitov goes beyond Dostoevsky. Moreover, as Morson and Emerson emphasize, Dostoevskian unpredictability is only one kind of unfinalizability discussed by Bakhtin, who finds another sort of unfinalizability in Goethe's intense sense of historical continuity and connection to everyday life (Morson and Emerson 419).[11]

If Dostoevsky's unpredictability undermines the Marxist vision of a predetermined conclusion to history, Goethe's sense of connection among past, present, and future directly contradicts the Soviet quest for a radical break in history with the revolution of 1917. Indeed, Bakhtin's readings of these two major literary figures seem designed specifically to challenge these two major tenets of Soviet ideology, just as his portrayal of the carnivalesque in Rabelais serves as a subtly subversive commentary on the prudery and sterility of the Stalinist era. Interestingly, *Pushkin House* partakes of both of the major kinds of unfinalizability discussed by Bakhtin: if Bitov's eccentric and unpredictable plot recalls Bakhtin's Dostoevsky, his extensive array of allusions to previous literary texts suggests an attempt to effect a connection with the historical past in the mode of Bakhtin's Goethe.[12]

Lyova Odoevtsev is a scholar of nineteenth-century Russian literature who is centrally concerned with uncovering a continuous tradition in that literature. A long description of Lyova's unpublished critical essay "The Three Prophets," which occupies a prominent place in *Pushkin House*, nicely illustrates the style of the protagonist's scholarly endeavors (225-242). In this essay Lyova reads three poems by Pushkin, Lermontov, and Tyutchev, and discusses the relationships among them. Lyova seems almost obsessed with finding connections among the three poems, as when he determines that all three poems were written when the poets were twenty-seven years old, not coincidentally the same age as Lyova when he writes the essay. Lyova, in fact, is not above doing considerable violence to the poems in order to reach conclusions that match his own preoccupations. Bitov's narrator several times points out errors in Lyova's analysis, concluding that "it's not about Pushkin, not about Lermontov, and especially not about Tyutchev, but about him, about Lyova . . . it bespeaks *his* experience" (104, Bitov's emphasis and ellipsis).

Alice Stone Nakhimovsky notes Bitov's dialogue with the past and suggests that Bitov participates in a trend of "cultural nostalgia" which has become prominent in recent Russian literature. Nakhimovsky diagnoses the central problem of *Pushkin House* as "the disorientation of the new generation, cut off irretrievably from its cultural past" (196). Nakhimovsky then discusses Lyova's attempts and subsequent failure to recover the past, pointing out that because of the events that separate the nineteenth and twentieth centuries Lyova and his generation are unable to bridge the gap between past and present despite all their efforts. Central among these events, of course, was the Bolshevik Revolution, which effected a radical cultural break with the past that was felt as early as 1920 when Zamyatin satirized this phenomena by having his D-503 refer to the "impassable abyss between the present and the past" that informs his One State (6).

For Nakhimovsky the embedded allusions to nineteenth-century literature in *Pushkin House* often "result in a parody of the present. It is a parody which is fully appreciated by the characters, who recognize the futility of their attempts at recreating the past" (198). Thus the disparity between past and present works entirely to the advantage of the former, with the Soviet present functioning as a poor and degraded echo of the greatest of nineteenth-century Russian culture: "The nineteenth century for Bitov is culturally alive, the twentieth is a cultural vacuum. Attempts at repetition are doomed to comic failure. For Bitov, the present is so banal that even a tragic ending is impossible" (203). For Nakhimovsky, then, Bitov builds *Pushkin House* from bits and pieces of nineteenth-century Russian literature in order to call attention to its own status as a product of the degraded culture of the contemporary Soviet Union: "*Pushkin House* is thus a novel which is intentionally unable to stand up by itself, propped up against the giants of the nineteenth century, which did not, needless to say, have that problem" (198).

But the lack of a "tragic ending" hardly separates Bitov from his nineteenth-century predecessors. *Evgeny Onegin*, like *Pushkin House*, has no real termination—the narrator simply drops the narrative in midstream just as a climactic confrontation between Tatyana's husband and Evgeny seems imminent; *Notes from Underground* ends with an editor's note suggesting that the Underground Man's diary goes on, but that the remainder is not particularly interesting; *War and Peace* ends with a peculiar metaphysical tract that for most readers obscures, rather than elucidates, the meaning of the preceding text; *Dead Souls* was never finished at all. Similarly, the failure of Bitov's hero to achieve his goals or to attain tragic dimensions is actually a common element of Russian fiction of the nineteenth century. Onegin fails to realize the life of an aloof Byronic hero when he falls madly in love with Tatyana; the Underground Man fails to assert his independence from his environment or to present convincing arguments for the superiority of the irrational; Chichikov neither becomes a successful landowner nor attains the Christian salvation that Gogol apparently intended for him.

Nakhimovsky reads Bitov almost as if he were T. S. Eliot, residing in a degraded present and frantically shoring fragments against the ruins of the golden past of Russian literature. But the degradation of contemporary Soviet culture is not nearly so complete as Nakhimovsky suggests. Certainly Russian literature and culture suffered during the Soviet years, especially during the period of Stalin, and it is not without reason that in *The Gift* Nabokov's Fyodor bemoans the fact that even by the mid-twenties "everything in Russia [had] become so shoddy, so crabbed and gray" (187). But the very existence of impressive works of twentieth-century Russian literature like *Pushkin House* and *The Gift* (not to mention the works of Zamyatin, Ilf and Petrov, Bulgakov, Olesha, Pilnyak, Zoshchenko, Aksyonov, Aleshkovsky, Voinovich, Sokolov, and others) indicates that even Stalin and decades of socialist realism were unable completely to extinguish the fires of Russian literary creativity.

Many of these writers, like Bitov, seem to have made it part of their project to attempt to salvage the great Russian literary past from oblivion. But any difficulty these writers might have in establishing a firm connection with the past is not strictly a modern (i.e., Soviet) phenomenon in Russian culture. As Holquist has emphasized, the great Russian writers of the nineteenth century were in much the same predicament. Thus, far from writing in a sterile and degraded environment relative to the great Russian writers of the nineteenth century, Bitov is in a sense in a far better position than were his predecessors—simply because he *has* them as predecessors.

In addition, Bitov's allusions to his literary predecessors are often parodic and highly irreverent, suggesting that, far from worshipping them as gods from the past, he in fact feels quite comfortable in their presence. The parodic texture of Bitov's treatment of his literary sources, along with his experimental form, might even suggest that *Pushkin House* is a sort of declaration of independence from the Russian literary past and an announcement that contemporary writers like Bitov have now moved beyond the shadow of Pushkin, Dostoevsky, et al. But a look at works of early nineteenth-century fiction like Pushkin's *Tales of Belkin* shows that Russian writers of that time were already using many of the same sophisticated self-conscious literary techniques as Bitov. Hellebust thus notes that Bitov "follows firmly in the tradition of classical Russian literature," and that *Pushkin House* "can be read as a continuation, rather than a subversion, of a tradition" (267). What Hellebust does not say, however, is that Bitov's participation in the tradition of "classical" Russian literature is in itself potentially a sign of subversion of yet another tradition in Russian literature, namely that of the Soviet tradition of socialist realism.

Bitov's very ability to construct a successful novel from mostly nineteenth-century materials suggests that the historical rupture represented by the Revolution did not break off all communication with the past. In addition, Bitov directly indicates at several points in the book his belief that the Russian cultural past was not obliterated or made irrelevant by the Revolution. In Lyova's meeting with his grandfather early in the book, the old man suggests that by disrupting the normal flow of cultural evolution, the Revolution did not destroy the past, but simply cut off dialogue with it, thereby preserving it intact, free of the usual rereadings and reevaluations that would otherwise have occurred:

What matters is the break, not the destruction. The authorities froze there untoppled, unmoving: they're all in their places, from Derzhavin to Blok—the sequel won't shake their order, because there won't be a sequel. (64)

At the end of the book Bitov presents a fragment of a text presumably written by this same grandfather in which a similar idea is expressed. Here the grandfather suggests that the killing of Pushkin by Baron George-Charles d'Anthès in a duel in 1837 paradoxically served to solidify and enhance Pushkin's reputation as a poet. D'Anthès himself played a role very much like that of the Revolution, a link Modest Platonovich points out by bestowing upon the baron an honorary Soviet title: "The People's Artist d'Anthès sculpted Pushkin from his bullet" (353).

D'Anthès, then, removed Pushkin from the land of the living and made him a sort of museum piece, as the 1917 Revolution did nineteenth-century Russian literature in general. It is no accident that Bitov builds his book around the central image of Pushkin House, itself quite literally a museum for the preservation of the Russian cultural past as a sort of quaint relic with no real relevance to the present—much in the vein of the "Ancient House" of Zamyatin's *We*. However, from the point of view of Bakhtin, with his central emphasis on the importance of a living contact between literature and the present, this sort of museum preservation has serious negative consequences. Through this process, nineteenth-century Russian literature is made into a dead specimen under glass, preserved intact but removed from contact with contemporary reality. Bitov's book, on the other hand, strives to achieve such close contact with reality that it might be mistaken for a newspaper. He notes in his prologue that he will try to construct his story in such a way that it is contiguous with contemporary reality, "So that, on putting aside the novel, you might read a fresh or stale newspaper and suppose that what is happening now in the newspaper—and consecʒently, to some extent, in the world at large—is happening in the time of the novel" (6-7). Moreover, through his dialogue with the Russian literary past Bitov attempts to bring it back into contact with reality as well, metaphorically smashing the glass cases that enclose Pushkin, Lermontov, Dostoevsky, Turgenev, and others and bringing them back to life much as he resurrects the "dead" Lyova. Indeed, the final paragraph of Modest Platonovich's inserted text (and of Bitov's novel) compares Russian culture to a phoenix, the suggestion of potential cultural rebirth being obvious. After all, d'Anthes may have made of Pushkin a statue, frozen in time, but we know from Pushkin's own *The Bronze Horseman* that statues sometimes come alive.

NOTES

1. Note that Bitov insists on referring to the city as "Petersburg" throughout the text, perhaps thereby providing a subtle commentary on the attempted Soviet break with the Russian past as embodied in the renaming of the city after Lenin, while calling attention to a similar historical discontinuity arising from the policies of Peter the Great.

2. The structural and conceptual similarities between *The Gift* and *Pushkin House* are in fact so strόng that one is tempted to see Nabokov's novel as a model for Bitov's. However, Hellebust notes that Bitov has denied any influence of Nabokov, whom "he simply had not read by the time he wrote his novel ('Kommentarii k obshcheizvestnomu'). It is only Nabokov's own overinsistent denial of non-Russian influences (e.g. Kafka) and the ponderous circumstantial (i.e. textual) evidence against both authors that tempt one to doubt. Compare *Pushkin House* (284) with Nabokov's *Invitation to a Beheading* (217-23)" (277).

3. As Donald Fanger notes, *Dead Souls* is narrated by two distinct voices on different levels. The "narrator" tells the story of the book, while the "author" is a sort of metanarrator who steps outside this narration and comments upon it (171).

4. Incidentally, the initials of the editor of these sections "(*Italics mine—A.B.)*" are also reminiscent of Pushkin's "editor" in *The Tales of Belkin* "A.P."

5. It may be significant that Bitov calls attention to the fact that Lyova is named after Tolstoy, the one major nineteenth-century Russian writer to whom Bitov does *not* overtly pay homage in the book.

6. See Clark and Holquist for an extensive discussion of this early work, much of which is now translated and published in the volume *Art and Answerability* (63-94).

7. Compare Fredric Jameson's contention that the process of narrative is "the central function or *instance* of the human mind" (*Political* 13, emphasis in original).

8. Note that Bitov begins *Pushkin House* with a quote from Pushkin that he identifies as the draft of an epigraph for the *Tales of Belkin*: "This is what will be: we, too, will not be." The similarities between this epigraph and the famous "I can't go on, I'll go on" constructions of Beckett is obvious.

9. Jameson suggests that literary texts participate in this loss of temporal continuity, since they themselves are the products of the labor of writers who are alienated from their own texts. See "Postmodernism and Consumer Society."

10. See Pearce for a discussion of the postmodern aspects of the epilogue to *V.*. One might also compare here Tolstoy's *War and Peace*, which ends with an epilogue that supposedly wraps up the narrative, followed by *another* lengthy epilogue in which Tolstoy expounds on his theory of history. As Morson notes, this second epilogue, which seems to bear very little relation to the preceding narrative, undermines the book's sense of closure, providing a conclusion that "fails to end anything" (*Hidden* 63).

11. Bakhtin's figuration of Goethe as the supreme "prosaic" writer may owe something to Russian predecessors like Pushkin, who came to appreciate Goethe's "all-encompassing view of life, to admire his sharp eye for the 'details of reality'" (von Gronicka 65).

12. Goethe himself drew heavily on existing literature to construct his own works. Thus Weisinger notes that "most of Goethe's greatest literary achievement is directly derived from literary works of the past. . . . This borrowing of earlier material to fashion new was by no means a naive borrowing; all of these works depend for their very sophisticated effect on our awareness of their status *as* appropriation and reworking of earlier material" (20).

7

All-Purpose Parody: Sasha Sokolov's *Astrophobia*

Sasha Sokolov's *Astrophobia* in many ways represents a culmination of the antiauthoritarian writings of Russian dissident and émigré writers of the past few decades.[1] The book is a genuine tour de force, a massive and riotously funny encyclopedic mock epic whose tremendous verbal energy is generated largely by parodies of other recent Russian fiction. Indeed, almost everything in this brilliant text is addressed in one way or another to previous texts and especially to the ways those texts address the events of Soviet history. At the same time, however, *Astrophobia* is far from derivative. Sokolov's use of his intertextual sources in highly inventive, not only making his own text a unique creation, but also renewing previous texts and asking readers to approach those texts in new and different ways. Thus, having just discussed *Astrophobia*'s reliance on the works of writers like Solzhenitsyn, Limonov, and Nabokov, D. Barton Johnson concludes that Sokolov is "the most original voice in contemporary Russian prose" ("Avant-Garde" 177).

Bakhtin provides an extremely useful framework within which to approach Sokolov's dialogue with other texts in *Astrophobia*, though at first glance *Astrophobia* seems to disavow the kind of political engagement that for Bakhtin is central to the novel. After all, much of *Astrophobia* seems designed to mock the efforts of recent dissident writers to challenge official Soviet ideologies, especially Stalinism, while much of Bakhtin's work can itself be read at least partially as a reaction against the oppressive policies of Stalin. Bakhtin's emphasis on the importance of dialogue and on the rich productivity of mixtures of multiple perspectives runs directly counter to the monological authoritarianism of the Stalin era. Bakhtin's comments on carnival and laughter take on special significance in light of the humorless and puritanical prudery of the Stalinist regime. And Bakhtin's continuing apotheosis of change, his vision of history as an ongoing and never-ending process, stands in stark contrast to the conservative support for the status quo that lay at the heart of the chronotope of Stalinism. These same aspects of Stalinism provided targets for a whole range of modern antiSoviet writers, so it is hardly surprising that the works of writers from Zamyatin to Voinovich—which themselves gain so much energy from their subversive dialogues with Soviet authority—respond so well to Bakhtinian readings.

Stalin recognized the power of literature: through his support for socialist realism sought to create a new literary tradition that would convey the official ideology of his regime. Paradoxically, however, the most important literary legacy of Stalinism may lie in the rich body of antiStalinist literature that it inspired. Indeed, Stalin remains a central figure in antiofficial Soviet literature decades beyond his death. It is certainly important that the lessons learned from Stalinism not be forgotten. On the other hand, one could argue that the continuing prominence of Stalin in contemporary Russian literature runs counter to Bakhtin's belief in ongoing historical change and in the ability of the novel to respond to this change.

Russian dissident literature is rich and—given its focus on a specific common target—relatively diverse. Phenomena like the very different treatments of religion by writers like Aleshkovsky and Voinovich and like Voinovich's parodic send-up of Solzhenitsyn in *Moscow 2042* indicate some of the rifts that have arisen within the antiSoviet literature of émigré writers. Still, there is a danger that an ongoing focus on the Stalinist past might deprive this literature of the close contact with contemporary reality that Bakhtin sees as the main source of the novel's generic energy. In addition, a number of recent antiofficial Soviet writings seem informed by a self-righteousness and sanctimoniousness that lend these writings their own authoritarian tone. Of course, writers like Aksyonov, with his strong focus on contemporary culture, and Voinovich, with his warnings against reactionary Russian nationalism, already work against the calcification of dissident literature. But the text that may do the most to counter any trend toward stagnation or authoritarianism in antiofficial Russian literature is Sokolov's *Astrophobia*, which also harkens back to the days of Stalin but whose satirical focus is not so much on Stalin as on the attacks on Stalinism that are so central to recent dissident and émigré literature.

For Bakhtin parody is the principal tool through which the novel updates itself and maintains its contemporaneity. And parody is certainly central to *Astrophobia*, which gains its energies from the parody of a wide range of literary and cultural targets. The scope of Sokolov's parody in the book encompasses virtually all Russian literature from Pushkin and Gogol forward. Moreover, it encompasses much of Western literature and culture as well. Olga Matich usefully summarizes the book's parodic targets:

Like *Eugene Onegin*, *Palisandriia* may be described as a post-modern encyclopedia of contemporary Russian literary life in its various discourses. Besides autobiographical writing and the retrieval of history, it spoofs Aesopian language, play with Soviet cliches, literary graphomania, the emigre novel and emigre nostalgia, the spy novel, dissident politics, Gulag, sensationalism, literary taboo-lifting, Aksyonov's superman hero, Limonov's sexual liberation, the Freudian craze or psychoanalytic mythology, Western liberalism, civil rights, Western popular culture, and so on. ("Context" 335)

Astrophobia is supposedly the story of Palisander Dahlberg, compiled by a biographer in the year 2757 A.D. from texts written by Palisander himself around the year 2044. Palisander is a larger than life character of Rabelaisian proportions. Immensely strong and capable of Gargantuan sexual exploits, he is absolutely irresistible to women, despite having seven fingers on each hand and being hairless, falsetto-voiced, and physically huge (in more ways than one). Moreover, he is the ultimate Kremlin insider, the grandson of the monk Rasputin and great-nephew of Stalin's security chief Lavrenty Beria. Indeed, Palisander is heir apparent to the leadership of the mysterious Order of the Watchmen, a hereditary organization in which (so *Astrophobia* tells us) lies the real political power in the Soviet Union. Orphaned at a young age, Palisander is so important that his upbringing and education are supervised by a Guardian Council that includes such eminent figures as Beria, Krushchev, Brezhnev, Andropov, and even Stalin himself.

Palisander's position thus makes him privy to the inner workings of the Kremlin hierarchy. As a result, his story sheds light on aspects of Soviet history that might otherwise have remained hidden. *Astrophobia* is in this sense somewhat reminiscent of the rewritings of Soviet history by writers like Solzhenitsyn and of the writings of memoirists like Evgenia Ginsburg or (especially) of insiders like

Svetlana Allilueva, Khrushchev, and Brezhnev. But *Astrophobia* is far from an earnest effort to recover the real truth of the Soviet past. Indeed, it is an outrageous parody of such efforts that ultimately suggests the impossibility of knowing the truth of history. At the same time that he mocks writers like Solzhenitsyn, however, Sokolov also sets his parodic sights on the sensationalism of writers like Edward Limonov, who have employed shock tactics like sexual explicitness and *mat* language to attack the fastidious prudery of Soviet censorship.

Critics of *Astrophobia* agree that dissident and émigré writers are the most direct objects of parody in *Astrophobia*. Johnson, for example, singles out Solzhenitsyn and Limonov among the targets of Sokolov's multifarious parodic assault:

Astrophobia is a multilevel parody of many things: the classic epic, the historical memoir, the pornographic novel, the spy thriller, and so on. Not least, however, is the deflation of two varieties of a recent literary phenomenon: the self-righteous, moralistic, semi-documentary memoir à la Solzhenitsyn and the nitty-gritty, pornographic, semi-autobiography à la Limonov. ("Avant-Garde" 174)

Elsewhere, Johnson suggests that certain motifs in *Astrophobia* can be taken as a commentary on "contemporary 'nationalist' writers, such as Solzhenitsyn, with their passion for cleansing Russian of foreign impurities" ("Galoshes" 170). Arnold McMillin notes that *Astrophobia* is driven by parody, especially of the "type of historical writing epitomised by Solzhenitsyn" (239). And Matich presents a brief summary of the relevance of Limonov's *It's Me, Eddie* to *Astrophobia* ("History" 424).

Sokolov's dialogue with Solzhenitsyn is especially overt. Solzhenitsyn is specifically mentioned at one point in the book, as Palisander reveals that "Solzhenitsyn" is in fact simply another name used by the reactionary nationalist writer Soloukhin (91). This identification illustrates Sokolov's view of Solzhenitsyn as "the leading representative of what Sokolov sees as the neo-monarchist, neo-Slavophile school" (Johnson, "Avant-Garde" 174). Other references to Solzhenitsyn in *Astrophobia* are only slightly less direct. Like Solzhenitsyn, Palisander receives the Nobel Prize for Literature late in the book, though Palisander goes Solzhenitsyn one better by receiving an additional Peace Prize for his work for hermaphrodites' rights. One section of *Astrophobia* is based on Palisander's *Prison Diaries*, written during his incarceration after an attempted assassination of Brezhnev at the instigation of Andropov. The echoes of Solzhenitsyn's novelizations of life in Soviet prison camps are obvious here, except that, far from the dire conditions depicted in Solzhenitsyn's works, Palisander (as fits his high station in life) is imprisoned in a luxurious palace formerly owned by Prince Yusupov. Another section of *Astrophobia* is based on a work by Palisander entitled *Reminiscences of Old Age, or, Candle in the Wind*. One of the book's many footnotes identifies *Candle in the Wind* as the title of a play by Maxwell Anderson, but the title in fact belongs to a play by Solzhenitsyn. And Palisander's text again bears certain resemblances to Solzhenitsyn's. For example, Solzhenitsyn's play features a licentious aunt who openly flirts with her nephew, while Palisander's *Candle in the Wind* tells the story of his seduction by Majorette, a woman whom he confuses with an elderly aunt who seduced him in one of his numerous previous incarnations. However, the religious conservative Solzhenitsyn uses this motif to criticize the hedonism and moral decay that he sees as rampant in modern society. Palisander's version, on the other hand, is a carnivalesque tale of outrageous sexual activity: not only does Majorette turn out to be a sadist, but we also learn in one scene from this chapter that Palisander is a hermaphrodite and witness his intercourse with both Majorette and the psychoanalyst Carl Jung.

Such direct references notwithstanding, Sokolov's most effective parody of Solzhenitsyn occurs in the way Palisander's memoirs carnivalize the efforts of writers like Solzhenitsyn to reveal the truth of Soviet history. From the first pages of *Astrophobia* Palisander challenges received versions of the Soviet past. For example, in the book's opening prologue he reveals that his famous great-uncle Beria was not shot on charges of conspiracy but actually committed suicide, hanging himself from the hands of the clock atop the Kremlin's Salvation Tower. Later, we learn that the reports of Beria's execution were fabricated in order to discredit him and others who had sought to reveal that the Soviet Union was secretly being ruled not by the Communist Party but by unspecified "Certain Powers" from abroad (67). Palisander's revelations lead to a number of other revisions of history as well. We also learn, for example, of a childhood prank in which Palisander and some friends (the sons of Soviet leaders like Molotov and Kaganovich) hide a dachshund in Stalin's closet. Stalin later opens the door and then dies from a stroke he incurs when the "Baskervillian hound" leaps out at him (100).

Palisander's continual suggestions that official reports of Soviet history were inaccurate could be taken as a commentary on the unreliability of official versions of history under the Soviet regime. However, far from replacing official proSoviet accounts of history with revelations of the antiSoviet "truth" à la Solzhenitsyn, Palisander produces a highly personal and eccentric account of events that is often quite sympathetic to the Soviet powers that were. Indeed, the nature of Palisander's revisions of history usually works to the advantage of the Soviet leaders, especially of Stalin. The report of Stalin's death from fear of a small pet might first seem designed to undermine the myth of Stalin as a fearless warrior and defender of Communism. But this death is in fact part of Palisander's general description of Stalin as a kind, gentle figure who spends his time playing with the children of the Kremlin entourage. On a personal level, in short, Palisander depicts a Stalin who is quite consistent with the representations of Stalin in stock socialist realist works of the time. And Palisander's Stalin is benevolent politically as well. He is a liberal who works to lift the Iron Curtain and to give greater freedom to the Russian people. Unfortunately, he is frustrated in his efforts at enlightened reform by the "Certain Powers" who are really in charge in the Soviet Union.

In the final analysis, it seems clear that Palisander's carnivalesque revisions of history in *Astrophobia* function not so much as a parody of official versions of Soviet history as of the recent retellings of that history by dissident writers like Solzhenitsyn. Indeed, Palisander's approach to historical reportage has a great deal in common with Solzhenitsyn's. Both, for example, focus on the prosaic details of everyday Soviet life in a semi-documentary style. Palisander explicitly calls attention to this approach at several points in *Astrophobia*. In the midst of his opening revelation of Beria's suicide he thus pauses for a digression on the life of lowly Horse Marine officer Yakov Nezabudka, who is identified as one of those innumerable common people whose lives are destined to go unrecorded in the annals of history. Then, as if to illustrate the point, Palisander devotes almost all of the remainder of his memoirs to stories of various famous and powerful figures from Soviet history. Even when dealing with such exalted figures, however, he maintains his focus on the prosaic, believing that "however the grudging may grumble, in the lives of the great every detail is tantalizing, all seeming minutiae titillating" (12). Indeed, explaining his relationship to history in a missive presumably written to the exiled Anastasia Romanova, Palisander proclaims his fondness for the great ideals of the noble past, but goes on to admit his irresistible attraction to the "paltry day-to-day" as well (20). For example, Palisander expresses his fondness for prosaic items like galoshes numerous times in the text, and indeed this footwear motif runs throughout Sokolov's fiction. As Johnson notes, this motif connects Sokolov's work to that of predecessors from Gogol and Pushkin to Bunin and Kataev. But galoshes serve most centrally in Sokolov's work as "an explicit symbol of mundane, sensory reality as opposed to the grandiose, abstract pseudo-ideal of History" ("Galoshes" 172).

Palisander's focus on "mundane, sensory" reality at first seems reminiscent of Solzhenitsyn, but Palisander in fact concentrates on aspects of this reality that differ dramatically from those emphasized by Solzhenitsyn. For example, Solzhenitsyn echoes Gogol in his concern for keeping the Russian language free from Western contamination, while Palisander recalls the narrator of *Dead Souls* in his belief that different national languages are informed by different worldviews. But Palisander, a linguist in the class of Rabelais's Panurge, in fact knows a wide variety of languages, including Greek, Latin, Russian, Georgian, Basque, Sanskrit, French, German, English, and even Berber, and can use them all with great facility.[2] Indeed, in contrast to the Russian purist Solzhenitsyn, Palisander is such a polyglot that he becomes almost a walking advertisement for Bakhtin's notion of heteroglossia. And despite Palisander's continual protestations of fastidiousness and squeamishness, the details of everyday life that he describes focus almost entirely on the sexual and the scatological. One of *Astrophobia*'s innumerable footnotes describes a text entitled *History of the Water Closet*, a massive encyclopedic survey of sewage systems from caveman times up to the present (213). Among other things, this text is reminiscent of Joyce's *Finnegans Wake*, a connection to which Sokolov calls attention by including a notation that the book had been dubbed "the next Iliad" by Dublin newspaper "*Finnegan's Week*."[3] But *History of the Water Closet* is also quite suggestive of *Astrophobia* itself. For example, the footnote in which the book is described comes directly after the recitation of a poem by Palisander entitled "Pushkin" that turns out to be about urination rather than poetry. And one of the most carnivalesque moments in *Astrophobia* occurs when Palisander has an attack of diarrhea while locked inside a prison tower. Because the tower contains no sanitary facilities, Palisander thrusts his posterior through a window to relieve himself. This operation is somewhat successful, though it is observed by Majorette and several others on the ground who yell mockingly at Palisander, whose position is then made even worse when he discovers that his largish rump has gotten stuck in the window, leaving him at the mercy of the derisive crowd below (358-9).

This scatological incident inflames Majorette's sexual interest in Palisander, and from that point on the two usually meet for their sexual encounters in the bathroom, suggesting a link between sex and excrement that is left unspecified in the text. Other sexual details included by Palisander in his memoirs are similarly outrageous, including Majorette's sadism and Palisander's hermaphroditism. Meanwhile, in his role as a male Palisander is an unparalleled sexual athlete with an impressive roster of sexual conquests, though these conquests tend to be of a rather unusual nature. He thus reveals in the course of the text that even as a young boy he had already been sexually involved with the wives of both Stalin and Brezhnev. Moreover, he hints that the relationship with Nadezhda Stalin led her husband to murder her and that the relationship with Victoria Brezhnev caused her husband to have an attack that finally killed him after years of near-death.

Palisander maintains a lifelong fascination with the wives of powerful men. The love of his life is Shaganeh Khomeini, Madame Superior of the Government Massage Parlor to which Palisander has been dispatched as steward in punishment for his role in Stalin's death. The decrepit Shaganeh, the former wife of the Ayatollah, is a rather unconventional dream girl, but Palinsander finds her decrepitude attractive. He is most drawn to Shaganeh because her sagging (and thus spacious) vagina can comfortably accommodate his huge penis and (especially) because she has been legless since birth. To add to the carnivalesque grotesquerie of this relationship, Palisander's favorite place to couple with the legless Shaganeh is amid the "moss and slime" of the crypts in the graveyard of the former Convent of the New Virgin that now houses the Government Massage Parlor (118).

Such carnivalesque details are hardly the kind to be found in Solzhenitsyn's revisions of Soviet history, though they do represent a rather logical extension of the focus by Solzhenitsyn and other dissident writers on the details of the lives of private individuals. The exaggerated sexual and excremental details of *Astrophobia* are at first glance more reminiscent of Rabelais than of Solzhenitsyn, and indeed Palisander describes himself late in the book as "a figure of Rabelaisian proportions" (379). Actually, though, the rather bizarre sexual incidents related in *Astrophobia* are probably aimed more directly at writers like Limonov, who have centrally focused on the description of presumably shocking sexual activities. Limonov is not mentioned directly in the book, but there are subtle gestures in his direction. During a stay in Paris, for example, Palisander lives on the Rue des Archives, the same street once inhabited by Limonov. Both Matich ("History" 424) and Johnson ""Avant-Garde" 174) thus conclude that *Astrophobia* is at least partially a response to Limonov's work, especially *It's Me, Eddie*.

The protagonist/narrator of *It's Me, Eddie* (clearly identified with Limonov himself) describes his experiences as a Russian émigré in

New York City. Among other things, the hardships and injustices encountered by Limonov's narrator counter the idealization of the West to be found in certain strains of Russian dissident literature. Indeed, this narrator anticipates Voinovich's *Moscow 2042* by suggesting that dissidents like Sakharov and Solzhenitsyn, widely admired in the West, are in fact right wing extremists who "would obviously pose a danger should they come to power" (89). But the aspect of Limonov's writing that has received the most attention is its graphic and explicit sex, rather in the mode of Henry Miller.

Palisander's outrageous sexual adventures often read almost as an attempt to out-Limonov Limonov, and indeed many aspects of *Astrophobia* can be read as parodic references to Limonov's work. For example, Palisander's hermaphroditism can be taken as a literalization of the bisexuality of Limonov's Edichka. However, just as Palisander presents material reminiscent of Solzhenitsyn in ways far different from Solzhenitsyn, so too does his presentation of graphic sexual material differ dramatically from Limonov's graphic, semi-autobiographical approach. For one thing, Palisander's carnivalesque escapades have a comic tone that is almost entirely lacking in Limonov's presentation. For another, despite his overtly sexual material the squeamish Palisander actually includes no graphic sexual descriptions in his memoirs at all. Instead, his sexual encounters are related through euphemism and indirection, up to and including the frequent use of Sternean gaps in the text at key sexual moments. In a sense, Sokolov seems to play Solzhenitsyn and Limonov off against one another, relating documentary history of the kind associated with Solzhenitsyn as it might be told by Limonov and revealing sexual details of the kind typical of Limonov as they might be described by a religious conservative like Solzhenitsyn.

The resultant dialogic confrontation between Solzhenitsyn and Limonov is highly effective at undermining the authority of either as a source of truth about Soviet history or about the dissident/émigré experience. For example, Palisander's fastidiousness suggests a revulsion at the physical that is characteristic of certain Christian traditions. Indeed, Palisander is so appalled by his own physicality that he spends most of his life refusing to view his own mirror reflection because he does not want to be reminded that his "typically repulsive exterior" is "endowed with the flaws of my fellowmen" (299). Because of this fastidiousness of the protagonist, the sexual and excremental imagery of *Astrophobia* is in fact far from Rabelaisian. Bakhtin emphasizes in his discussion of Rabelais in the chronotope essay that the Rabelaisian worldview, with its open acceptance of the physical realities of life, is diametrically opposed to medieval

Catholicism, "whose ideology of the human body is perceived solely under the sign of decay and strife, where in real-life practice, there reigned a crude and dirty physical licentiousness" (*Dialogic* 171). Rabelais's emphasis on the physical is in no way "dirty" or perverse. On the contrary, Rabelaisian motifs like sex and defecation merely represent a healthy acknowledgment of human participation in the physical and temporal world. For Bakhtin it is medieval Catholicism, with its rejection of the physical in favor of a focus on the ideal and timeless other world of heaven, that displays a perverse attitude toward human physicality.

In *Astrophobia* it is the ostensibly Rabelaisian Palisander who rejects the physical in the way that Bakhtin associates with medieval religion. For example, Palisander is so divorced from physical and temporal reality that he has no idea of his own age. Believing that he is still a teenager, he is shocked to discover late in the book that he has become an old man. In short, he lacks precisely the engagement with temporal history that Bakhtin associates with the material lower bodily stratum of Rabelais. Within the complex intertextual context of *Astrophobia* Palisander's rejection of the physical has numerous implications. For one thing, medieval Catholicism always functions in Bakhtin's work at least partially as a cipher for Stalinism, and Palisander's fastidiousness is certainly reminiscent of the priggishness of the Stalinist era. But Solzhenitsyn and Limonov are implicated in this motif as well. Palisander's disengagement from the passing of time can be taken partially as a reference to the inability of the reactionary Solzhenitsyn to move with the times. Further, if Palisander's squeamishness echoes both the Christian tradition and Stalinism, there is a suggestion that the religiosity of Solzhenitsyn may not differ all that dramatically from Stalin's attempts to surround his regime with a religious aura and to establish his government as an unchallenged moral authority. Meanwhile, Palisander's dialogue with Limonov calls attention to the fact that the sexual "liberation" depicted in works like *It's Me, Eddie* is a far cry from the celebration of physicality that Bakhtin associates with Rabelais and may instead be informed by a belief that an emphasis on sex is revolting in more ways than one.

This suggestion that the ideology of dissident and émigré writers may not be all that different from that of the Stalinists they so abhor is also made in *Astrophobia* in other ways, as when Andropov reveals to Palisander that the many Soviet émigré writers in the West are mostly agents of the KGB who only pretend to be antiSoviet in order to be able to operate more freely (75). And Palisander makes his own distaste for the works of dissident and émigré writers quite clear when he attempts to contrast the honesty of his revelations with the writings of certain other memoirists:

I could of course deceive you. I could concoct a cockamamie canard like the ones served forth by those multitudes of memoirists—traitors and hangmen, bandits and usurpers, the lackeys of highnesses brought low and nonexistent national minorities, suffragans and suffragettes, schoolgirls and callgirls, sons and lovers, willowy widows and will-hungry minions (chaffering their hands over urns still warm with eminent ashes), and other such riffraff weighted down with an excess of memory. (30)

Of course, Palisander himself is rather weighted down with memory, often waxing nostalgic in his own days of exile from Mother Russia late in the text. Moreover, despite his condemnation of the dishonesty of his fellow memoirists, Palisander himself is hardly a bastion of veracity. For example, many of his rewritings of the reported facts of Soviet history smack simply of misinformation, as when he reveals that Trotsky died of a tarantula bite in Uruguay (94). At times Palisander seems to suggest (à la Solzhenitsyn) that his unofficial history will replace the bogus official versions of the past with the "truth," as when he claims early on that his confessions will be entirely authentic and objective: "With my innate sincerity I shall tell the whole truth—yes, humiliating and heartrending as it is. And as if it had happened to someone else. A couple of toads, say." Yet he immediately undercuts this claim to truthfulness by admitting that he will relate his past "not as it actually happened. Or even not at all" (16). Indeed, Palisander often openly contradicts himself, calling attention to the unreliability of his information. For example, he introduces a steward called Sibelius as the twin brother of another character called Truhilde (287). He then later describes Sibelius as a tutor but admits in a footnote that "other sources" list Sibelius as a steward (334). He then claims that Sibelius is Truhilde's son and then calls attention to the discrepancy by adding in a footnote: "Other sources claim he was her brother" (335). If such reversals undermine the authority of Palisander's narrative, he himself warns early on that all versions of history (including his own) are to some extent unreliable. He confesses his youthful fascination with the facts of history, but then openly questions whether such facts can actually be known (19).

In general, Palisander's complete lack of any sense of time makes him the most unreliable historian imaginable. Indeed, beginning with Beria's hanging from the Kremlin clock in the book's opening episode,

time is very much out of joint throughout *Astrophobia*. Palisander
seems almost oblivious to chronological sequence, sometimes having
characters discuss events well before those events have actually
occurred. He calls attention to one of these moments in a footnote,
describing the phenomenon as a "reminiscence of the future" and
noting that "[w]e are visited by such reminiscences much more often
than we think, or rather, so often that we have learned to forget them
long before they occur" (165). He also suggests that his great-
grandfather's legendary resistance to poison can be attributed to the
fact that he took an antidote just before his famous poisoning because
of his "unbeatable intuition and knowledge of history" (199). In short,
Rasputin apparently "remembered" the attempt on his life even before
it happened and therefore took steps to prevent it. Palisander himself
seems to have a similar ability, often experiencing the phenomenon of
uzhe bylo (*déjà vu*) so vividly that he takes it as "proof of our regular
comings and goings along the circular paths of being" (288). The
result of this circularity is a narrative so scrambled that it becomes
virtually impossible to track coherently, even (and perhaps especially)
for readers who are relatively familiar with the events of Russian
history. For example, events from different historical periods are
often telescoped into near simultaneity, as when Stalin's death and the
rule of an ancient and failing Brezhnev occur at about the same time.
Thus the aged Brezhnev is already the ruler ("Locum Tenens") of the
Soviet Union when he founds the euphemistically named Government
Massage Parlor to provide a sexual release for Kremlin officials after
he himself is inspired by a particularly stimulating experience while
on a trip to Finland (81-2). But Palisander is then "exiled" to this
institution after the 1953 death of Stalin, placing Brezhnev's rule even
before Stalin's demise even though Brezhnev was in fact a rising and
relatively young Party official in 1953.

The sense of passing time in *Astrophobia* is further complicated by
the fact that Palisander apparently remembers events from several
different previous incarnations (ranging back to his days as Catherine
the Great's horse, and even before) but sometimes confuses events
from different reincarnations. In keeping with the motif of advance
memory, some of these reincarnations are even in the future. In the
midst of Palisander's story of his adventures with Majorette in the
fictional European country of "Belvedere," the narrative suddenly
leaps into the future to relate an anecdote concerning Palisander's
involvement with Québec's secession from Canada in the 1990s, an
event that seems somewhat conflated in Palisander's memory with the
French Revolution. The narrator (who usually seems to be Palisander,
but who often refers to Palisander in third person) then admits the

difficulties inherent in the lack of temporal order, or "anachrony," of his text:

Anachrony is harmful, disastrous. It eats away at the structure of a narrative, robbing it of its clarity, its very identity. Like Palisander, we began to wonder in which of his incarnations all this occurred. Who was he? An orphan boy of the Middle Ages, a youth of the Iron Age, or an old man of the Age of Transition seeking refuge in the castle where he had—once, at least—been born and grown to maturity? (347)

Clearly, Palisander's most direct predecessor as a chronicler of events is not so much Solzhenitsyn as Laurence Sterne, whose *Tristram Shandy* is evoked at numerous points in the text. At one point, Palisander's "aunties" (the staff of the Government Massage Parlor) accuse him (with obvious sexual innuendo) of threatening them with his imposing nose. Palisander somewhat confusingly tries to defend his behavior (and his disconnection from time) by explaining that a grandfather clock weight fell on his "nose" when he was a baby. In addition to those of Sterne, there are echoes of Gogol in this episode, and indeed Palisander refers explicitly to Gogol's story "The Nose" in the continuation of this conversation on the very next page. There are, in fact, numerous echoes of Gogol in *Astrophobia*, as when the exiled Palisander recalls the project of Chichikov in *Dead Souls* by accumulating a collection of the bodies of Russians who have been buried abroad while in exile.[4] But the motifs of the nose *double entendre*, of the replacement bridge, and of the grandfather clock all make it obvious that *Tristram Sandy*, rather than Gogol, is the most direct referent of Palisander's "nose" episode.[5]

The structural similarities between *Astrophobia* and *Tristram Shandy* are obvious as well. Tristram and Palisander have a great deal in common as confused and incompetent narrators who have considerable difficulty getting their stories straight. These difficulties present both Sterne and Sokolov with numerous opportunities to parody more conventional narrative structures. Indeed, parody lies at the heart of both novels. It is no accident that *Tristram Shandy* was such a favorite of the Russian Formalists, with their central emphasis on parody as a device for the renewal of literature. And Viktor Shklovsky's famous claim that Sterne's apparently chaotic work was in fact the "most typical novel in world literature" is clearly relevant to *Astrophobia* as well (57). However, the more clearly political (or perhaps one should say antipolitical) intonation of the parodies in Sokolov's book make it stand even more obviously than Sterne's as an exemplification of Bakhtin's emphasis on parody, an emphasis that echoes the Russian Formalists but with an additional insistence on the ideological (rather than purely formal) implications of parody.

The link to *Tristram Shandy* is, among other things, helpful for identifying the genre of *Astrophobia*, which is closely related to Menippean satire. The fragmented narrative with inserted texts from numerous other genres, the concern with contemporary political issues, the reliance on comic effects, the use of fantastic elements, the inclusion of sometimes scandalous sexual and excremental imagery, and various other elements of *Astrophobia* make it an almost classic example of the Menippean genre, especially as described by Bakhtin in the Dostoevsky book and elsewhere. Of course, for Bakhtin, one of the most crucial indicators of a genre is its chronotope, or attitude toward space and time. And one of the most obvious similarities between *Tristram Shandy* and *Astrophobia* is their scrambling of chronology, a scrambling so ostentatious that it clearly calls attention to the importance of time in both books. Indeed, the complex treatment of time is probably the most interesting formal feature of both books. Mendilow, for example, has argued that a study of *Tristram Shandy* "could almost serve as a summary of all the problems involved in the consideration of the time factors and values of the novel" (161). And time is certainly central to *Astrophobia* as well, despite Palisander's attempted rejection of it through most of his life. Indeed, when Palisander returns from exile to assume political power as the culmination of the novel's events, his official title becomes "Witness of the Russian Chronarchiate," and he admits that the real ruler of Russia is not he, but Time itself (146).

It is important, however, to recognize that the chronotope of *Astrophobia* (like almost everything in the book) is largely parodic. In short, *Astrophobia*'s chronotope does not directly represent a specific worldview as much as it parodies certain other worldviews. For example, the anachronisms, inaccuracies, and confused chronologies that inform Palisander's narrative clearly challenge the self-seriousness of recent writers like Solzhenitsyn who have claimed access to the truth of history. At the same time, Sokolov's parodic assault on Solzhenitsyn can in no way be taken as a defense of the official histories of a Stalinist regime that blatantly claimed the right constantly to revise the past. Instead, the ostentatious unreliability of Palisander's memoirs simply calls attention to the fact that Sokolov is not writing history at all. He is writing fiction, and as such he is under no obligation of strict fidelity to the truth. Nor should he be. If the power of fiction lies, as the Russian Formalists argued, in its ability to create new and defamiliarizing perspectives on the world, then that power requires an ability to go beyond the normal confines of reality.

Astrophobia is filled with characters and events from Soviet history, though the historical material imported into the book is usually transformed in strange and highly defamiliarizing ways. Contrary to the attempts at overt reproduction of political reality in the work of so many of his contemporaries among émigré writers, Sokolov insists on maintaining a clear distinction between fiction and reality, no matter how engaged with reality that fiction might be. Bakhtin's comments on the relationship between fiction and reality in the novel are again quite relevant here. Despite his consistent emphasis on the necessity of close contact between the novel and the social world outside the novel, Bakhtin insists that "there is a sharp and categorical boundary line between the actual world as source of representation and the world represented in the work." And he goes on to urge readers and critics to remain ever-aware of this boundary:

We must never forget this, we must never confuse—as has been done up to now and as is still often done—the *represented* world with the world outside the text (naive realism); nor must we confuse the author-creator of a work with the author as a human being (naive biographism). (*Dialogic* 253)

For Bakhtin, however, fiction and reality remain "indissolubly tied up with each other and find themselves in continual mutual interaction" (*Dialogic* 254). Indeed, it is the firm boundary line between fiction and reality that allows this interaction to be productive and that gives the novel the critical distance it needs to be able to engage in a genuinely effective dialogue with the historical world. Bakhtin explains the relationship between fiction and the real world with a metaphor from biology, noting that living organisms by their very nature resist fusion with their environment, but that they must maintain contact with that environment in order to stay alive.

It is not hard to find examples of literary works that clearly illustrate Bakhtin's insistence that a strict distinction between fiction and reality can in fact facilitate dialogic contact between the two. For example, in Emma Bovary Flaubert depicts perhaps *the* classic example of a literary character whose own attitudes erode the boundary between fiction and reality. But he does so as part of a network of images that serve as a powerful critical commentary upon the bourgeois society of his contemporary France. In more recent times the Russian émigré Nabokov provides a striking illustration of Bakhtin's thesis. Nabokov maintained throughout his career a fierce

commitment to separation between fiction and reality, going so far as
to say in one of his lectures (on *Madame Bovary*, interestingly enough)
that "literature is of no practical value whatsoever, except in the very
special case of somebody's wishing to become, of all things, a
professor of literature" (*Lectures* 125).

Nabokov then digresses in this lecture (constructed during his
American exile in the Stalinist 1940s) into a diatribe against the
philistinism of Soviet society and culture. In short, his declaration of
the apolitical nature of literature turns out to be highly political. And
a similar doubleness informs Nabokov's fiction, which is characterized
by an allusiveness, linguistic virtuosity, and formal brilliance that call
attention to its status as fiction, while still often providing powerful
commentaries on political reality. Indeed, Nabokov provides frequent
reminders that political messages can be found in ostensibly apolitical
works, as when the protagonist of *The Gift* claims to find a
representation of Stalin amid the ancient Persian miniatures pictured
in a book in the St. Petersburg Public Library (83).

The formal complexity and linguistic experimentation of
Nabokov's fiction can themselves be taken at least partially as a
reaction against socialist realist demands for simplicity and
accessibility. Meanwhile, dystopian works like *Bend Sinister* and
Invitation to a Beheading, both of which depict in excruciating detail
the horrifying human cost of totalitarian political regimes, have
obvious political implications. Yet these works are also highly literary,
and Nabokov has disclaimed political relevance in both cases, as in the
introduction to *Bend Sinister*:

I have never been interested in what is called the literature of social
comment . . . I am neither a didacticist nor an allegorizer. Politics and
economics, atomic bombs, primitive and abstract art forms, the entire
Orient, symptoms of "thaw" in Soviet Russia, the Future of Mankind,
and so on, leave me supremely indifferent. (vi)

Nabokov, apparently sitting atop the Olympus of "pure art," here
seems to deny that he has any interest in real world events at all. He
goes on to proclaim that *Bend Sinister* bears no relationship to the
political and historical context within which it was written:

Similarly, the influence of my epoch on my present book is as
negligible as the influence of my books, or at least of this book, on my
epoch. There can be distinguished, no doubt, certain reflections in the
glass directly caused by the idiotic and despicable regimes that we all
know and that have brushed against me in the course of my life:

worlds of tyranny and torture, of Fascists and Bolshevists, of Philistine thinkers and jack-booted baboons. No doubt, too, without those infamous models before me I could not have larded this fantasy with bits of Lenin's speeches, and a chunk of the Soviet constitution, and gobs of Nazist pseudo-efficiency. (vii)

But this denial is curious indeed, as it calls specific attention to the "reflections" of specific totalitarian regimes in his book, even signalling the reader to be on the alert for specific allusions to the authoritarian practices of both Soviet Russia and Nazi Germany.

In a similar way *Astrophobia*, which openly mocks the political engagement of recent Soviet dissident and émigré writers, still calls attention to some of the same issues addressed by those writers. Indeed, Nabokov may the one writer whose work *Astrophobia* most closely resembles, especially in terms of stylistic and formal characteristics. Nabokov himself was an enthusiastic supporter of Sokolov's work, and numerous critics have remarked parallels between the two writers. Matich, for example, suggests that Nabokov, along with Bely, provides "an essential context in which to view Sokolov's literary development," despite the fact that Sokolov himself discounts the importance of Nabokov's direct influence on his work ("Context" 303). Johnson, meanwhile, concludes that of the important recent Russian émigré writers only Sokolov seems to show any marked affinity with Nabokov in terms of style and technique ("Sokolov and Nabokov" 153).

Critics like Matich and Johnson have called particular attention to the intertextual dialogue between *Astrophobia* and Nabokov's *Lolita*. *Lolita* is directly mentioned at one point in *Astrophobia* (338), and numerous aspects of Sokolov's book recall Nabokov's novel. For example, both Palisander and Nabokov's Humbert Humbert are extremely fastidious and squeamish about the physical aspects of human life, yet both become involved in scandalous sexual situations. However, in keeping with his strategy of parodic reversal, Sokolov often reverses the Nabokovian motifs that his work recalls. Thus Humbert's enthrallment to young girls is inverted in Palisander's fascination with old women. But the most important parallel between *Lolita* and *Astrophobia* probably resides in the way both address the relationship between fiction and reality. Nabokov's Charlotte and Dolores Haze have their expectations of reality conditioned largely by American popular culture, while Humbert's view of the world is derived largely from his readings in European literature. Meanwhile, *Lolita* itself is composed largely of a patchwork of allusions to other literary works, as is *Astrophobia*. Sokolov's Palisander, like Nabokov's

Humbert, is a great reader who seems familiar with a virtually unlimited range of literature and often approaches reality through that reading. For example, at one point he tells Andropov that he learned to use firearms by reading *The Count of Monte Cristo*, the book so important to Aleshkovsky's Bashov—and, for that matter, Joyce's Stephen Dedalus (74).

As with *Madame Bovary* itself, the bovarystic motifs in *Lolita* and *Astrophobia* warn against a confusion of fiction and reality. For both Sokolov and Nabokov this warning has a special resonance within the context of Soviet history, especially during the Stalin years, where the boundary between fact and fiction was obscured as a matter of official government policy. In short, even when Sokolov and Nabokov construct fictions that attempt clearly to set themselves off as different from reality, that very difference establishes a close contact with the social world. But the implicit social commentary in Nabokov's work is not limited to the Soviet regime he so despised. Much of *Lolita* can be read as a scathing condemnation of the misleading view of reality derived from advertising, film, magazines, and other elements of popular culture in America. On the other hand, Nabokov does not hold up "high" art as a privileged alternative to popular culture. Though Humbert appears to see through the way the Americans he encounters are being duped by their culture, his view of reality (derived mainly from French "high" literature) is at least as distorted as theirs, and this distortion leads in his case to even more horrific results.[6] As Ellen Pifer puts it, "If Lolita is the victim of American pop culture, she is even more cruelly the victim of Humbert's aesthetic proclivities" (170). Indeed, there is a close correlation between Humbert's belief that he can possess in reality what his imagination has envisioned as the ideal nymphet and Lolita's belief that she can possess the idealized consumer goods presented in advertising. As Dana Brand notes, "[b]elief in the possibility of the actual possession of an image is . . . the means by which advertisements reduce people to thralldom" (19).

But Nabokov is not suggesting that we put aside all representations of reality in exchange for the thing itself. On the contrary, everywhere in his fiction Nabokov makes clear his belief that there is no unmediated access to reality. As he puts it in his postscript to *Lolita*, "reality" is "one of the few words which mean nothing without quotes" (314). Our access to reality is always belated, always filtered through our own expectations and interpretations. Pifer has discussed in some detail this aspect of Nabokov's work as part of her strong argument for Nabokov's ethical and moral commitment. She notes that it is not mediation to which Nabokov objects, but rather mediation that attempts to pass itself off as direct access to reality. This attitude explains Nabokov's antipathy toward realistic fiction and the highly artificial quality of his own work: "Nabokov, who found that even recorded history may be a kind of romance, or fiction, was understandably averse to *any* literary method that aspires to the authenticity of ultimate and objective reality" (Pifer 129, her emphasis).

This description of Nabokov's attitude toward history as mediation is obviously quite relevant to Sokolov's project in *Astrophobia*. And Nabokov's own statement elsewhere that "I do not believe that 'history' exists apart from the historian" even more directly recalls the intrusive historical method of Sokolov's Palisander (*Strong* 138). This view of history also recalls the efforts of Van Veen, the narrator/protagonist of Nabokov's *Ada*, to construct a coherent narrative of his past. Indeed, though the links between *Ada* and *Astrophobia* have received little critical attention, *Ada* may ultimately be the Nabokov work that is most relevant to Sokolov's book. *Astrophobia* and *Ada* are formally quite similar. Both are parodic memoirs whose twisted chronologies and densely allusive textures put heavy demands upon reader memory and ingenuity. And both are highly entertaining comic works that still manage to make serious statements about fundamental literary and philosophical issues.

Nabokov's Van Veen and Sokolov's Palisander Dahlberg have many similarities as the central figures in the two texts. Both, for example, are impressive sexual athletes a large percentage of whose sexual escapades are incestuous. But Van is a handsome Adonis whose incestuous energies are directed at a beautiful sister his own age (whom he does not even initially realize is his sister), while the grotesque sexual escapades of the bizarre-looking Palisander can be read as a parody of Van. Van and Palisander are also both prolific and successful writers of both fiction and memoirs, and they have a great deal in common as chroniclers of the past. The often nostalgic tone of Van's remembrances of things past (a feature of much of Nabokov's work) is echoed in Palisander's own fond recollections of his childhood. However, the most obvious referent of nostalgia in Nabokov's work is an idyllic version of tsarist Russia that was destroyed by the Bolshevik Revolution, while Palisander's memories arise from within the walls of the Communist Kremlin, described as a "horn of plenty" where "[e]veryone led a happy, gay, carefree existence" (97). Meanwhile, both Van and Palisander are philosophers of time, though their specific philosophies differ dramatically. Palisander views time as circular, leading him to question conventional notions of sequence. Van is a strong proponent of linear time whose faith in conventional notions of sequentiality and simultaneity leads him violently to reject concepts like Einstein's theory of relativity that would challenge such notions.

Noting the many points of similarity between Sokolov and Nabokov, Johnson nevertheless concludes that "the differences between Sokolov and Nabokov are ultimately far more important than their similarities" ("Sokolov and Nabokov" 159). The same can certainly be said of the relationship between Nabokov's Van and Sokolov's Palisander, though it is important to recognize that the differences between Sokolov and Nabokov can often be interpreted as parodic. That *Astrophobia* can resemble Nabokov's work in so many ways and yet also take such a parodic attitude toward that work is particularly significant from a Bakhtinian point of view. If parody is the central driving force for innovation in literature, *Astrophobia* might appear to be a virtual dead end. It is difficult to see how Sokolov's book itself could be parodied effectively, as it is itself already so purely parodic. Indeed, *Astrophobia* is to a certain extent already self-parodic. Yet Nabokov's work is highly parodic (and self-parodic) as well, and Sokolov is still able to make it a rich source of material for his own parodies. Moreover, *Astrophobia* is far more than a simple parody of any given text or author, directing its parodic energies at a wide variety of targets. Novelists who come after Sokolov may in fact not find it very fruitful simply to write parodies of *Astrophobia*, but they might learn valuable lessons from Sokolov's text about the power of parody, especially when that parody derives from multiple sources—one of which could be *Astrophobia* itself. *Astrophobia* nicely illustrates Bakhtin's insistence on the impossibility of a "last word." It thus serves as a strong reminder of the ability of literature to renew itself and countering what might be seen as certain tendencies toward petrification in recent Russian émigré literature. Given the dramatic changes now under way in what was the Soviet Union, dramatic changes can be expected in Russian literature in the near future. *Astrophobia* suggests that those changes might be exciting indeed.

NOTES

1. *Astrophobia* is the title of the English translation. Sokolov's Russian original is entitled *Palisandriia*.

2. Panurge figures for Rabelais as a similar image of linguistic multiplicity, as when he shifts among German, Italian, Dutch, Spanish, Danish, Hebrew, Greek, Latin, and invented nonsense

languages in his initial encounter with Pantagruel in Chapter 9 of Book II of *Gargantua and Pantagruel*.

3. See Hart and Solomon for discussions of the sexual and scatological imagery in *Finnegans Wake*. *Astrophobia* frequently makes reference to the works of nonRussian writers like Joyce and Beckett (who at one point even appears as a character).

4. Numerous critics have noted the importance of Gogol in Sokolov's work. See, for example, Matich ("Context" 303) and Johnson ("Galoshes" 155 and "Sokolov and Nabokov" 158-9). Aleksei Cvetkov has gone so far as to claim that Gogol is Sokolov's "only direct precursor" (cited in Johnson, "Sokolov and Nabokov" 162n.20).

5. Of course, these two influences cannot be entirely separated; Sterne's book was a major influence on Gogol and many other Russian writers.

6. For a discussion of this aspect of *Lolita* see *Literature and Domination*.

Works Cited

Adorno, Theodor. *Minima Moralia: Reflections from a Damaged Life*. Trans. E. F. N. Jephcott. London: NLB, 1974.

Aksyonov, Vassily. "Back in the USSR." Review of *Songs to Seven Strings* by Gerald Stanton Smith. *TLS* (March 28, 1986): 338.

Aksyonov, Vassily. *The Burn*. Trans. Michael Glenny. New York: Vintage, 1985.

Aksyonov, Vassily. *"The Destruction of Pompeii" and Other Stories*. Various translators. Ann Arbor, Michigan: Ardis, 1991.

Aksyonov, Vassily. *In Search of Melancholy Baby*. Trans. Michael Henry Heim and Antonina Bouis. New York: Vintage, 1989.

Aksyonov, Vassily. *The Island of Crimea*. Trans. Michael Henry Heim. New York: Random House, 1983.

Aksyonov, Vassily. *Say Cheese!* Trans. Antonina W. Bouis. New York: Random House, 1989.

Aleshkovsky, Yuz. *The Hand, or, Confession of an Executioner*. Trans. Susan Brownsberger. London: Peter Halban, 1989.

Aleshkovsky, Yuz. *Kangaroo*. Trans. Tamara Glenny. New York: Farrar, Straus and Giroux, 1986.

Alexandrova, Vera. *A History of Soviet LIterature: 1917-1964, From Gorky to Solzhenitsyn*. Trans. Mirra Ginsberg. New York: Doubleday, 1964.

Arendt, Hannah. *The Origins of Totalitarianism*. Second Edition. Cleveland: World Publishing, 1958.

St. Augustine. *Confessions*. Trans. R. S. Pine-Coffin. New York: Dorset, 1961.

Bakhtin, M. M. *Art and Answerability: Early Philosophical Essays*. Ed. Michael Holquist and Vadim Liapunov. Trans. Vadim Liapunov and Kenneth Brostrum. Austin: U of Texas P, 1990.

Bakhtin, M. M. *The Dialogic Imagination.* Ed. Michael Holquist. Trans. Caryl Emerson and Michael Holquist. Austin: U of Texas P, 1981.

Bakhtin, M. M. Preface to *Resurrection* by Leo Tolstoy. Trans. Caryl Emerson. Reprinted in *Rethinking Bakhtin: Extensions and Challenges.* Ed. Gary Saul Morson and Caryl Emerson. Evanston, Illinois: Northwestern UP, 1989, 237-57.

Bakhtin, M. M. *Problems of Dostoevsky's Poetics.* Trans. and Ed. Caryl Emerson. Minneapolis: U of Minnesota P, 1984.

Bakhtin, M. M. *Rabelais and His World.* Trans. Helene Iswolsky. Bloomington, Indiana: Indiana UP, 1984.

Bakhtin, M. M. *Speech Genres and Other Late Essays.* Trans. Vern W. McGhee. Ed. Caryl Emerson and Michael Holquist. Austin: U of Texas P, 1986.

Berczynski, T. S. "Kavalerov's Monologue in *Envy:* A Baroque Soliloquy." *Russian Literary Triquarterly* 1 (Fall 1971): 375-85.

Bernstein, Michael André. "The Poetics of *Ressentiment*." *Rethinking Bakhtin: Extensions and Challenges.* Evanston, Illinois: Northwestern UP, 1989. 197-223.

Berrong, Richard M. *Rabelais and Bakhtin: Popular Culture in "Gargantua and Pantagruel."* Lincoln: U of Nebraska P, 1986.

Billington, James H. *The Icon and the Axe: An Interpretive History of Russian Culture.* New York: Knopf, 1967.

Bitov, Andrei. *Pushkin House.* New York: Farrar, Straus and Giroux, 1987.

Blackall, Eric A. *Goethe and the Novel.* Ithaca: New York: Cornell UP, 1976.

Booker, M. Keith. *The Dystopian Impulse in Modern Literature: Fiction as Social Criticism.* Westport, Connecticut: Greenwood P, 1994.

Booker, M. Keith. *Literature and Domination: Sex, Knowledge, and Power in Modern Fiction.* Gainesville: UP of Florida, 1993.

Booker, M. Keith. "'A War Between the Mind and Sky': Bakhtin and Poetry, Stevens and Politics." *The Wallace Stevens Journal* 14 (1990): 71-85.

Brand, Dana. "The Interaction of Aestheticism and American Consumer Culture in Nabokov's *Lolita*." *Modern Language Studies* 17 (Spring 1987): 14-21.

Brown, Edward J. "Zinoviev, Aleshkovsky, Rabelais, Sorrentino, Possibly Pynchon, Maybe James Joyce, and Certainly *Tristram Shandy:* A Comparative Study of a Satirical Mode." *Stanford Slavic Studies* 1 (1987): 307-325.

Brownsberger, Susan. Translator's afterword to *Pushkin House* by Andrei Bitov. New York: Farrar, Straus and Giroux, 1987, 359-63.

Bulgakov, Mikhail. "The Fatal Eggs." *"Diaboliad" and Other Stories.* Trans. Carl R. Proffer. Bloomington: Indiana UP, 1972. 48-134.

Bulgakov, Mikhail. *Heart of a Dog.* Trans. Michael Glenny. New York: Harcourt, Brace, and World, 1968.

Bulgakov, Mikhail. *The Master and Margarita.* Trans. Mirra Ginsberg. New York: Grove Weidenfeld, 1987.

Bullock, Allan. *Hitler and Stalin: Parallel Lives.* New York: Alfred A. Knopf, 1992.

Burbank, Jane. *Intelligentsia and Revolution: Russian Views of Bolshevism, 1917-1922.* Oxford: Oxford UP, 1986.

Chapple, Richard L. *Soviet Satire of the Twenties.* Gainesville: UP of Florida, 1980.

Clark, Katerina. "Political History and Literary Chronotope: Some Soviet Case Studies." *Literature and History: Theoretical Problems and Russian Case Studies.* Ed. Gary Saul Morson. Stanford, California: Stanford UP, 1986. 230-46.

Clark, Katerina. *The Soviet Novel: History as Ritual.* Chicago: U of Chicago P, 1981.

Clark, Katerina and Michael Holquist. *Mikhail Bakhtin.* Cambridge, Massachusetts: Belknap P, 1984.

Clowes, Edith W. *Russian Experimental Fiction: Resisting Ideology after Utopia.* Princeton, New Jersey: Princeton UP, 1993.

Conquest, Robert. *The Great Terror: A Reassessment.* Oxford: Oxford UP, 1990.

Conrad, Joseph. *Under Western Eyes.* New York: New American Library, 1987.

Dirscherl, Denis, S.J. *Dostoevsky and the Catholic Church.* Chicago: Loyola UP, 1986.

Domar, Rebecca A. "The Tragedy of a Soviet Satirist, or the Case of Zoshchenko." *Through the Glass of Soviet Literature.* Ed. Ernest J. Simmons. New York: Columbia UP, 1953. 201-43.

Dostoevsky, Fyodor. *The Brothers Karamazov.* Trans. Richard Pevear and Larissa Volokhonsky. San Francisco: North Point P, 1990.

Dostoevsky, Fyodor. *Devils.* Trans. Michael R. Katz. Oxford: Oxford UP, 1992.

Dostoevsky, Fyodor. *Notes from Underground.* Trans. Mirra Ginsburg. New York: Bantam Books, 1976.

Eagleton, Terry. *Walter Benjamin: Towards a Revolutionary Criticism.* London: Verso, 1981.

Eaton, Katherine. "Brecht's Contacts With the Theater of Meyerhold." *Drama in the Twentieth Century: Comparative and Critical Essays.* Ed. Clifford Davidson, C. J. Gianakaris, and John H. Stroupe. New York: AMS P, 1984. 203-21.

Edwards, T. R. N. *Three Russian Writers and the Irrational: Zamyatin, Pil'nyak, and Bulgakov.* Cambridge: Cambridge UP, 1982.

Emerson, Caryl. "The Outer Word and Inner Speech: Bakhtin, Vygotsky, and the Internalization of Language." *Bakhtin: Essays and Dialogues on His Work.* Ed. Gary Saul Morson. Chicago: U of Chicago P, 1986. 21-40.

Fanger, Donald. *The Creation of Nikolai Gogol.* Cambridge, Massachusetts: Harvard UP, 1979.

Feuchtwanger, Lion. *Moscow 1937: My Visit Described for My Friends.* Trans. Irene Josephy. New York: Viking, 1937.

Fitzpatrick, Sheila. *The Cultural Front: Power and Culture in Revolutionary Russia.* Ithaca, New York: Cornell UP, 1992.

Fitzpatrick, Sheila. *The Russian Revolution: 1917-1932.* Oxford: Oxford UP, 1984.

Foucault, Michel. *The History of Sexuality, Volume I: An Introduction.* Trans. Robert Hurley. New York: Vintage Books, 1980.

Foucault, Michel. *The Use of Pleasure.* Trans. Robert Hurley. New York: Vintage, 1986.

Freud, Sigmund. *Civilization and Its Discontents.* Trans. James Strachey. New York: Norton, 1961.

Gardiner, Michael. *The Dialogics of Critique: M. M. Bakhtin and the Theory of Ideology.* London: Routledge, 1992.

Ginzburg, Eugenia. *Within the Whirlwind.* Trans. Ian Borland. New York: Harcourt Brace Jovanovich, 1981.

Gogol, Nikolai. *Dead Souls.* Trans. David Magarshack. London: Penguin, 1961.

Gogol, Nikolai. *"Diary of a Madman" and Other Stories.* Trans. Ronald Wilks. New York: Penguin, 1972.

Graff, Gerald. *Literature Against Itself: Literary Ideas in Modern Society.* Chicago: U of Chicago P, 1979.

Graham, J. W. "Point of View in *The Waves*: Some Services of the Style." *University of Toronto Quarterly* 39 (1970): 193-211.

Hart, Clive. *Structure and Motif in* Finnegans Wake. Evanston, Illinois: Northwestern UP, 1962.

Hellebust, Rolf. "Fiction and Unreality in Bitov's *Pushkin House*." *Style* 25 (1991): 265-279.

Holquist, Michael. "Answering as Authoring: Mikhail Bakhtin's Trans-Linguistics." *Bakhtin: Essays and Dialogues on His Work.* Ed. Gary Saul Morson. Chicago: U of Chicago P, 1986. 59-71.

Holquist, Michael. "Bakhtin and Rabelais: Theory as Praxis." *boundary 2* 11.1-2 (Fall-Winter, 1982-3): 5-19.

Holquist, Michael. *Dialogism: Bakhtin and His World.* London: Routledge, 1990.

Holquist, Michael. *Dostoevsky and the Novel.* Princeton, New Jersey: Princeton UP, 1977.

Holquist, Michael. Prologue. *Rabelais and His World.* By Mikhail Bakhtin. Bloomington: Indiana UP, 1984. xiii-xxiii.

Huyssen, Andreas. *After the Great Divide: Modernism, Mass Culture, Postmodernism.* Bloomington: Indiana UP, 1986.

Ilf and Petrov. *The Golden Calf.* Trans. John H. C. Richardson. New York: Random House, 1962.

Ilf and Petrov. *The Twelve Chairs.* Trans. John H. C. Richardson. New York: Vintage Books, 1961.

Jackson, Robert Louis. *Dostoevsky's Underground Man in Russian Literature.* The Hague: Mouton, 1958.

Jameson, Fredric. *Marxism and Form: Twentieth-Century Dialectical Theories of Literature.* Princeton, New Jersey: Princeton UP, 1971.

Jameson, Fredric. *The Political Unconscious: Narrative as a Socially Symbolic Act.* Ithaca, New York: Cornell UP, 1981.

Jameson, Fredric. "Postmodernism and Consumer Society." *The Anti-Aesthetic: Essays on Postmodern Culture.* Ed. Hal Foster. Port Townsend, Washington: Bay P, 1983. 111-26.

Jameson, Fredric. "Postmodernism, or, the Cultural Logic of Late Capitalism." *New Left Review* 145 (1984): 53-91.

Jameson, Fredric. *Postmodernism, or, The Cultural Logic of Late Capitalism.* Durham: Duke UP, 1991.

Johnson, D. Barton. "The Galoshes Manifesto: A Motif in the Novels of Sasha Sokolov." *Oxford Slavonic Papers* 22 (1989): 155-79.

Johnson, D. Barton. "Sasha Sokolov and Vladimir Nabokov." *Russian Language Journal* 41.138-9 (1987): 153-62.

Johnson, D. Barton. "Sasha Sokolov: The New Russian Avant-Garde." *Critique* 30.3 (1989): 163-78.

Johnson, J. J., Jr. "V. P. Aksënov: A Literary Biography." *Vassily Pavlovich Aksënov: A Writer in Quest of Himself.* Ed. Edward Mozejko. Columbus, Ohio: Slavica, 1986. 32-52.

Joravsky, David. *Soviet Marxism and Natural Science 1917-1932.* New York: Columbia UP, 1961.

Joyce, James. *Finnegans Wake.* New York: Viking, 1939.

Works Cited

Karpov, Lena. Introduction to *The Destruction of Pompeii and Other Stories* by Vassily Aksyonov. Ann Arbor, Michigan: Ardis, 1991, vii–x.

Kearney, Richard. *The Wake of Imagination: Toward a Postmodern Culture*. Minneapolis: U of Minnesota P, 1988.

Kern, Gary. "After the Afterword." *Before Sunrise* by Mikhail Zoshchenko. Ann Arbor, Michigan: Ardis, 1974. 345–66.

Kern, Gary. "*Youth Restored*: Before the Introductions." *Youth Restored* by Mikhail Zoshchenko. Ann Arbor, Michigan: Ardis, 1984. 1–5.

Kershner, R. B. *Joyce, Bakhtin, and Popular Literature: Chronicles of Disorder*. Chapel Hill: U of North Carolina P, 1989.

Kinser, Samuel. *Rabelais's Carnival: Text, Context, and Metatext*. Berkeley: U of California P, 1990.

Kristeva, Julia. *Desire in Language: A Semiotic Approach to Literature and Art*. New York: Columbia UP, 1980.

Lauridsen, Inger and Per Dalgård. "Interview with V. P. Aksënov." *Vassily Pavlovich Aksënov: A Writer in Quest of Himself*. Ed. Edward Mozejko. Columbus, Ohio: Slavica, 1986. 14–25.

Limonov, Edward. *It's Me, Eddie: A Fictional Memoir*. Trans. S. L. Campbell. New York: Grove, 1983.

Loseff, Lev. *On the Beneficence of Censorship: Aesopian Language in Modern Russian Literature*. Munich: Verlag Otto Sagner, 1984.

Lunacharsky, Anatoly. *On Literature and Art*. Ed. K. M. Cook. Trans. Avril Pyman and Fainna Glagoleva. Moscow: Progress, 1973.

Maguire, Robert. *Red Virgin Soil: Soviet Literature in the 1920s*. Princeton, New Jersey: Princeton UP, 1968.

Matich, Olga. "Sasha Sokolov and His Literary Context." *Canadian-American Slavic Studies* 21.3–4 (1987): 301–319.

Matich, Olga. "Sasha Sokolov's *Palisandriia*: History and Myth." *The Russian Review* 45 (1986): 415–26.

Matich, Olga. "Vasilii Aksenov and the Literature of Convergence: *Ostrov Krym* as Self-Criticism." *Slavic Review* 47.4 (1988): 642–51.

McGann, Jerome. *Historical Studies and Literary Criticism*. Madison, Wisconsin: U of Wisconsin P, 1985.

McHale, Brian. *Postmodernist Fiction*. New York: Methuen, 1987.

McHugh, Roland. *The Sigla of "Finnegans Wake."* Austin: U of Texas P, 1976.

McLean, Hugh. Introduction to *Nervous People and Other Satires* by Mikhail Zoshchenko. Bloomington: Indiana UP, 1975, vii–xxvii.

McMillin, Arnold. "Aberration or the Future: The Avant-Garde Novels of Sasha Sokolov." *From Pushkin to "Palisandriia": Essays on the Russian Novel in Honor of Richard Freeborn.* Ed. Arnold McMillin. New York: St. Martin's, 1990. 229-43.

Mendilow, A. A. *Time and the Novel.* London: P. Nevill, 1952.

Meyer, Priscilla. "Aksenov and Stalinism: Political, Moral, and Literary Power." *Slavic and East European Journal* 30.4 (1986): 509-25.

Meyer, Priscilla. "*Skaz* in the Work of Juz Aleshkovskij." *Slavic and East European Journal* 28.4 (1984): 455-61.

Mills, Judith M. "Of Dreams, Devils, Irrationality and *The Master and Margarita.*" *Russian Literature and Psychoanalysis.* Ed. D. Raucour-Laferriere. Amsterdam: Bejamins, 1989. 303-27.

Morson, Gary Saul. *Hidden in PLain View: Narrative and Creative Potentials in "War and Peace."* Stanford, California: Stanford UP, 1987.

Morson, Gary Saul and Caryl Emerson. *Mikhail Bakhtin: Creation of a Prosaics.* Stanford, California: Stanford UP, 1990.

Mozejko, Edward. "*The Steel Bird* and Aksënov's Prose of the Seventies." *Vassily Pavlovich Aksënov: A Writer in Quest of Himself.* Ed. Edward Mozejko. Columbus, Ohio: Slavica, 1986. 205-23.

Murphy, A. B. *Mikhail Zoshchenko: A Literary Profile.* Oxford: Meeuws, 1981.

Nabokov, Vladimir. *The Annotated Lolita.* Ed. Alfred Appel, Jr. New York and Toronto: McGraw-Hill, 1970.

Nabokov, Vladimir. *Bend Sinister.* New York: Henry Holt, 1947.

Nabokov, Vladimir. *The Gift.* Trans. by Michael Scammel with the collaboration of the author. New York: Wideview/Perigee Books, 1963.

Nabokov, Vladimir. *Invitation to a Beheading.* Trans. Dmitri Nabokov and Vladimir Nabokov. New York: Putnam, 1959.

Nabokov, Vladimir. *Lectures on Literature.* Ed. Fredson Bowers. San Diego: Harcourt Brace Jovanovich, 1980.

Nabokov, Vladimir. *Strong Opinions.* New York: McGraw-Hill, 1981.

Nakhimovsky, Alice Stone. "Looking Back at Paradise Lost: The Russian Nineteenth Century in Andrei Bitov's *Pushkin House.*" *Russian Literature Triquarterly* 22 (1989): 195-204.

Nietzsche, Friedrich. *On the Genealogy of Morals. Basic Writings of Nietzsche.* Trans. and ed. Walter Kaufmann. New York: Modern Library, 1968. 439-599.

O'Brien, Flann. *At Swim-Two-Birds.* 1939. New York: New American Library, 1976.

Orwell, George. *1984.* New York: New American Library, 1961.

Patterson, David. *Literature and Spirit: Essays on Bakhtin and His Contemporaries*. Lexington: The UP of Kentucky, 1988.

Pearce, Richard, "Pynchon's Endings." *Novel* 18 (1985): 145-53.

Peppard, Victor. *The Poetics of Yury Olesha*. Gainesville: U of Florida P, 1989.

Phillips, William, ed. "Writers in Exile: A Conference of Soviet and East European Dissidents." *Partisan Review* 50 (1983): 487-525.

Pifer, Ellen. *Nabokov and the Novel*. Cambridge, Massachusetts: Harvard UP, 1980.

Polan, Dana B. "Daffy Duck and Bertolt Brecht: Toward a Politics of Self-Reflexive Cinema?" *American Media and Mass Culture*. Ed. Donald Lazere. Berkeley: U of California P, 1987. 345-56.

Proffer, E. "Bulgakov's *The Master and Margarita*: Genre and Motif." *Canadian Slavonic Studies* 3.4 (1969): 431-44.

Proffer, Ellendea. "The Prague Winter: Two Novels by Aksyonov." *The Third Wave: Russian Literature in Emigration*. Ed. Olga Matich and Michael Heim. Ann Arbor, Michigan: Ardis, 1984. 131-7.

Pynchon, Thomas. *Vineland*. Boston: Little, Brown, 1990.

Rabelais, François. *The Histories of Gargantua and Pantagruel*. Trans. J. M. Cohen. London: Penguin, 1955.

Ricoeur, Paul. *Time and Narrative*. Vol. III. Trans. Kathleen Blamey and David Pellauer. Chicago: U of Chicago P, 1988.

Roman, Gail Harrison and Virginia Hagelstein Marquardt, eds. *The Avant-Garde Frontier: Russia Meets the West, 1910-1930*. Gainesville: UP of Florida, 1992.

Scatton, Linda H. "Zoshchenko's Lenin Stories: The Pitfalls of Hagiography in a Secular Context." *New Studies in Russian Language and Literature*. Ed. Anna Lisa Crone and Catherine V. Chvany. Columbus, Ohio: Slavica, 1987. 253-57.

Sharratt, B. K. "Narrative Techniques in *The Master and Margarita*." *Canadian Slavonic Papers* 16.1 (1974): 1-13.

Shklovsky, Viktor. "Sterne's *Tristram Shandy*: Stylistic Commentary." *Russian Formalist Criticism: Four Essays*. Ed. Lee Lemon and Marion Reis. Lincoln: U of Nebraska P, 1965, 25-57.

Shragin, Boris. *The Challenge of the Spirit*. Trans. P. S. Falla. New York: Alfred A. Knopf, 1978.

Siegle, Robert. *The Politics of Reflexivity: Narrative and Constitutive Poetics of Culture*. Baltimore: Johns Hopkins UP, 1986.

Singer, Alan. "The Dis-position of the Subject: Agency and Form in the Ideology of the Novel." *Novel* 22 (1988): 5-23.

Sinyavsky. Andrei (as Abram Tertz). *Goodnight!* Trans. Richard Lourie. New York: Viking, 1989.

Sinyavsky, Andrei (as Abram Tertz). "On Socialist Realism." Trans. George Dennis. *"The Trial Begins" and "On Socialist Realism."* Berkeley: U of California P, 1982. 147-219.

Sinyavsky, Andrei. *Soviet Civilization: A Cultural History.* Trans. Joanne Turnbull with the assistance of Nikolai Formozov. New York: Little, Brown, 1988.

Skvorecky, Josef. *The Engineer of Human Souls.* New York: Pocket Books, 1985.

Slonim, Marc. *Soviet Russian Literature: Writers and Problems, 1917-1977.* Second Revised Edition. New York: Oxford UP, 1977.

Sokolov, Sasha. *Astrophobia.* Trans. Michael Henry Heim. New York: Grove Weidenfeld, 1989.

Solomon, Margaret. *Eternal Geomater: The Sexual Universe of Finnegans Wake.* Carbondale: Southern Illinois UP, 1969.

Stallybrass, Peter and Allon White. *The Politics and Poetics of Transgression.* Ithaca, New York: Cornell UP, 1986.

Stenbock-Fermor, Elisabeth. "Bulgakov's *The Master and Margarita* and Goethe's *Faust.*" *Slavic and East European Journal* 13.3 (1969): 309-25.

Stites, Richard. *Revolutionary Dreams: Utopian Vision and Experimental Life in the Russian Revolution.* New York: Oxford UP, 1989.

Striedter, Yurij. "Three Postrevolutionary Russian Utopian Novels." *The Russian Novel from Pushkin to Pasternak.*" Ed. John Garrard. New Haven, Connecticut: Yale UP, 1983. 177-201.

Struve, Gleb. *Soviet Russian Literature, 1917-50.* Norman: U of Oklahoma P, 1951.

Thomson, Boris. *The Premature Revolution: Russian Literature and Society 1917-1946.* London: Weidenfeld and Nicolson, 1972.

Titunik, I. R. "The Baxtin Problem: Concerning Katerina Clark and Michael Holquist's *Mikhail Bakhtin.*" *Slavic and East European Journal* 30.1 (1986): 91-95.

Titunik, I. R. "Mikhail Zoshchenko and the Problem of *Skaz.*" *California Slavic Studies* 6 (1971): 83-96.

Vishevsky, A. and T. Pogacar. "The Function of Conventional Language Pattern in the Prose of Vasiliy Aksënov." *Vassily Pavlovich Aksënov: A Writer in Quest of Himself.* Ed. Edward Mozejko. Columbus, Ohio: Slavica, 1986. 131-46.

Voloshinov, V. N. *Freudianism: A Critical Sketch.* Trans. I. R. Titunik. Ed. I. R. Titunik and Neal H. Bruss. Bloomington: Indiana UP, 1987.

Voloshinov, V. N. *Marxism and the Philosophy of Language*. Trans. Ladislav Matejka and I. R. Titunik. Cambridge, Massachusetts: Harvard UP, 1986.

von Gronicka, André. *The Russian Image of Goethe. Volume One: Goethe in Russian Literature of the First Half of the Nineteenth Century*. Philadelphia: U of Pennsylvania P, 1968.

Weisinger, Kenneth D. *The Classical Facade: A Nonclassical Reading of Goethe's Classicism*. University Park: Pennsylvania State UP, 1988.

Williams, Raymond and Edward Said. "Media, Margins, and Modernity." *The Politics of Modernism: Against the New Conformists* by Raymond Williams. Ed. Tony Pinkney. London: Verso, 1989. 177-97.

Wise, Jennifer. "Marginalizing Drama: Bakhtin's Theory of Genre." *Essays in Theatre* 8.1 (1989): 15-22.

Woolf, Virginia. "Modern Fiction." *The Common Reader*. New York: Harcourt, Brace and Company, 1948. 207-18.

Woolf, Virginia. *A Room of One's Own*. New York: Harcourt Brace Jovanovich, 1929.

Woolf, Virginia. *The Waves*. New York: Harcourt, Brace, Jovanovich, 1931.

Woolf, Virginia. *A Writer's Diary*. Ed. Leonard Woolf. New York: Harcourt, Brace and Company, 1954.

Wright, A. Colin. *Mikhail Bulgakov: Life and Interpretations*. Toronto: U of Toronto P, 1978.

Yaeger, Patricia. *Honey-Mad Women: Emancipatory Strategies in Women's Writing*. New York: Columbia UP, 1988.

Zamyatin, Evgeny. *A Soviet Heretic*. Ed. and Trans. Mirra Ginsberg. Chicago: U of Chicago P, 1970.

Zamyatin, Evgeny. *We*. Trans. Mirra Ginsberg. New York: Avon, 1983.

Zholkovsky, Alexander. "Dreaming Right and Reading Right: Five Keys to One of Ilf and Petrov's Ridiculous Men." *Slavic Review* 48.1 (Spring 1989): 36-53.

Zinoviev, Alexander. *The Yawning Heights*. Trans. Gordon Clough. New York: Random House, 1979.

Zoshchenko, Mikhail. *Before Sunrise*. Trans. Gary Kern. Ann Arbor, Michigan: Ardis, 1974.

Zoshchenko, Mikhail. *"Nervous People" and Other Satires*. Trans. Maria Gordon and Hugh McLean. Ed. Hugh McLean. Bloomington: Indiana UP, 1975.

Zoshchenko, Mikhail. *Youth Restored*. Trans. Joel Stern. Ann Arbor, Michigan: Ardis, 1984.

Index

About the Authors

M. KEITH BOOKER is Associate Professor of English and director of Graduate Studies at the University of Arkansas. He has published numerous articles on literature and literary theory and is the author of several books, including *The Dystopian Impulse in Modern Literature* and *Dystopian Literature*, both published by Greenwood Press in 1994.

DUBRAVKA JURAGA is a doctoral candidate in Comparative Literature at the University of Arkansas. A former Fulbright Scholar from Yugoslavia, she has published numerous translations and articles on literature and culture in both the United States and Europe.

ISBN 0-313-29526-3

90000>

EAN

9 780313 295263

HARDCOVER BAR CODE